The Collected Poems

Giorgio Bassani in 1988 in his study in via Carissimi 28, Rome. In the background, drawings by his uncle Giacomo (see "Family History" in *Epitaph*) and a stuffed heron, symbol for the fifth novel in *The Novel of Ferrara*. (Photo Gigi Danieli)

Giorgio Bassani

The Collected Poems

Translated with an Introduction and Notes
by Roberta Antognini and Peter Robinson

Agincourt Press
New York, 2023

Translation, Introduction, and Notes
copyright © Roberta Antognini and Peter Robinson 2023
Foreword copyright © Paola Bassani 2023

Opuntia is an imprint of Agincourt Press
Luigi Ballerini and Gianluca Rizzo, Editors
Agincourt Press is a non-profit organization chaired by Berardo Paradiso

All manuscripts are subject to peer review.

All rights reserved.

ISBN: 978-1-946328-36-6

AGINCOURT PRESS
P.O. Box 1039
Cooper Station
New York, NY 10003
www.agincourtbooks.com

© 2023 by Agincourt Press

Table of Contents

15 *Foreword* by Paola Bassani
19 *Translators' Note*
23 *Introduction*
37 *Chronology*

IN RIMA / IN RHYME

STORIE DEI POVERI AMANTI / POOR LOVERS' STORIES

52 Preludio / Prelude
52 Sera sul Po / Evening on the Po
54 Pontelagoscuro / Pontelagoscuro
54 Sulla baia / On the Bay
54 I gabbiani / The Seagulls
56 Il balcone / The Balcony
56 Piazza d'Armi / Piazza d'Armi
56 Serenata / Serenade
58 I crisantemi / The Chrysanthemums
58 Pavana / Pavan
58 Dai bastioni orientali / From the Eastern Bastions
60 I girasoli / The Sunflowers
60 Dopo la sagra / After the Feast
60 Di settembre a San Giorgio / In September at San Giorgio
62 Verso Ferrara / Towards Ferrrara
62 Sera a Porta Reno / Evening at Porta Reno
62 Marina d'ottobre / Seaside in October
64 Punta marina / Punta Marina

64 Chiaro di luna / Clair de Lune
64 Variazione sul tema precedente / Variation on the Preceding Theme
66 Immagine / Image
68 Monselice / Monselice
68 Nel suo compleanno / On His Birthday
68 Storie dei poveri amanti / Poor Lovers' Stories
74 I giocatori / The Players
76 Cena di Pasqua / Easter Supper
76 Mascherata / Masquerade
76 Emilia / Emilia
78 I Campi Elisi / The Elysian Fields
78 Imitazione da Orazio / Imitation of Horace
78 Epitaffio per un tipografo / Epitaph for a Typographer
80 Saluto a Roma / Salute to Rome
82 I carbonai / The Coalmen
82 Non piangere / Don't Weep
84 Retrovia / Behind the Lines

TE LUCIS ANTE / TE LUCIS ANTE

I
90 Valle dell'Aniene / Valle dell'Aniene
90 Dal carcere / From Prison

II
94 1 E riapprodi, ogni notte, / And you resurface, every night,
94 2 Dormo: o sei tu che pungi / I sleep: oh is it you sting
94 3 Dunque lascia il tuo regno / So then leave your reign
96 4 «Chissà», tenti; «e se questo / "Who knows," you try; "and if
96 5 Un ultimo segnale, / A very last signal,
96 6 Un fischio era (o mi parve / A whistle it was (or seemed
98 7 Luce che i caldi tetti / Light, you're saluting
98 8 Quando più ero solo, / When I was more alone,
100 9 Pur se m'eri vicino, / Though were you near me,
100 10 E sei tu che ove aggiorni, / And it's you where it dawns,
100 11 E voi, labbra ch'io volli / And you, lips I desired
102 12 Da me, da me attendevi / From me, from me you awaited

102 13 Mi avessi da bambino / If only when a child
102 14 Stesa eri, sul prato, / Lain you were, on the meadow,
104 15 D'oltre il passo del vento / Beyond the wind's tread,
104 16 Sei venuto alla porta. / You came to the door.

III
108 Vide cor meum / Vide Cor Meum
108 Venuto con la notte / Come with the Night
108 Dove sei? / Where Are You?
108 Il velo di fiamma / The Veil of Flame
110 Per un quadro di Morandi / For a Picture by Morandi
110 Ars poetica / Ars Poetica
110 Canzone / Song
110 Per il parco di Ninfa / For the Parco di Ninfa
112 Villa Glori / Villa Glori
112 Sera a Montesacro / Montesacro Evening
112 Angelus / Angelus
112 L'alba ai vetri / Dawn at the Panes
114 L'orto / The Garden
114 I fiori / The Flowers
114 La campana / The Bell
116 Sogno / Dream
116 A mio padre / To My Father
116 Qualche volta / Sometimes
118 Stella / Star
118 Commiato / Leave-Taking

SENZA / WITHOUT

EPITAFFIO / EPITAPH

124 Foro Italico giugno '72 / Foro Italico June '72
124 Negli anni d'oro / In the Golden Years
124 Ormai lo so / By Now I Know
126 Da quando / From When
126 Gli ex fascistoni di Ferrara / Ferrara's Ex-Fascists

130 A un'amica / To a Lady Friend
130 Invettiva / Invective
132 A un professore di filosofia / To a Professor of Philosophy
134 Conversazione letteraria / Literary Conversation
134 A un critico / To a Critic
136 A un altro critico / To Another Critic
136 A Franco Fortini / To Franco Fortini
138 Anche tu / You Too
138 Nudo / Naked
138 4 marzo '73 / 4 March '73
140 I due sangui / The Two Bloods
140 All'amata / To the Loved One
142 No non aggiungerò / No I'll not Add
142 All'addiaccio / In the Open
144 Da Hofmannsthal / From Hofmannsthal
144 L'ho già detto / I've Already Said It
146 Mi chiedi perché mai e quando / You Ask Me Whyever and When
146 La cuginetta cattolica / My Little Catholic Cousin
148 Dai giornali / From the Newspapers
150 Al telefono / On the Phone
150 Rolls Royce / Rolls Royce
154 Promenade des Anglais / Promenade des Anglais
154 A letto / In Bed
156 Indovinello / Guessing Game
158 Lettera / Letter
162 Ninfa rivisitata / Ninfa Revisited
164 Le leggi razziali / The Racial Laws
166 Alla periferia / On the Outskirts
168 Di profilo / In Profile
168 Arrivo mia madre non sta bene / I Arrive My Mother's Not Well
170 Storia di famiglia / Family History
176 Davvero cari non saprei dirvelo / Really My Dears I Wouldn't Know How
176 La bocca / My Mouth
178 Santa Severa / Santa Severa
178 Isola Bisentina / Isola Bisentina
180 Molto pacatamente / Very Calmly
182 Dalla Sicilia / From Sicily

182 Danse macabre / Danse Macabre
184 Villino tricamere / Three-Bedroom Cottage
184 Per scherzo e per gioco / As a Joke and for Fun
186 Carta igienica / Toilet Paper
186 Salto di Fondi / Salto di Fondi
186 Forte Antenne / Forte Antenne
188 Bocca Trabaria / Bocca Trabaria
188 Tennis Club / Tennis Club
190 Odradek / Odradek
190 Passo veloce come il vento / I Go by Quickly Like the Wind
192 Les adieux / Les Adieux
192 Sul Pollino / On the Pollino
194 Lo so quel che significa / I Know What It Means
194 Di ritorno da Bucarest / Returning from Bucharest
196 Saturnia / Saturnia
196 In memoria / In Memory
198 Per una macchiolina / For a Little Spot
198 La Porta Rosa / Porta Rosa
202 Ars dictandi / Ars Dictandi
202 Valzer / Waltz
204 In capelli / Bareheaded
204 I grandi / The Grown-Ups
212 Marg / Marg
216 Parafrasando Engels / Paraphrasing Engels

IN GRAN SEGRETO / IN GREAT SECRET

I
222 Attenti! / Careful!
222 Vigilia di festa / Holiday Eve
224 A Momi / To Momi
224 Tale e quale / Exactly Like
226 A Natalia Ginzburg / To Natalia Ginzburg
226 Alla stessa / To the Same
226 A un letterato / To a Literary Man
228 Allo stesso / To the Same
228 Muore un'epoca / An Era Dies

230 Orly / Orly
232 Congedo / Farewell
232 Sangue e buio / Blood and Dark
232 Da Villon / From Villon
234 I congiurati / The Conspirators
234 Piazza Indipendenza / Piazza Indipendenza
236 Al critico d'un rotocalco / To a Magazine Critic
238 Quartiere Salario / Quartiere Salario
238 Campagna romana / Roman Countryside
238 Dove vivi? / Where Do You Live?
240 In collera col più grande amico / Angry with His Best Friend
240 A Franco Fortini / To Franco Fortini
242 Lo so perché / I Know Why
242 Se ho cambiato! / If I Have Changed!
244 Domenica mattina / Sunday Morning

II
248 Racconto / Story
248 15 giugno 1975 / 15 June 1975
250 Modena Nord / Modena Nord
250 A casa / At Home
252 In vacanza / On Holiday
252 Al telefono / On the Phone
254 Da Orazio / At Orazio's
254 In un orecchio / In One Ear
256 Ciampino / Ciampino
256 Da Alceo / From Alcaeus
256 Per cartolina / By Postcard
258 Ut pictura / Ut Pictura
262 Compleanno / Birthday
262 Campus / Campus
264 Visitando l'Indiana / Visiting Indiana
264 Per lettera / By Letter
266 A un giovane giornalista indiscreto / To an Indiscreet Young Journalist
268 Da Machado / From Machado
268 Shattuck Hotel / Shattuck Hotel
268 In gran segreto / In Great Secret

272 In Maremma / In Maremma
272 Parla il depresso / The Depressed Man Speaks
274 Padre e figlio / Father and Son
276 La capanna dell'ortolano / The Market-Gardener's Shed

III
282 Brindisi per l'anno nuovo / Toast for the New Year
282 Amori impossibile / Impossible Loves
284 Raccordo anulare / Raccordo Anulare
284 Da ballare / For Dancing
286 Negli spogliatoi del tennis / In the Tennis Changing Room
286 A mia figlia per il suo compleanno / To My Daughter for Her Birthday
286 Gli spettri (frammento) / The Ghosts (Fragment)
290 In sogno / In Dream

295 *Postscript*
301 *Notes*
339 *Bibliography*

Se tradurre è masochistico, tradurre poesia in poesia è disciplina da fachiri e da contorsionisti, da aspiranti suicidi come il mago Houdini. Farsi ingabbiare avvinti da mille catene, liberarsi e uscirne vivi per arrivare a porgere una trappola altrettanto bella, ardua, avvincente, in dono al lettore: è questa la sfida per il traduttore.

If translating is masochistic, translating poetry as poetry is a practice for fakirs and contortionists, for would-be-suicides like the escapologist Houdini. Having yourself imprisoned, entangled in a thousand chains, freeing yourself and getting out alive so as to offer an equally beautiful, difficult, captivating trap as a gift to the reader: this is the challenge for the translator.

Ottavio Fatica, *Lost in Translation*

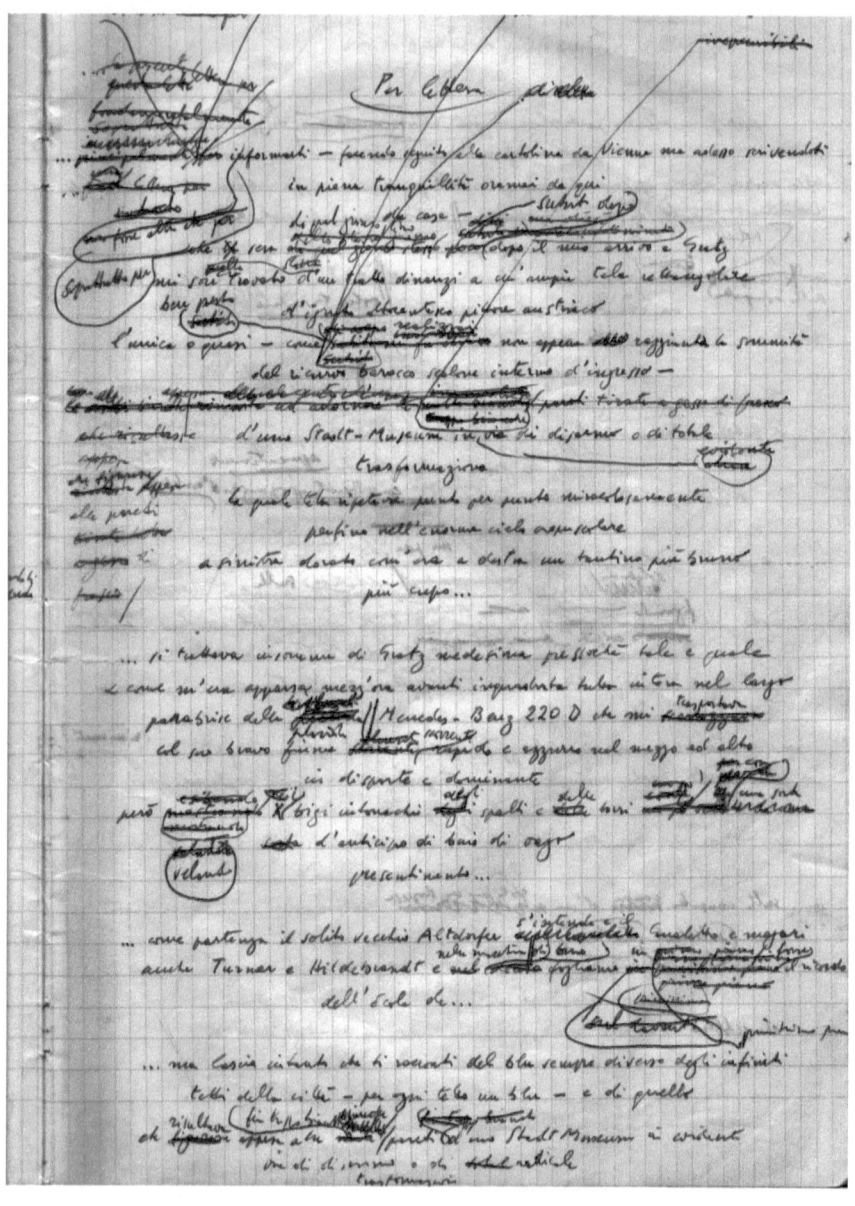

One of the manuscript versions of "Ut Pictura" (in *In gran segreto*) with numerous corrections and revisions, including the provisional title "Per lettera." (Fondo manoscritti Eredi Paola e Enrico Bassani)

Foreword
Giorgio Bassani's A Bigger Splash

Paola Bassani

Everything is connected in Giorgio Bassani's work, everything articulated through the first verses in *Poor Lovers' Stories* to the last in *Epitaph* and *In Great Secret* and through his entire lyrical and narrative production. And yet, there are twists, major fractures, starting with perhaps the most critical and poignant of all, the author's last production in verse, in which Bassani most likely reaches the apex of his artistic expression.

"Father," we children, still very young at the time and whom he always considered among his first readers and confidants, "why in these poems do you keep taking us to cemeteries, why this passion of yours for tombstones?" we would ask in an apparently light and absent-minded tone but in truth, very concerned. In an even lighter and more distracted tone, thus avoiding any real explanation, he would answer: "That's how... I like it, I found my way..."

It would be – as we know now – his last. His way as a man, of course, but also above all his way as an artist, leading him to the most perfect, absolute and at the same time most unsettling expression of his creation.

Despite his frantic will to live, to immerse himself in reality, something that always distinguished the man and artist my father was, despite his passionate struggle in the world and the civic and moral commitment that cost him so much, despite the urgency to give voice to the past in rich and constructive terms, the dialogue with death – primarily with his own – represents the central theme of his inspiration.

But never before did this dialogue become so intimate and persistent as in the poems of *Epitaph* and *In Great Secret*, written during the 1970s and early 1980s, giving way to absolutely new and unsettling expressive solutions.

Actually, already in *The Heron*, released in 1968, the dialogue with death takes on an entirely different shape. The *no man's land* evoked in the novel, the desolate land that opens up just outside Ferrara and which Edgardo Limentani travels and measures in vain, is a large, immense cemetery: the world's cemetery. But the *no man's land* of *The Heron* is above all America – New York, Indiana, California, and Ontario – which Bassani had assiduously visited since the early 1960s, and where he had many friends and taught several times. The *no man's land*, so dear to the writer now, and which inspires in him a sort of anxiety, an obsession for cemeteries, feeds above all on the atmosphere and taste – primarily on a figurative level – dominant in the United States at the time.

As we know, Nicolas De Staël's *Nu Couché* published on the cover of Bassani's novel *The Garden of the Finzi-Continis*, despite being chosen by his publisher, fully satisfied the writer (in an interview, he offered the following penetrating comment: "She is a woman waiting"); yet beyond the painting of a Nicolas De Staël now, above all, there remain the images offered by *pop art* as stimulus for the author's imagination.

In *The Heron*, as we know (and Bassani himself was the first to emphasize it), the influence of a certain French writing then in vogue, the *école du regard*, was absolutely crucial. In Bassani's later poetic collections, *Epitaph* and *In Great Secret*, the dialogue with this writing, though present, weakens, becomes less incisive, and the general orientation leads elsewhere: here, in my opinion, the predominant and therefore more productive and creative graft is offered precisely by *pop art*. To put it plainly in the style of Giorgio Bassani, a disciple of the philosopher Benedetto Croce and art historian Roberto Longhi, his last poems are a "critical essay" on *pop art*.

"Here," my father wrote to his assistant and dear friend Bruna Lanaro from Bloomington in 1976, "time passes very slowly. I live in a small town made up almost exclusively of cottages with backyards, pretty enough, taking them one by one, but all together, rather funereal. At the center of this small-town encampment, a complex of large buildings in a style between Neo-Gothic and E.U.R., where, among the trees, the actual and true university city is located. I live there. And in practice, I never go beyond the limit of the so-called 'campus.' A great bore." Bloomington is for him, then, a cemetery with grave-cottages next to each other. A very precise and at the same time hallucinated, fluctuating, and obsessive reality, much like Andy Warhol's or David Hockney's or the last Bacon paintings (though in Bacon – as indeed in my father – the representation very often borders on the tragic and desperate)...

Bloomington's anonymous and funereal cottages, therefore, as well as the image of the "Iron Detroit" in "By Letter," or the "white parallelepiped" of "Shattuck Hotel," which stands tall on the edge of San Francisco, all offer, in

Bassani's poems, "the illusion of being able straight away to start the sweetest / and longest / possible sleep" (in "In Great Secret").

But the places arousing in Bassani this sweet and at the same time obsessive image of death can be far more intimate and familiar. It is in fact in his Maratea, between Cersuta, Filocaio, and the harbor, by the sea or perhaps near some swimming pool in the area, that Bassani builds his California and responds in such a personal way to David Hockney, for example, and to his hallucinated *A Bigger Splash*. The characters evoked here, in Maratea and its surroundings, but also elsewhere, in completely anonymous areas, such as the bespectacled and "half-bald" owner of the "Arabianizing three-bedroom cottage" (in "Three-Bedroom Cottage"), or the "tall and thin / unknown forty-year-old lingering this side of the threshold / to an electrician's or body shop's shutter / half bald in blue jeans" (in "On the Outskirts"), are mannequin-figures, serial figures, just as David Hockney's, or Tom Wesselmann's or Andy Warhol's, they are ghosts immersed in their impassive and absurd quotidian lives.

But that's not enough. Like the artists just mentioned and many others from the same circle, Bassani too in his last poems wants hypnotically to convince us of the non-symbolic, but effective, absolutely tangible, and real presence of the things he evokes. He wants to convey the sense of their accumulation, of their ruthless and absurd repetition and massification. And he does it with graves. Ultimately, the graphic shape, the peculiar metric system he adopted, the funeral inscriptions, do nothing but visually restore the shape of the tombstone, of the marble "large white open page" (in "Waltz") within which words are inscribed and in front of which, as readers, we suddenly find ourselves. At the same time, this structure allows us to capture the object-tomb in its entirety, in its general composition, i.e., in terms of perspective, material, volume and weight.

Tombs, therefore, next to each other, repetitive, all the same masses lost in the vastness of the world, useless objects also for consumption: Bassani, poet but painter as well, sculptor, architect, and photographer, shows them in their hypnotic and suffocating presence together with their chilling estrangement.

Inside them, however, the dead are more alive than ever. They are "Dantesque" dead, waiting (like the woman in Nicolas De Staël's *Nu Couché*) to be freed, to emerge into the light, finally to return among us. The lyrics of Bassani's last phase actually express the opposite of a taste for accumulation, for mortuary massification, for the photographic and serial nothingness, all motifs so dear – we repeat – to *pop art*. Bassani's lyrics bring to the stage stories and characters full of extraordinary tension and vitality. It is the strength of poetry that performs this miracle, it is poetry which is able to resurrect those who are no longer with us.

The miracle of this resurrection takes on truly palpable substance, being translated into entirely visual terms, especially when one considers the particularly suggestive handwriting of certain Bassani's manuscripts. Take, for example, one of the drafts of "By Letter" (published in *In Great Secret* with a different title, "Ut Pictura" [p. 14]). Here the pen corrections become sparks, gushes, bursts of life that suddenly emerge from the tombstone-page, peeking and pressing from behind the dense grain of the text, in short, they are voices calling us and imploring "we're here!".

These revisions are in fact entirely different from those in his first poetic collections (as the examples of "Easter Supper" [p. 306-307] or "Villa Glori" [p. 311] illustrate). In them the appearance and handwriting are much more static and circumscribed, similar in this to the revisions in the prose manuscripts.

Gushes, sparks, leaps of life, then: Giorgio Bassani in his last poems realizes his own very personal *Bigger Splash*.

Welcome back to life, dear Father, welcome back among us!

Translators' Note

For anglophone readers it has been possible for quite some time now to gain a good sense of Giorgio Bassani's career as a novelist, the various renderings of his fiction culminating in 2018 with the publication of *The Novel of Ferrara*, their integrated edition, translated by Jamie McKendrick. However, the situation for his poetry has been very different, and apart from a handful of poems available in various anthologies, magazines and one long-out-of-print small press edition of later work, a reader without Italian would have little to go on to construct a full picture of Bassani's creative achievement. The purpose of *The Collected Poems*, the first translation in English of Bassani's authorized poetic oeuvre, is to give readers access to the distinctly contrasting styles of poetry that he wrote early and late in life, and to allow readers of Bassani's fiction to place his prose oeuvre within the framing publications of the early and late collections of poems.

The first of Bassani's novels to be translated into English was also his first, *Gli occhiali d'oro* (*The Gold-Rimmed Spectacles*), which appeared in 1960 only two years after the original, in both Great Britain and the United States, translated by Isabel Quigly. After the *Gli occhiali d'oro*, Quigly translated *Storie ferraresi* (*A Prospect of Ferrara*) in 1962 and *Il giardino dei Finzi-Contini* (*The Garden of the Finzi-Continis*) in 1965. With the exception of *Gli occhiali d'oro*, William Weaver then translated all of Bassani's fiction: *L'airone* (*The Heron*) (1970), *Cinque storie ferraresi* (*Five Stories of Ferrara*) (1971), *Dietro la porta* (*Behind the Door*) (1972), *L'odore del fieno* (*The Smell of Hay*) (1975), and *Il giardino dei Finzi-Contini* (1977). As mentioned above, the English poet Jamie McKendrick has now completed an entirely new translation of these six key volumes.

By contrast, during the same period, only a few of his poems have been attempted, not only in English but also in other languages. Until now there have been no other collected editions of his poetry in translation (the recent French edition, *Poèmes*, is a selection [Gallot 2021]). Such English translations as exist are scattered in periodicals and anthologies, often difficult to locate. Readers interested in these previous renderings will find them collected in Roberta Antognini's "Traduzione e ricezione dell'opera poetica di Giorgio Bassani in Nord America" (Antognini 2020a; 2020b). What's more, his poems' being so hard to find has made their impact and influence in the English-speaking world very limited indeed. In our Introduction below we include an account of the tenuous route by which Bassani's work came to Peter Robinson's attention in England during the latter quarter of the twentieth century. Lately, however, a new interest in his poetry has resulted in plentiful scholarship (see Bibliography), culminating in 2021 in the annotated edition by Anna Dolfi, one of his most eminent scholars (Dolfi 2021). In light of this fresh attention to his oeuvre as a poet and given his interest and involvement in translations of his work, Bassani would surely have felt vindicated.

For this bilingual volume of Giorgio Bassani's poems, we follow the texts as they appear in the first collected edition, *In rima e senza* (In Rhyme And Without) (Milan: Mondadori, 1982), and as reproduced in Giorgio Bassani, *Opere* (Milan: Mondadori, 1998), which "represents the final considered arrangement of his entire poetry" (Dolfi 2021: 363). We have omitted *Traducendo* (Translating), the third section of *In rima*, which contains versions from the French of Paul-Jean Toulet and René Char and the English of Robert Louis Stevenson. The most recent and complete translation of the fiction to which we refer is Giorgio Bassani, *The Novel of Ferrara*, trans. Jamie McKendrick (New York: Norton, 2018). We have provided notes for those poems where readers would benefit from some contextual explanation. They are much indebted to those by Anna Dolfi in Dolfi 2021. We have also made grateful reference for our Chronology to the outline of his life on the Fondazione Bassani website, to which we refer readers for further information and the bibliography: www.giorgiobassani.it/cronologia.htm. All translations from Italian are ours unless otherwise stated.

Given that there are not many Italian poets from the twentieth century whose work has been fully translated into English, we are particularly grateful for the help we have received in being able to bring this project to completion. Our special thanks go to Paola Bassani, the poet's daughter, president of the Fondazione Bassani, whose generous, unwavering commitment and enthusiastic support have been invaluable. We would like to thank Marcello Azzi, Luigi

Ballerini, Valerio Cappozzo, Anna Dolfi, Antonella Guarnieri, Gaia Litrico, Berardo Paradiso, Amanda Thornton, and Ornella Trevisan for their contributions to this work. We would also like to express our gratitude to Gianluca Rizzo of Agincourt Press for the care and attention given to our typescript by a publisher who continues to believe in the lasting power and value of poetry. Finally, we are grateful to all the various translators of Bassani's poetry, whose work we have read and carefully studied.

A few of the translations collected here have appeared in earlier versions in the following publications: Peter Robinson, *The Great Friend and Other Translated Poems* (Tonbridge, Kent: Worple Press, 2002); *The Faber Book of 20th Century Italian Poems*, ed. Jamie McKendrick (London: Faber & Faber, 2004); *The FGS Book of 20th-Century Italian Poetry*, ed. Geoffrey Brock (New York: Farrar, Straus & Giroux, 2012); *Raceme* no. 5 (Autumn 2016); *University of Reading Creative Arts Anthology* no. 10 (June 2017); and Antognini 2020b. A slightly longer version of the Foreword by Paola Bassani in its original Italian was first published as the Premessa to Giorgio Bassani, *Poesie complete* (Dolfi 2021).

This publication was made possible in part by a grant from the Fondazione Bassani and from the Mellon Foundation Career and Curricular Transitions Endowment Fund. We are most grateful to both the Fondazione Bassani and Vassar College for their generous support.

Roberta Antognini and Peter Robinson, June 2023

Introduction

1

Giorgio Bassani, internationally celebrated as a novelist, more than once commented on the importance of his poetry, both for himself and for his work as a whole. Indeed, he considered himself above all a poet and in the course of his life felt the need to remind his readers: "Now, I am quite well known as a novelist, but less so as a lyric poet" (Mosena 2015: 77). In "Down There, at the End of the Corridor," the final chapter to *The Smell of Hay*, the last volume in *The Novel of Ferrara*, he recounts the difficult genesis of "The Stroll Before Dinner," one of his most famous short stories, and explains the creative struggle he had with it: "wasn't I after all a poet?" (*The Novel of Ferrara*: 737). This can mean both that he began as a poet and that, even when writing in the prose for which he is better known, he has never been anything but a poet.

What's more, in the volume's very last sentence the author states that to continue to write beyond his third-person short stories he had to "try to surface from his lair" and "dare finally to call himself 'I'" (*The Novel of Ferrara*: 741). The first-person subject that he would include in his next three novels is the young poet who in the fourth part of *The Garden of the Finzi-Continis*, chapter 7, cites Apollinaire and Ungaretti, discusses Montale, and is accused of "second-hand Crepuscularism" by his friend Malnate. He recites to him "a poem of mine" in a series of conversations about poetry, literature, and politics occurring in cityscapes that re-evoke those of these same early poems (*The Novel of Ferrara*: 426-427). This pointedly draws attention, then, to the first emergence of his poetic oeuvre, and its necessary connection to the prose fiction.

Indeed, the publishing history of the early Bassani focuses primarily on his poetry: "between 1942 and 1947, the years in which I'd move from Ferrara to Rome, I had almost exclusively composed poems" (*The Novel of Ferrara*: 736). After the 1940 collection of short stories published under the pseudonym of

Giacomo Marchi, *Una città di pianura* (A City of the Plain), his first published books were collections of verse: in 1945, *Storie dei poveri amanti e altri versi* (Poor Lovers' Stories and Other Verses), in 1947, *Te lucis ante (1946-47)*, and in 1951, *Un'altra libertà* (Another Freedom). It was only in 1956 that his short stories, *Cinque storie ferraresi* (*Five Stories of Ferrara*), appeared, followed in 1958 by his first novel, *Gli occhiali d'oro* (*The Gold-Rimmed Spectacles*). And, in his life's work, it is poetry that frames the more celebrated prose, for, after the 1972 *L'odore del fieno* (*The Smell of Hay*), Bassani would no longer write fiction, and his final two volumes of new work would be poetry: *Epitaffio* (Epitaph) in 1974 and *In gran segreto* (In Great Secret) in 1978. Then, having brought together his narrative production under the title *Il romanzo di Ferrara* (*The Novel of Ferrara*), its definitive edition appearing in 1980, Bassani collected his entire poetic production, early and late, under the title *In rima e senza* (In Rhyme and Without), which appeared in 1982. This volume established his poetic oeuvre as shaped around the two distinct styles and periods in which it had emerged: 1939-1951 for the *In rima* section, and 1973-1981 for *Senza*. The more than twenty years separating these two phases of poetic activity are those in which Bassani composed and revised his series of fictions.

The widely accepted centrality of Bassani's fiction has recently been underlined with the 2018 publication, by Norton in the US and Penguin Books in the UK, of *The Novel of Ferrara*. Published separately over the years, the author's prose works have now been presented in an edition described on the Penguin website as "Bassani's six classic books, collected for the first time in English as the epic masterwork they were intended to be." At the heart of this sequence of publications is *The Garden of the Finzi-Continis*, the book which cemented his international reputation, not least when discovered by an American audience thanks to Vittorio De Sica's Oscar-winning film of 1970.

Yet the significance of poetry in Bassani's life and literary formation can be sensed by reflecting on the ways his most famous novel revisit and elaborate both the overall atmosphere and particular moments evoked in his early poems. Also of cardinal importance for an understanding of Bassani's works is the fact that this early poetry was composed during key years for his life and writing: those which included the Racial Laws introduced by Mussolini's fascist government in the summer and autumn of 1938; then the earlier, superficially successful period of Italy's war as an ally of Nazi Germany leading to the fatal setbacks, for that cause, of late 1942, the invasion of Sicily in July 1943 and Mussolini's fall from power. This moment would have a direct impact on Bassani's fate because the collapse of the regime would lead to his release from prison in Ferrara, after an incarceration of three months following his arrest in May for anti-fascist activities.

The Italian leader's rescue by German paratroopers from Gran Sasso, and the establishment of the puppet Salò Republic on Lake Garda, and with it the years of, in effect, civil war from September 1943 until April 1945, brought in the worst times of all for the fate of the Jewish population in Northern Italy, and among them some of the writer's relatives. As noted above, Bassani's first books of poetry were published in Rome during the immediate post-war, a time when revelations about the extent of the attempted final solution for the Jews of Europe emerged, initiating the long aftermath of those events, an aftermath within which Bassani's oeuvre in both poetry and prose takes its rightful place.

2

Reflecting on that moment of his first poetic inspiration in "Postscript", his important self-commentary published as an afterword to his early poems in the 1963 volume *L'alba ai vetri* (Dawn at the Panes), Bassani contrasts his own mood at that moment with the state of the world: "The spring of '42! Stalingrad, El Alamein, and the future uncertain, dark... Even so, despite everything, life has never again appeared so beautiful to me, so beautiful and tender as then" (p. 295). The poems from *Poor Lovers' Stories* (1945) are largely inspired by the period leading up to May 1943, though a number of them are touched with a knowledge of what the Racial Laws indicated was to come. "Easter Supper," for instance, which would be returned to in prose for *The Garden of the Finzi-Continis* (for further details, see note to this poem). Similarly, poems such as "Towards Ferrara" have the curious air of a haunted idyll, a first draft, as it were, not only for the doomed pleasures and obsessions of his most famous novel but also the train journeys to and from Bologna central to *The Gold-Rimmed Spectacles*.

These poems were followed by *Te Lucis Ante 1946-47* (1947), whose title sequence, along with "From Prison," centers upon the months from May 1943 to Mussolini's fall in July when Bassani was imprisoned in Ferrara for his anti-fascism. Released on the collapse of the government, the writer was able, extraordinarily enough, during the summer before General Badoglio's cessation of hostilities with the Allies, to marry Valeria Sinigallia and have a two-week honeymoon at Marina di Ravenna. Leaving Ferrara, he made it first to Florence, where he lived under the assumed name of Giacomo Marchi, then

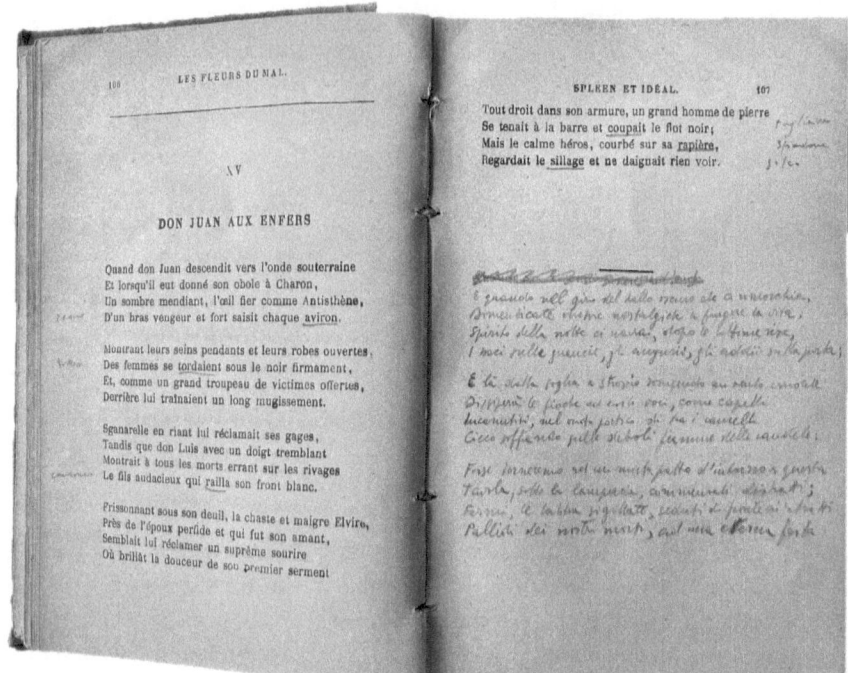

A draft of "Cena di Pasqua" ("Easter Supper") from *Storie dei poveri amanti*, c. 1942, in Charles Baudelaire, *Le fleurs du mal* (Paris: Calmann-Lévy, [no date]). (Fondazione Bassani, Ferrara)

to Rome – experiences which, while prompting some of the brief lyrics in his early collections, pointed towards the need to explore those occasions and their consequences in the more capacious forms of his fiction.

In his "Postscript", Bassani would evoke that moment of early poetic production by citing the great art historian from Bologna University: "Critics are born: poets emerge – Roberto Longhi said. In the spring of 1942, the first impulse to write verses came to me from art, from culture, more than from life and reality" (p. 295). This may be true enough, given the life and reality surrounding the poet early in that year of the war, but the poems he wrote also evoke details from his immediate surroundings, whether it be a train journey from Bologna towards Ferrara, a restaurant at Porta Reno, the rural life of the Po valley, or the seaside of the Adriatic coast. If his poetry was emerging marginally in extremely uncertain times, it was also making a first attempt at the scenery that would feature in much of his life's work. As with most of Bassani's writings, the early poetry reached its final form through a series of publications that reveal a degree of evolving uncertainty about details of the work and how it should properly sound.

Reviewing *Storie dei poveri amanti e altri versi* (Poor Lovers' Stories and Other Verses), in *Il Mondo* (Florence, 1 Dec 1945), Eugenio Montale recognized Bassani's combination of an inter-war style learned from various crepuscular, impressionist and hermetic poets, and an impulse to narrative that had already resulted in the stories for his first collection *Una città di pianura* (A City of the Plain): "In him, then," Montale wrote, "the prose writer lets us know about himself even in the weave of the verse which flees every sonorous abstraction and takes advantage of a language that is realistic, but which never contradicts the tonal possibility of lyric." The future Nobel laureate then correlates this early style to the landscapes in the Po valley where it first arose:

> And Giorgio Bassani reveals himself in perfect possession of an instrument that he hasn't invented but which shows itself sympathetic to his possibilities; he has knowledge of caesuras, of false rhymes, and of assonances; always knows how to lift from the level of flat prose the wearier and more precarious cadence. And particularly adept this artistry seems at low intonations when he comes to make use of them to give us motifs and pictures of his Ferrara countryside.
>
> (Montale 1996: 638)

Bassani's early poems conjure up that painterly landscape, the temperature and sensibility of the Po valley in summer, within unusually constraining forms, quietly expressive as they are of other surrounding constrictions, so that the packed capaciousness of their paired quatrains contain a perpetual struggle between a vividly prose-like descriptiveness and rhyme-punctuated rhythmic hesitancy – which is what contributes so much to giving these early poems their unique timbre and flavour. (For Bassani's response to this review, see "Postscript", p. 297.)

With the exception of the unusually expansive "Valle dell'Aniene" and "From Prison," the compacted lyrics in the *Te Lucis Ante* sequence, and the poems written in the earliest post-war years develop a style that would grow ever more laconically compressed, with its narrative elements reduced under the pressure of circumstances, as if this mode, widely shared among poets of the inter-war period, was itself compelled towards silence. And it is perhaps that fate for this style which will have prompted the eloquence first provided by the development of his fiction. Some ten years later, Bassani reissued his early poetry, again with adjustments, in *L'alba ai vetri* (Dawn at the Panes), a collection of poems dated 1942-1951, which appeared from Einaudi in 1963. The definitive 1982 version of these works, the *In rima* (*In Rhyme*) section of what is in effect a collected early poems, was largely an editorial restoration in which some of the poems excluded from the 1963 edition were brought back, and further revisions made to some of the texts. The early poetry can thus be seen both to establish the character of his major themes (with intuitions of the persona that would largely narrate them), and to make first sketches of the landscapes, the cityscapes, and some of the events that would take narrative form in such novels as *The Gold-Rimmed Spectacles* and *The Garden of the Finzi-Continis*, works in which the narrator allows himself to be referred to as a poet and combines his own inspiration with that of his fictional narrator: "'Like truth itself / like her, sad and beautiful...': these first two verses of a poem I never finished, though they were written much later, in Rome, soon after the war, refer back to that Micòl of August 1939, and the way I saw her then" (*The Novel of Ferrara*: 416). Never finished or not, these lines, referring to the heroine in *The Garden of the Finzi-Continis*, appear at the start of the final stanza to part 16 of the "Te Lucis Ante" sequence. Thus, aside from the interest of these early poems in their own right, they form an essential and founding element in the work of this major twentieth-century Italian writer.

3

Yet the Bassani who concluded *The Smell of Hay* and his collected fiction by daring "finally to call himself 'I'," (*The Novel of Ferrara*: 741) deploying the poet that he was back then to enable his major fiction, this writer had already begun to compose the poems of his final two collections. In dramatic contrast to the early verse, the poetry he completed after having published his key fictional works takes the form of a freely lineated postscript to the themes he had established and explored over the previous quarter century. The two volumes, *Epitaffio* (Epitaph) and *In gran segreto* (In Great Secret), collected under the title *Senza* (Without), are direct and telling, in both senses, whereas the earlier work is oblique and showing. The poetic diction of the early verse was carefully selected to sustain a tone in evoking the landscapes and people of Ferrara and the Po valley, to characterize the experience of imprisonment in terms that remained all but choked by that experience, or to initiate fleeting encounters and intimately elegiac reflections in the Roman environs of the early post-war years.

By contrast, the later poems are colloquially flexible with no clear limit to the vocabulary that could be employed.

Individual pieces range from short, satiric epigrams, to extended evocations, posthumous returns, family histories, touristic encounters, often combining a strange nostalgia with an unflinching memory. They are the work of a survivor, with his share of survivor guilt, also coming to terms with the inevitability of his own eventual death. The tones of voice in these late poems can be dryly sardonic, as in his *risposte* to Natalia Ginzburg's negative review of *Epitaffio* ("To Natalia Ginzburg," "To the Same," "On Holiday"). They can be fondly paternal, as in the poem for his daughter Paola's birthday ("To My Daughter for Her Birthday"), or wittily tender, as in "Marg." They can be angrily unforgiving, as when he addresses the ex-fascists of Ferrara ("Ferrara's Ex-Fascists"), and they can comment on the literary world ("To Franco Fortini," "The Conspirators"), or report on his visits as a literary celebrity to the United States, as in "Campus." These late poems of an established literary figure, with their variety of colloquial tones, greater range of diction, more unpredictable states of mind and feelings, add up to a multi-faceted self-portrait of the writer in later life.

Introducing a selection of Bassani's work for *Poeti italiani del secondo Novecento 1945-1995* Stefano Giovanardi observes:

> If the layout of the verses is constantly "in epigraph," as if to stress the solemnity like *monumentum aere perennius* of the components (a choice in itself not devoid of irony), the style assumes by contrast much more prosaic forms: obviously not only from the absence of rhyme, but also the decidedly "atonal" versification which dilutes the rhythmic cadences all but finally rendering them imperceptible, and which then powerfully alludes to a sort of slow dissolution of the poetic institution, coinciding dramatically with the exhaustion of narrative force, in a parabola destined unfailingly for silence.
> (Cucchi & Giovanardi 1995: 753)

This highly suggestive interpretation of the implications in Bassani's design for his later poems nonetheless underplays the ambivalence of these gestures, an ambivalence whereby what has been called "anti-poetry" with its atonal free-verse rhythms, aversion to rhyme, to narrative, and noble feeling, nonetheless evokes the institutions of poetry by their very absence. It is also far from obvious that the narrative force in Bassani is exhausted in the longer poems gathered in these last two collections, poems such as "Rolls Royce," "The Grown-Ups," or "The Market-Gardener's Shed." Here too, and not for the first or last time, the inevitable pull toward silence calls forth an unusually intense burst of eloquence.

Bassani in 1956, with Pier Paolo Pasolini and Niccolò Gallo, on the occasion of the Strega Prize for *Cinque storie ferraresi*. (Archivio RCS)

Yet one way to see Bassani's early and later poetry talking to each other, as it were, would be to note the different ways both kinds of poetry combine a rhythmic intensification of speech with a differently inflected narrative thread. In the earlier poetry the forward movement is syntactic and rhythmical, and the narrative component implied in the chosen detail – the hands and lips of the young lovers in "Towards Ferrara," the songs of workers on their bicycles in "Pontelagoscuro," the servant girls called from their beds in "Variation on the

Preceding Theme," the restaurant tables in "Evening at Porta Reno," and stretches of farmland or beach in "Clair de Lune" and "Emilia." In the later poems, it is the urgency of telling, of narrating, which drives the poems forward, as if dragging moraines of imagery, evocation, and description along with it, as can be felt in "Letter" or "Family History."

The role of these poems, written after the completion of his fictional oeuvre, draws upon the new freedoms of expression won by Pop Art, as Paola Bassani has suggested in her Foreword, or the Confessional and Beat poets in America – while their centered layout may also have been drawn from such examples as the poetry of Michael McClure. By contrast with the dramatized indirection and implication of fictional narrative, these poems speak directly to issues that figure centrally in the fiction, as for example in his address to "Ferrara's Ex-Fascists." Here too, the shift in conventions as regards the limit between public and private life redrawn in mid-century anglophone writing may have encouraged Bassani to comment on his affective life, his literary reputation, family history, and friendships with colleagues such as Franco Fortini and Mario Soldati in ways that his earlier styles of writing poetry would not have allowed. These later poems are also, then, an unusually frank recapitulation and development of themes that had engaged him throughout his writing life.

4

Producing a poetic oeuvre in two such contrasting styles presents an unusual challenge to its translators, especially if the task of translating poetry is agreed to require, despite the usual taunts about its impossibility, both a fidelity to the sense of the original and a commitment to representing in the second language the experience of the original as being one of reading poetry. For then the challenge is to find means in English for representing the experience first of a poetry committed to the styles developed during the interwar years in Italy, one which has its own rhythmical, syntactic, and stanzaic conventions, such as those sketched by Montale in his review of Bassani's first publication. Secondly, translators need to develop a style for the "anti-poetry" of the final two collections with their sustained, yet eccentrically unpredictable rhythmic impulse, their direct and often outspoken range of tones, from the sardonic and satiric to the fond, the elegiac, and familial.

In this endeavor, we follow in the footsteps of some distinguished translators. A fragment of the poem "Non piangere" ("Don't Weep") from *Storie dei poveri amanti e altri versi* (1945) was most probably the first English translation of a text by Bassani. It appeared in an essay published in 1946 and was the work of the Scottish poet and writer Hamish Henderson. After this fragment, the next of Bassani's works to be translated into English, together with the short story, "Storia d'amore" ("Love Story") (the future "Lida Mantovani" and the first narrative in the first book of *The Novel of Ferrara*), were once again poems: eight translated by a young William Weaver, "Valle dell'Aniene", "Dalla prigione ("From Prison"), "Vide Cor Meum," "Per un quadro di Morandi" (For a Picture by Morandi"), "Ars Poetica", "L'alba ai vetri" ("Dawn at the Panes"), "Sogno" ("Dream"), and "Commiato" ("Leave-Taking"). Both "Love Story" and these poems appeared in *An Anthology of New Italian Writers* in 1950, a compilation from the magazine *Botteghe Oscure* aimed at the British and American markets. This international, multilingual literary review was founded and owned by Marguerite Caetani, an American-born publisher, journalist, art collector, patron of the arts, and aristocrat upon marriage to Roffredo Caetani, prince of Bassiano. Bassani worked in Rome at *Botteghe Oscure* as the Italian editor for as long as the publication existed (1948-1960). *New Italian Writers* was favorably received and opened the way for a wider circulation of contemporary Italian literature in the Anglophone world. For Bassani, it was the first of his many encounters with an American audience culminating in the 1970s with his frequent visits to the United States and Canada, where he was a visiting professor in various institutions (see Chronology, and Bibliography for details).

One outcome of these sojourns across the Atlantic was the appearance, more than thirty years after the *Anthology of New Italian Writers*, of twelve poems (all from the two later collections, *Epitaffio* and *In gran segreto*) gathered in *Rolls Royce and Other Poems*, edited and translated by Francesca Valente and published by Aya Press, Toronto, in 1982, with an authoritative introduction by Northrop Frye and the collaboration of Valente with two distinguished Canadian poets, Greg Gatenby and Irving Layton (to which must be added the supervision of Portia Prebys, the poet's last companion, and Bassani himself). These two publications – both long out of print, featuring just a few poems from, respectively, the *In Rhyme* and *Without* phases of his work – were until now among the few places Anglophone readers might go to get an idea of Giorgio Bassani, the poet.

For our book, the challenge of representing both Bassani's poetic styles has been addressed by collaborators who came at his oeuvre from quite distinct directions. Peter had encountered the early poetry in his middle twenties through reading versions of two early poems rendered by Donald Davie in the "Los Angeles Poems" section of his 1972 *Collected Poems*. A graduate student at the University of Cambridge in the late 1970s, he was attempting to write poetry and, as a part of that apprenticeship, to translate where he could from French and Italian. Over the following twenty years and more, he would occasionally encounter other early poems by Bassani, making versions of a few for a projected anthology of translations that were not to see the light of day.

Then, in August 2015, inspired to write a sequence called "The Ringstead Poems" (Robinson 2017) deriving from the fate of the British poet John Cornford, killed fighting for the loyalists in the Spanish Civil War in December 1936, and conscious not only that a year hence would be the eightieth anniversary of the Spanish Civil War's outbreak but also the centenary of Giorgio Bassani's birth, he took as model the formal repertoire of his early poetry – the eight-line landscape pieces, sonnets, and slightly longer quatrain poems, with varying degrees of rhyme – as a means for organizing the flood of material emerging. Moreover, because Bassani had proved such a prompt to his inspiration, Peter decided to include a poem in the series that would be an acknowledged imitation. Then, out of gratitude for the outcome and aware of the approaching centenary, he began translating more of those early poems along with the "Postscript" to Bassani's 1963 collection *L'alba ai vetri* (Dawn at the Panes) – publishing some of this material obscurely in two very small English magazines.

Yet it was thanks to these publications, both extremely hard to find, though one advertised on the internet, that, out of the blue, he received a message from Roberta, an Italianist at Vassar specializing in Petrarch, requesting to see scans of the relevant pages. She had an interest in translation, had collaborated on versions from Amelia Rosselli, and was researching an essay on the translation and reception of Bassani's poetry in English, which would be accompanied by an anthology of translations published in *Dal particolare all'universale. I libri di poesia di Giorgio Bassani* (see Antognini 2020a; 2020b). By this point, Peter had a complete draft of the early poetry, and, in light of their discussions over a lunch in Zurich, they agreed to collaborate on a collected edition of Giorgio Bassani's verse.

Together they set about bringing their distinctive tastes and skills to rendering these markedly different ways of writing verse. The aim was to convey in English the qualities of both early and late work. To this end, the translations from *In rima* attempt to respect the rhythmical shaping of the rhymed quatrains that largely make up the formal resource employed by Bassani, finding rhymes and assonances where it is possible to combine them with a respect for the sense of the original, without any Quixotic attempt to match the rhymes where that would require a paraphrastic rewriting and a complete abandonment of the syntactic ordering of the Italian poems. The language of the originals with its careful sustaining of a measured tone was then calibrated in the translations to evoke an equivalent of that mid-century Italian poetic diction, but one nevertheless sensitive to the tones of contemporary English.

By contrast, translating the later poems has required finding an English which catches appropriately that greater range of tones, idioms, vocabularies, and rhythms. The last of these have been addressed by treating the freely lineated stanza, or verse paragraph, as the rhythmic unit, attempting to achieve a certain integrity for the individual lines linked together with flowing enjambments to produce a decided forward drive within unpredictable variations and evolutions. Bassani's manuscripts show that these poems were composed to have a centered layout and, while not always being able, for syntactical reasons, to follow the exact lineation of the originals, the translators have attempted, wherever possible, to respect it.

In this bilingual edition we offer translations that can be read as poems in their own right, with the aim of giving readers with no Italian an experience as analogous as possible to that of reading Bassani's originals. For readers with a little Italian, these translations can function as guides to the complexities which the poems themselves present. To readers more familiar with or fluent in Italian, we offer, along with a text of the complete authorized poetry, solutions to the challenges in how these poems can be rendered, always aware that there can be no definitive translation and that the readings offered by such a text almost always suggest other possible solutions to those very problems. We have provided informative notes on poems where necessary, indicating briefly, for instance, the locations of placenames and some information on persons addressed or evoked. We occasionally provide details of usage or reference that do not readily come over in translation, or other help where it is thought useful.

Commenting on translations from Luciano Erba that Peter made with the support of the poet and his wife Mimia, Matthew Reynolds in *The Poetry of Translation* observed that those versions "achieve the strangeness and complexity of poetry by interpreting as little as possible." In offering a bilingual edition of Giorgio Bassani's poetry, whether in translations or notes, we have tried to do the same. Nevertheless, translating involves tacit interpretation; but the translation, if it is to represent the poetics of the original, cannot take the form of an expansion or commentary explaining it. For that would be to take away one of the key experiences involved in reading such poems. Often the urge to translate arises from a need to understand a work, but, oddly enough, the outcome, if it is to be successful, has to imitate the experience of that encounter with the initial difficulty. Whatever else it achieves, a translation of modernist or hermetic poetry, or "anti-poetry" for that matter, must not remove that essential resistance to ready interpretation – because that is one of poetry's key resources as regards its inexhaustibility and thus its continuing value in survival.

Giorgio Bassani's work in poetry exemplifies an unusually sustained and varied trust in the expressive capacities of distinctive modes for composing verse. In doing so, it tests and extends poetry's ability to encapsulate lived moments and remembered conditions of both individual and collective lives, whether it be those of the twenty-six-year-old poet in Ferrara and environs, or the same writer's final, until recently uncollected, "The Old Man's Song", dated 4 October 1984 on the manuscript (Dolfi 2021: 321 and 616):

IL CANTO DEL VECCHIO

Canta il vecchio lo so lo
capisco
non c'è più tempo per avere
tempo
da
perdere

eppure sarebbe stato bello averne
svegliarsi una mattina e dirsi dunque
la amo dirle
girandomi dunque sì
ti
amo

THE OLD MAN'S SONG

The old man sings I know I
    get it
there's no time left to have
    time
    to
    lose

    yet it would be good to have some
awaking one morning and telling yourself well then
    I love her tell her
turning around well then yes
    I love
    you

The intimacy and directness of this late poem, its informality and improvised form, when placed next to the earliest work collected here, further illustrate a distinctively individual thread through the crisis and evolution of twentieth-century Italian poetry. In bringing together both these different seasons of his lyric impulse, Bassani didn't so much offer a transition from an outmoded style committed to the institutions of time-honored poetic formality to one superficially freed from those constraints, as rather invite readers to recognize the co-dependence of such ways of composing verse. In doing so, Giorgio Bassani's poetry summons us to open ourselves to the full range of the art's possibilities and, as both readers and writers, to ourselves take up and carry them forward. Just as in "To Momi" Bassani refers to "Poetry" with a capital P, addressing, in Italian, that feminine noun with the female pronoun "her," thus personifying it, so it's perhaps not fanciful to suggest that in "The Old Man's Song" the third-person love object at its close may be read, when this unnamed interlocutor is finally addressed by that second person pronoun, as the poet Bassani speaking to his last poem and to poetry itself.

Chronology

1916-1933 Giorgio Bassani is born in Bologna on 4 March 1916 into a wealthy family of Jewish origin resident in Ferrara for many generations. Giorgio's parents had met because Cesare Minerbi, the father of his mother Dora, was the Bassani family doctor. They married in 1915 and, besides Giorgio, had two further children, Paolo and Jenny. In Ferrara, where the writer would spend his childhood and adolescence, the family-owned house in via Cisterna del Follo 1 would be Bassani's home until 1943.

1934 Bassani enrolls at the University of Bologna. In studying literature, he breaks with family tradition: his father and both his grandparents were doctors. At university, he meets the poet Attilio Bertolucci, with whom he will maintain a lifelong friendship.

1935 In the autumn, attends the art historian Roberto Longhi's classes for the first time and establishes a deep and lasting friendship with him. Publishes his first short story, "III Classe" (Third Class) in the *Corriere Padano*.

1936 Publishes two other short stories in the *Corriere Padano*: "Nuvole e mare" (Clouds and the Sea) and "I mendicanti" (The Beggars).

1938 The imposition of the Racial Laws has an impact on his habits and acquaintances. "My father was Jewish, probably of Ashkenazi origin," recalls his daughter Paola, "but of secular faith. He considered himself first and foremost an Italian, an Italian like anyone else." And the writer Pietro Citati observes: "When he was rejected by all his Catholic friends, a wound opened in him that I believe has never healed." In "Ferrara's Ex-Fascists" (from *Epitaph*), Bassani would revisit this wound. In April, publishes the short story "Un concerto" (A Concert), later included in his first collection, *Una città di pianura* (A City of the Plain) in Bassani 1998: 1521-1580.

1939 Graduates with a thesis on the eighteenth-century linguist and writer Niccolò Tommaseo. The racial laws force Jewish students and professors at the Liceo Ariosto, Ferrara's high school, where Bassani teaches, to move to the old kindergarten at via Vignatagliata 79 in the ancient Ferrara ghetto.

1940 Publishes his short story collection, *Una città di pianura*, in Milan, under the pseudonym Giacomo Marchi because "at that time, we had the Racial Laws, so it was forbidden by the police, to any Jew, to exist. I therefore called myself Giacomo Marchi because I could not be called Giorgio Bassani. If I became Giacomo Marchi, it was not from my choice, ideological, psychological, etc., but for political and racial reasons" (Bassani 1998: 1341). For his pseudonym, he chooses his Catholic grandmother's surname, and the given name of a much-loved uncle to whom he would dedicate some lines in "Family History" (from *Epitaph*). In Ferrara, in September, Bassani meets Valeria Sinigallia, his future wife. Also of Jewish origin from Ferrara, she lives in Venice. Her mother, Enrichetta Sullam, is descended from the poetess Sara Copia Sullam, whose life and work Bassani will later research in the Marciana Library.

1942 Devotes himself assiduously to lyric poetry. His clandestine political activity intensifies both in Bologna and Ferrara. Continues to teach in the Jewish school.

1943 Arrested in May for anti-fascist activity. From prison writes to Valeria and his family. Fourteen letters are collected under the title "Da una prigione" (From a Prison, in the collection *Di là dal cuore* [Beyond the Heart] in Bassani 1998: 947-962). Following the fall of Mussolini's regime, Bassani is released from prison on 26 July. He marries Valeria Sinigallia on 4 August in Bologna, and they spend their honeymoon in Marina di Ravenna. Bassani decides not to return to Ferrara and to live in Florence. At the end of August, the couple arrive in Florence with little money and rent a room under a false name. In desperate need of income, Bassani translates Hemingway's *Farewell to Arms* (never published), James Cain's *The Postman Always Rings Twice* (1945) and works from the French, including Voltaire's *Private Life of Frederick II* (1945). Continues his political activity. Relatives who remained in Ferrara are deported to Buchenwald. His parents and sister save themselves by going into hiding. On 6 December, the Bassanis leave Florence for Rome.

1944 Bassani describes the expectation of Liberation and many upheavals from the situation in Rome between 25 January and 19 February in "Pagine di un diario ritrovato" (Pages from a Rediscovered Diary), now in *Di là dal cuore* (in Bassani 1998: 965-983). In the summer, goes to Naples, where many Italian intellectuals have gathered, including Mario Soldati and Leo Longanesi. Also visits the house of Benedetto Croce, where he becomes friends with the philosopher's daughters, the writers Elena and Alda.

1945 On 1 September, his daughter Paola is born. After graduating in Art History from the University of Bologna under Francesco Arcangeli, one of Bassani's greatest friends, she will specialize at the Sorbonne, live first in Brussels and then Paris, teaching at the universities of Tours and Rennes. Bassani publishes with Astrolabio in Rome *Storie di poveri amanti e altri versi* (Poor Lovers' Stories and Other Verses) containing poems written between 1939 and 1945.

1946 A second edition of *Storie di poveri amanti e altri versi* is brought out by the same publisher. Adapting to various jobs to support his family, Bassani is employed at the Ministry of Labor, the War Veterans office, and works in a library.

1947 The poetry collection *Te lucis ante. 1946-47* comes out in Rome from Ubaldini. He meets the American Princess Marguerite Caetani di Bassiano, a great patron of the arts, who intends to continue in Italy the work begun in France with the magazine *Commerce*. She turns to Bassani in search of collaborators. In March, meets Pier Paolo Pasolini.

1948 Becomes editor of *Botteghe Oscure*, the magazine founded by Princess Caetani in the same year, and works for it until its closure in 1960. In *Botteghe Oscure*, Caetani and Bassani publish the best of Italian and international literature, through which Italian readers discover writers such as Ingeborg Bachmann, Dylan Thomas, René Char, Henri Michaux, Roger Caillois, Maurice Blanchot, Georges Bataille, Antonin Artaud, W. H. Auden, Truman Capote, and Robert Graves. Among the Italian writers published are Mario Soldati, Carlo Cassola, Italo Calvino, Attilio Bertolucci, Giorgio Caproni, and Pier Paolo Pasolini. His father Enrico dies at the age of sixty-three.

1949 On 29 June, his second child is born, to whom Bassani gave his father's name. Enrico would graduate in veterinary medicine from the University of

Bassani in 1956 in Ostia antica, with Elisabeth Bowen, Alberto Moravia and Attilio Bertolucci. (Archivio Eredi Paola e Enrico Bassani)

Bologna and, like his father, become involved in environmental protection. In the autumn, begins teaching literature at the Nautical Institute of Naples.

1951 Leaves the Nautical Institute to teach at the Velletri Art School. In December, publishes the poetry collection *Un'altra libertà* (Another Freedom) with Mondadori.

1952 Collaborates on the screenplay for Mario Soldati's film *Le avventure di Mandrin* and Michelangelo Antonioni's *I vinti*. Bassani has a small part in Luciano Emmer's film *Le ragazze di Piazza di Spagna*.

1953 Publishes the short story "La passeggiata prima di cena" ("The Stroll Before Dinner"). Becomes editor of *Paragone*, the magazine founded by the writer Anna Banti and her husband Roberto Longhi, with which he collaborates until 1971. In this period, Pasolini and Bassani spend a good deal of time together.

1954 Continues to write screenplays. Has various contacts with the film industry, but writing screenplays is always a secondary activity for Bassani.

1955 Publishes the short story "Gli ultimi anni di Clelia Trotti" ("The Final Years of Clelia Trotti") for which in May 1957 he wins the international Veillon Prize. Together with a group of intellectuals, he founds Italia Nostra. Through this association, Bassani will support the protection of the Italian coastline against speculative building and the safeguarding of national parks. His actions are linked to the belief that "the Italian artistic and natural heritage belongs to the whole world and is therefore in some sense sacred" (Bassani 2018: 266).

1956 The collection *Cinque storie ferraresi* (*Five stories of Ferrara*) comes out from Einaudi. The book wins the prestigious Strega prize: "I am very much in favor of literary awards. [....] In a few months almost ten thousand copies (3 editions) were sold. Before then, one hundred, two hundred copies of my books were sold at the most... In reality, a public like ours, devoid of cultural traditions, needs guidance" (Bassani 2019: 45). Bassani becomes a consultant and then editorial director of the Feltrinelli publishing house.

1957 Visits the necropolis of Cerveteri with his wife, children and friends Niccolò Gallo, Cesare Garboli and Pietro Citati. He will recount this trip in the Prologue to *The Garden of the Finzi-Continis*. Teaches Theater History at the Silvio D'Amico National Academy of Dramatic Arts in Rome until November 1967. Many of his students will become important figures in Italian theater. With his student directors he studies the authors of the French Grand Siècle, Racine, Corneille, Molière.

1958 The novel *Gli occhiali d'oro* (*The Gold-Rimmed Spectacles*) is published by Einaudi. Alberto Moravia judges it his best story "in which there is a very acute comparison of Jews' and homosexuals' 'diversity'." For Feltrinelli, he discovers and publishes *The Leopard* by Giuseppe Tomasi di Lampedusa. Bassani's Preface defines it as a "national poem." During the summer, he is in Liguria, where he visits Franco Fortini, Enzo Siciliano, Roberto Longhi and Anna Banti, Mario Soldati, and Attilio Bertolucci.

1959 On 6 November, with Giuseppe Ungaretti, Giacomo Debenedetti, Alberto Moravia, and Emilio Gadda, Bassani is on the jury for the Città di Crotone Prize, awarded to Pasolini for *Una vita violenta* (*A Violent Life*).

1960 Publishes with Einaudi *Una notte del '43* (A Night in '43) and *Le storie ferraresi* (Stories of Ferrara). The director Florestano Vancini begins to work on the film version of "A night in '43." Bassani follows all stages of its production but is not involved in the screenplay. He likes the film, but not its altered title, "The Long Night of '43."

1961 On 15 October he is in Venice for the inauguration of the exhibition organized by Italia Nostra in defense of the city. On 3 November, in Rome, participates in the Round Table organized by the International Pen Club on the subject of Literary Translation and Translator Issues. There are writers and translators from twenty-two countries. Intervenes to request the oversight and consent of authors for the translation of their works.

1962 Einaudi publishes *The Garden of the Finzi-Continis*, which wins the Viareggio Prize. The novel, in addition to a large number of important reviews, has a sensational sale by Italian standards (one hundred thousand copies in five months) which – added to the success derived from being the "discoverer" of *The Leopard* – gives Bassani undisputed celebrity. Elected to the ranks of the Socialist Party, he becomes a city councilor in his city and, in this capacity, delivers the speech "In defense of Ferrara" where he argues that the greatest danger for a city is to lose its relationship with its culture, and therefore the task of city administrators is to preserve the historic center from those who speak of renewal but think above all of their own interests. Echoes of this controversy can be found in some lines for the poem "Porta Rosa" (in *Epitaph*).

1963 Publishes the collected edition, *L'alba ai vetri. Poesie 1942-'50* (Dawn at the Panes. Poems 1942-'50). Due to disagreements with the publisher, he ceases his activity at Feltrinelli. At the center of a violent controversy unleashed by the avant-garde literary movement Gruppo '63, which accuses him (he and another writer, Carlo Cassola) of writing like Liala, a prolific "women's fiction" author of the previous generation. The two facts are linked. Feltrinelli wants a changing of the guard in his publishing house and surrounds himself with intellectuals close to the neo-experimentalism of the avant-garde.

1964 Publishes the novel *Dietro la porta* (*Behind the Door*) with Einaudi. In the autumn, as a candidate for the socialists, he becomes vice president of RAI, the Italian state television. He resigns two years later in protest against excessive political interference, thus moving away from the socialists and growing nearer to the Republican party. Gallimard in Paris publishes the French translation of *Gli occhiali d'oro* (*The Gold-Rimmed Spectacles*). Thus begins the international diffusion of Bassani's work. His books will be translated into Catalan, Czech, Danish, Dutch, English, Finnish, French, German, Hebrew, Hungarian, Japanese, Norwegian, Polish, Portuguese, Romanian, Serbo-Croat, Slovenian, Spanish, Swedish and Turkish.

1965 Becomes President of Italia Nostra.

1966 In February, he travels to Israel at the invitation of the Italian Cultural Institute and gives presentations in Tel Aviv and Jerusalem. Publishes with Einaudi *Le parole preparate* (Prepared Words), in which he collects his essays.

1967 For Italia Nostra, presents the exhibition "Italia da salvare" (Italy to Be Saved) in Venice. In October, buys a house in Maratea, which he keeps until 1980. For Maratea, see note to "In the Open" from *Epitaph*.

1968 Publishes with Mondadori *L'airone* (*The Heron*), his last novel.

1969 *The Heron* wins the prestigious Campiello Prize. On 7 December he is in Dortmund to receive the international Nelly Sachs Prize for his entire oeuvre.

1970 The film based on *The Garden of the Finzi-Continis* directed by Vittorio De Sica is released. The history of this film's production extended over many years with a different director and different screenwriters, including Bassani himself. In the end, objecting to the final screenplay, Bassani withdraws his signature and demands that the title be changed: the film becomes *The Garden of the Finzi Continis*, without the hyphen. He judges De Sica's work thus: "That it derives in some way from my novel is not disputable, nor have I ever dreamed of disputing it. But that it betrays my novel, in substance and above all in spirit, no one, I believe, will be able to deny" (Bassani 1998: 1262). In Munich and Zurich for a series of lectures.

1972 Publishes *L'odore del fieno* (*The Smell of Hay*) with Mondadori. In February makes a trip to Northampton, Massachusetts, to give some lectures at Smith College.

1973 Under the title *Dentro le mura* (*Within the Walls*), publishes with Mondadori a new, entirely revised edition of the Ferrara stories.

1974 Publishes with Mondadori the collection of poems *Epitaffio* and assembles in a single volume his stories and novels as *Il romanzo di Ferrara* (*The Novel of Ferrara*). In February, Bassani is made an honorary member of the American Academy of Arts and Letters in New York.

1975 In the fall, he gives a series of lectures at Northwestern University, Illinois. Visits New York for the release of an English translation of the *L'odore del fieno* (*The Smell of Hay*).

1976 From March to April, teaches at Indiana University in Bloomington. In July, is in Vienna at the invitation of the Italian Cultural Institute. In October, moves to California and teaches at Berkeley until November. In December he is in Toronto.

1978 Publishes the collection of poems *In gran segreto* (In Great Secret) with Mondadori. Wins the Todi prize for his contribution to environmental protection. Appointed councilor emeritus of the Dante Alighieri society.

1979 From September to October, teaches in Canada at the University of Toronto.

1980 Mondadori publishes the definitive version of *The Novel of Ferrara*. Becomes honorary president of Italia Nostra. On March 8, Saint Mary's College of Notre Dame, Indiana, awards him an honorary degree in Letters. From November to December, teaches in Canada at Queen's University, Kingston, Ontario.

1981 Lectures at the universities of Paris, Poitiers, and Bordeaux.

1982 In November, receives the prestigious Bagutta prize for *In rima e senza* (In Rhyme and Without), a complete collection of his poetry published by Mondadori. Wins the Penna d'oro award of the Presidency of the Council of Ministers for his entire work as a writer. In Brussels at the invitation of the Italian Cultural Institute, then in Paris.

1983 Between 19 and 21 March, he participates in a conference on his work organized by André Sempoux at the Catholic University of Louvain-la-Neuve in Belgium. In October, wins the Mediterranean International Prize for fiction in Palermo.

1984 From 21 to 29 October, Bassani is in San Francisco where he presents the exhibit "Italia da salvare." Publishes with Mondadori *Di là dal cuore* (Beyond the Heart) a collected edition of his entire non-fictional production. Writes his last poem, "Il canto del vecchio" ("The Old Man' Song").

1985 In February, Bassani writes the introduction to the catalog for an exhibit of the Italian American painter Richard Piccolo – at the art gallery Il Gabbiano in Rome, which specialized in American art, and has only recently closed. It is the last new work published during his lifetime.

1987 His mother Dora Minerbi dies at the age of 94. Giuliano Montaldo's film *Gli occhiali d'oro*, based on Bassani's novel of the same title, is released. On 10 December he wins the Pirandello prize.

1988 With the paperback edition of *Gli occhiali d'oro* (*The Gold-Rimmed Spectacles*) he wins the Riviera delle Palme prize.

1992 Wins the Antonio Feltrinelli prize for fiction awarded by the Accademia Nazionale dei Lincei. The University of Ferrara awards him an honorary degree in Natural Sciences for his commitment to environmental protection.

1993 Fifty-five years after his expulsion from the Biblioteca Ariostea in Ferrara on account of the Racial Laws, the library organizes a ceremony in his honor.

2000 On 31 March Bassani is admitted to the San Camillo hospital in Rome, where he dies on 13 April. On 17 April he is buried in the Jewish cemetery of Ferrara. On 9 June a memorial event for Giorgio Bassani is held in Rome, organized by Italia Nostra.

IN RIMA E SENZA / IN RHYME AND WITHOUT

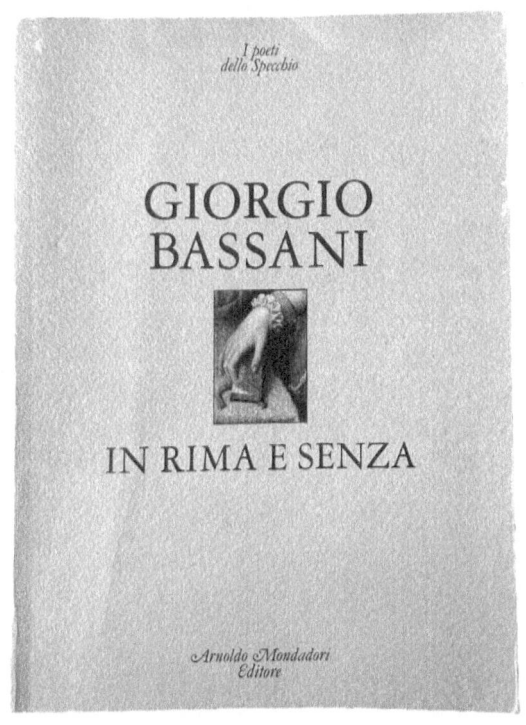

Cover of *In rima e senza*, Milan: Mondadori, 1982. (Fondazione Bassani, Ferrara)

I
IN RIMA / IN RHYME

STORIE DEI POVERI AMANTI / POOR LOVERS' STORIES

Cover of *Storie dei poveri amanti e altri versi*, Rome: Astrolabio, 1946, second edition. (Fondazione Bassani, Ferrara)

PRELUDIO

Lascia ch'io ti ricordi
se ritarda l'inverno,
se ancora mi rimordi,
se mi tiene il tuo inferno.

Trascorre il fuoco crudo
della luna sul grano.
Nel folto, ascoso e nudo,
il tuo riso arde piano.

Lascia ancora la voce
tua chiamarmi: io ti sento.
O mi porga un'atroce
speranza il tuo silenzio.

Calda nei tuoi capelli
come un mite tesoro
tu respiri coi cieli,
dormi serena in loro.

Lascia che nel profilo
che ti chiude io colga
la cifra che risolva
in un canto il mio grido.

Ma tu calma fermenti
pigra e opaca dal cuore.
Sei muta come un fiore.
Non odi, non rammenti.

SERA SUL PO

Sei solo, ormai: in un fumo amaro sopra funeste
solitudini d'acque arrossa languido il fuoco
di nostalgici incendi le solenni foreste.

PRELUDE

Let me remember you
if winter lingers,
if you gnaw me still,
if I'm held by your hell.

The moon's raw fire
passes over the wheat.
In the thickets, hidden, bare,
your smile burns quiet.

Let your voice still
call me: it's you I sense.
Or it offers a dreadful
hope to me, your silence.

In your tresses, warm
like a mild treasure,
you breathe with the skies,
serenely sleep in them.

Let me, in the profile
enclosing you, seize
the figure resolving
a song from my cries.

But you calm, idle, dull,
you ferment from the heart.
Like a flower you're mute.
You don't hear, don't recall.

EVENING ON THE PO

By now, you're alone: in bitter smoke above grim
solitudes of waters languidly the fire's reddening
solemn forests with nostalgic flames.

PONTELAGOSCURO

Dimenticami, se alla ruota sfavillante di raggi
ti affidi lungo gli asfalti dorati nella brezza
celeste che ti spalanca a sogni di giovinezza
infinita la fresca sera dei sottopassaggi.

Verso un borgo d'obliqui camini fumiganti,
bassi sull'erba madida della sgombra pianura,
emergi tu e ti dilegui. Vengono per l'aria scura
angeli in tuta azzurra, a sciami, in un fuoco di canti.

SULLA BAIA

Le languide fanfare d'uno sbarco di eroi
sommuovono i verdi campi del sole nella mattina
tranquilla: come tra polvere trepida la marina
di dolcissimi lampi d'armi ignude entro i tuoi

semichiusi occhi d'idolo, delusa mitologia.
Potessi tu ai richiami dei nostalgici e rauchi
corni di guerra emergere con malinconia
intatta vergine d'oro per quegli stanchi argonauti!

I GABBIANI

Vengono nel mattino i canti esili dei gabbiani,
neve e dardi sono per l'aria le loro voci serene.
Teneramente ti chiamano! Nel vento delle golene
col braccio li saluti al passaggio come assorti aeroplani.

E già lontani oltre l'argine del fiume che s'incurva,
li vedi perdersi nell'azzurra foschia bassa dei salici
controcorrente. La libera memoria di quelle fragili
ali è ancor qui che ti palpita nei grigi occhi, ti turba.

PONTELAGOSCURO

Forget me, should you trust along the gilded asphalt
in celestial breeze to the wheel glittering with rays
throwing you open to dreams of infinite youth
the fresh evening of the under-passageways.

Towards a village of oblique smoking chimneys,
low on the damp grass of the open plain,
you emerge and fade. Through the dark air
come blue-smocked angels, swarming, in a song-blaze.

ON THE BAY

Languid fanfares of a heroes' landing stir
the green fields in tranquil morning sun:
as fearful of softest flashes from bare weapons
is the shoreline through dust within your

half-closed idol's eyes, deluded mythology.
At the calls from nostalgic and hoarse horns
of war, if only you could emerge with melancholy,
intact gold virgin, for those tired Argonauts!

THE SEAGULLS

In the morning come the slender cries of seagulls,
snow and arrows their calm voices through the air.
Tenderly they call you! In wind from the floodplains
you salute them with your arm as if pensive planes.

And already far beyond the riverbank's curving away,
you see them lost in the low blue mist of willows
against the current. The free memory from those
frail wings still unsettles, beating in your grey eyes.

IL BALCONE

E ancora monterà dai viali odorosi e celesti
di vespero come un giovane vino l'amore. Ma sola
ti troverà se la fronte notturna t'arda, se la viola
profumi di memoria i transiti delle meste

meteore, nell'ora che più lacrima gli amanti
dimenticati e trascorsi il cielo consapevole.
Ascolterai derelitta spegnersi come una debole
minaccia il tuo sorriso nell'ombra folta di canti.

PIAZZA D'ARMI

Oltre le mura invisibili, al cielo basso, ai lampi,
fischiano lungamente i merci, con grida rauche
cercano l'orizzonte, le torri azzurre e labili
della pioggia che cade tiepida sopra i campi.

Si spengono i loro fuochi sulla tua fronte (una stella
triste) che inclini nell'ombra della stanza in silenzio.
Sei sola ormai, assediata nella tua casa di cemento.
I tuoi pensieri si perdono adagio nella nebbia.

SERENATA

Ora che in lenti vortici, come una chioma di neve
che oscure dita tormentano, la nebbia delle paludi
fuma alla tua finestra, e una bufera di buie
lacrime ti ridesta dentro sudate e grevi

coltrici, ora che è gelo e tenebra, da' voce,
chiusa forma in ascolto, a quel tuo tetro grammofono.
Uscita dalla nube al vetro, atroce
calma mano salutami, amaro riso sepolto.

THE BALCONY

And again, like a young wine, love will rise
from perfumed sky-blue avenues at dusk. But alone
it will find you if your nighttime forehead burns,
if the violet scents with memory the transits of sad

meteors, at the hour when the knowing sky
most mourns the vanished and forgotten lovers.
You'll listen to your smile fade like a weak threat,
saddened, in the shadow thick with songs.

PIAZZA D'ARMI

Beyond the invisible walls, to the low sky, the flashes,
freight trains are whistling long, with hoarse cries
they search the horizon, the blue and fleeting towers,
some rain falling lukewarm over fields.

Their fires go out on the forehead (a saddened
star) you lower in the shadow of the silent room.
By now you're alone, besieged in your cement home.
Gently in the fog your thoughts lose themselves.

SERENADE

Now that in slow vortices, like a mane of snow
tormented by murky fingers, fog from the marshes
smokes at your window, and a storm of dark tears
awakes you in heavy and sweat-soaked

blankets, now that it's ice and shadow, give voice,
closed listening form, to your grim gramophone.
Come out from the cloud at the glass, greet me,
you dreadful calm hand, bitter buried smile.

I CRISANTEMI

Fino a te non salivano i canti dei crisantemi
attraverso i fuochi ed il fumo d'un domestico inferno;
tu non udivi, ignara, le loro voci, il lieve
fruscìo delle loro chiome dentro il silenzio dell'inverno.

Fedeli a te sparita essi soli rimasti,
qui, da questo vecchio orto, rammemorano la tua dolcezza.
Innocente, di te, che ancora nei loro casti
profumi torni, sorride in lacrime la giovinezza.

PAVANA

Al ritmo lento, instancabile, di una triste pavana
sfiorivi. Nella stanza non c'eri che tu fra morte,
cieche cose. Smettevi. Filtrando dalla persiana
il sole un po' ti abbagliava. Basta col pianoforte.

Ma eccoti poi già tornata solitaria e insistente
a suonare, a suonare. Oh la noia, il novembre
della tua noia... Però infine era sempre
di nuovo notte. E ti alzavi, ormai indifferente.

DAI BASTIONI ORIENTALI

Approdano alla Mura degli Angeli con perse voci di campane
i grigi morti da est, si arenano i sarcofaghi d'oro
ai cumuli azzurri del fieno, un ultimo treno viola
palpita nei vetri sfavillanti delle fabbriche suburbane

quando malinconica grida la sirena della sera.
E son così tiepide e rosa d'asfalti corsi le gote
delle virili operaie, che il lume del giorno di primavera
arde d'amore sotto quegli occhi fino in fondo alla notte.

THE CRYSANTHEMUMS

The chrysanthemum's songs wouldn't rise
to you through a domestic hell of smoke and fires;
you didn't hear, unaware, their voices, the slim
rustle of their manes in the winter's silence.

Faithful to you, vanished, only these remaining,
here, from this old garden, remember your sweetness.
Innocent, of you, who still come back in their
chaste perfumes, youth's smiling in tears.

PAVAN

To the slow, inexhaustible rhythm of a sad pavan
you withered. In the room there was no one but you
among the dead, blind things. You'd stop. The sun
faintly dazzled, filtering through blinds. Enough piano.

But here you are then already alone again and insistent
on playing, on playing. Oh, the boredom, the November
of your boredom... But in the end it was always
night once more. And up you stood, by now indifferent.

FROM THE EASTERN BASTIONS

With lost voices of bells to the Mura degli Angeli
from the east the grey dead reach, the golden sarcophagi
are beached with the haystacks' cloud-blue, a last violet train
shudders in the outskirts factories' glittering panes

when the melancholy evening siren whines.
And so pink and warm are strong factory girls' cheeks
from pedalled asphalt that the light in springtime
under those eyes burns deep into the night with love.

I GIRASOLI

Non spira incenso più grato a Dio
quaggiù del canto sommesso e pio
dei girasoli che vivono un'estate
sola, lunghesso le strade ferrate.

Le loro voci son tutta una lode.
Quando discende la sera, e s'odono
campane, e s'alzano nebbie leggere
di là, e sfilano fumo le ciminiere

lontane, e l'erba è calda d'amanti,
durano per l'aria bruna i lor canti.
Nel sonno piegano i volti sereni
al lungo bacio d'addio dei treni.

DOPO LA SAGRA

Non resti nella piazza che un bimbo, che al nembo lontano
turchino e obliquo sopra le piccole fattorie luminose
della piana sorrida, e distacchi dalla torre bruna le rose,
dolci campane immense con l'esile addio della sua mano.

S'apra dalle vie l'ombra dell'umile, vecchio sobborgo più tardi
al sussurrato pegno d'un lungo vento di primavera,
che ci riporti dai campi l'infanzia assonnata, i carri
caldi d'oscura erba e di amari papaveri ad alta sera.

DI SETTEMBRE A SAN GIORGIO

Mai più ti abbatterai in lacrime su queste
arse erbe di schianto. Grandi tra le bandiere
tremano sul ponte candidi angeli nei volti a meste
luci di lontananza, s'apre dalle brughiere

desolate un'umana solitudine... È tempo
di caccia: e spari trasalgono fiochi nella tua pietra

THE SUNFLOWERS

No incense blows more grateful to God
down here than the subdued and pious
song of the sunflowers living for one
summer, down along the railway lines.

Their voices are all an act of praise.
When evening falls, and you hear
bells, and light fogs rise over there,
and smoke from far chimneys

unthreads, and grass is warm with lovers,
their songs endure in the darkened air.
In sleep their calm faces fold over
at the long goodbye kiss of the trains.

AFTER THE FEAST

May only a child remain in the piazza, smiling at the distant
nimbus, turquoise and slanting, over small luminous farms
in the plain, and from the brown tower detaching the roses,
immense soft bells with the slender farewell of his hands.

Later from the streets the shadow of the humble, old township
may open to the whispered token of a long spring wind
bringing us back our sleepy childhood from the fields, the carts
warm with dark grass and bitter poppies at late evening.

IN SEPTEMBER AT SAN GIORGIO

No longer upon these scorched grasses will you
break down in tears. Great between banners
on the bridge shiver white-faced angels to sad
distant lights, a human solitude opens

from the desolate moorlands… It's hunting season
time: and gunshots give a faint start to your stone,

o mia chiusa città, remoti dentro l'attento
stupore in cui tu duri implacabile, tetra.

VERSO FERRARA

È a quest'ora che vanno per calde erbe infinite
verso Ferrara gli ultimi treni, con fischi lenti
salutano la sera, affondano indolenti
nel sonno che via via là spegne pievi rosse, turrite.

Dai finestrini aperti l'alcool delle marcite
entra un po' a velare il lustro delle povere panche.
Dei poveri amanti in maglia scioglie le dita stanche,
fa deserte di baci le labbra inaridite.

SERA A PORTA RENO

Io solo di qua dai vecchi archi le assorte,
grame tovaglie a numerare. Ma laggiù i gentili
zingari fanno il fuoco, caldi da puerili
bocche van canti, si alza adagio dagli aeroporti

ancora azzurri l'ombra, annotta, e un dolce vento
porta con sé i motori, li sperde nel firmamento.

MARINA D'OTTOBRE

Che la pioggia dilavi il cielo, e il sole
basso d'autunno vermiglio sfavilli,
viola si curverà la spiaggia al lieto
urto della risacca.

E andremo dentro la bruma, noi, nel lieve
sonno che su dal buio, dal segreto
sciacquio fuma, fidando che per noi e basta
un faro alfine brilli.

o my closed city, remote in your watchful stupor
within which, implacable, gloomy, you endure.

TOWARDS FERRARA

It's at this hour through endless warm grasses
towards Ferrara the last trains run, with slow
whistles they greet the evening, indolently drown
in sleep slowly snuffing red, turreted churches.

From open windows the meadow's ferment
faintly enters to veil the shine of poor benches.
It loosens weary fingers of poor lovers in singlets,
renders the parched lips empty of kisses.

EVENING AT PORTA RENO

This side of the old arches I'm alone numbering
rapt wretched tablecloths. But down there gentle
gypsies set their fire, from childish mouths go
warm songs, from the still blue aerodromes

the shadow slowly rises, night falls, and a soft wind
carries off the engines, in the firmament disperses them.

SEASIDE IN OCTOBER

Should rain cleanse the sky, and the sun
low in autumn sparkle vermilion,
the beach will curve violet at a joyous
crashing of the backwave.

And us, we'll go within the haze, in the faint
sleep that smokes up from the dark,
from the secret rinsing, trusting that for us alone
finally a lighthouse shines.

PUNTA MARINA

Un'ombra sola trascorse sottovento, un piatto
ventre di tavole grondanti se la raffica tornava.
Fieno e papaveri per il mare nero portava
cinta la testa di zanzare l'ortolano distratto.

CHIARO DI LUNA

Questa luna che varca
alta i corsi sereni,
rosa al margine appena
da un'ombra, l'ansietà

della sua faccia vuota
è materna, una fioca
lampada sulla città.
Fuori porta è una brina

ma calda, così in pace
schiarando morta e mite
le sonore e infinite
strade della campagna,

così semplice, calma,
questa luna che bagna
dolcemente la salma
della contrada scura,

spegne rulli lontani
di carri, doma i cani
persi nella pianura…

VARIAZIONE SUL TEMA PRECEDENTE

Se un corno alto di luna varca i corsi sereni
e scalda della sua mite brace i glauchi selciati
escono i cavallanti tra il sonno ammantellati
alle strade che affondano tiepide in mezzo ai fieni.

PUNTA MARINA

A single shadow passed downwind, a flat belly
of tables dripping should the wind-gusts return.
His head mosquito-ringed, the distracted gardener
would bear towards the black sea hay and poppies.

CLAIR DE LUNE

This moon that crosses
high above serene streets,
barely gnawed at the edges
by a shadow, the fret

in its empty face
is maternal, a weak
lamp above the city.
Out of town it's a frost

but warm, so at peace,
dead and meek, making bright
the resonant and infinite
roads in the country,

so simple, calm,
this moon that's gently
washing the corpse
of the dark region,

drowns remote drumrolls
of carts, tames hounds
lost out on the plain...

VARIATION ON THE PRECEDING THEME

If a high horn-moon crosses the serene streets
and with its faint glow heats the glaucous stones
out come mantled horsemen through sleep
to warm roads that drown amongst the hay.

Calma e chiara è la notte, dal madore dei prati
sale un latte leggero che ondeggia a soffi leni
di vento, si ode a tratti la cieca ansia dei treni
lontani che precipitano verso i folti mercati.

Ma tu, dio che sorridi al profitto e alla perdita,
incanta lungo il cammino i tuoi neri protetti,
lungo il dolce cammino che sfiora i campi già verdi!

Socchiudi la finestra dell'ostessa, dai letti
odorosi richiama sulla porta le serve,
splendi nel vino, accendi nell'ombra occhi diletti!

IMMAGINE

Ti consuma
d'amore
quest'aria
vivo cuore,

terrestre
patimento
il sole
ti fa festa,

precaria
sul tuo stelo
il vento
ti consola,

una cosa
che brucia
nella luce
del cielo,

una rosa.

The night's calm and clear, wavering in slight
wind-gusts a pale milk rises from the meadows,
you hear at intervals the far trains' blind fright
as headlong towards packed markets they descend.

But you, god who smiles at the loss and the gain,
enchant your black flock along their path,
along the sweet path skirting fields already green!

The hostess's window half-open, call servant girls
back to the door from their odorous beds,
shine in the wine, sparkle loved eyes in the shadow!

IMAGE

It consumes
you with love
this air
live heart,

terrestrial
suffering
the sun
celebrates you,

the wind
consoles you
precarious
on your stem,

a thing
that glows
in light from
the sky,

a rose.

MONSELICE

A Monselice il vento va
sempre come dal mare.
Gira il treno al largo, non sa
forse come approdare.

Monselice, colle celeste,
fonte pura e lontana,
ricordo di te fra le meste
casupole una fontana.

A Monselice anche di giugno
la primavera non è senza nebbie.
Con foglie e foglie l'autunno.
L'inverno è tutto una sera.

Ma l'estate i tigli lungo il rettifilo
per Ferrara? Al loro quieto
stormire la luna mi amava,
quand'ero ragazzo, in segreto.

NEL SUO COMPLEANNO

E brilla ancor di pianti non trattenuti il sole
ultimo? E vanno amanti d'erba in cerca, erba e viole?

STORIE DEI POVERI AMANTI

Il giovane che conoscemmo
con la fosca pelliccia dal bavero rialzato,
e quel volto pallido, smagrato, e quegli occhi,
quegli occhi così simili alla luna che ami;

quel giovane che ci passò accanto in una
notte invernale umida e tiepida;
che sorrideva alla gomma dei suoi passi senza rumore
(che impensabile sorriso sotto la tesa del cappello!);

MONSELICE

At Monselice, the wind blows
always as from the sea.
The train turns offshore, doesn't know
how to make landfall maybe.

Monselice, celestial hillside,
clear brow far and pure,
of you, I recall through poor
dwellings, a fountain.

At Monselice, even in June,
not without fogs is the spring.
Leaf upon leaf the autumn.
Winter's all an evening.

But, summer, lime trees on the stretch
towards Ferrara? To their quiet
rustling the moon would love me,
when I was a boy, in secret.

ON HIS BIRTHDAY

And does it still shine with unrestrained tears, the sunset's
last ray? And do lovers go in search of grass, grass and violets?

POOR LOVERS' STORIES

The young man we met
with raised collar of dark fur,
and that pale face, grown thin, and those eyes,
those eyes so like the moon you love;

that young man who went by beside us
one warm and damp winter's night;
who smiled at the rubber of his soundless steps
(what unthinkable smile beneath his hat brim!);

quello che ti offerse il braccio e tu tremavi
per troppo amore; e ti condusse, e fu
senza pietà; che non è tornato mai
più, come le nebbie caldi orsi di pelo e gomma e neve;

e aveva dita e saliva ed occhi e sorriso di luna
sotto la tesa del cappello; e per la neve pelliccia: oh luna,
m'ha inseguito fin qua col coltello degli occhi,
ha voluto, luna, che ti chiamassi
con l'amoroso flauto delle memorie,

luna di queste notti.

*

Quel nostro bambino non nato
che ci guardò derelitto
con i suoi occhi d'aria, zitto,
ma che spesso si lamenta
adesso, agitando il braccino
spezzato, da una sua spenta
primavera lontana e solitaria,

il suo pianto come un belato,
esitando lieve nel vento
della notte, ecco ha rideste
su noi stesi a fumare nel prato
appena respirando, quasi da un mare
soffocato di palafitte,
le campane dirotte, le meste
voci delle nostre sconfitte.

Dimenticati sopra l'erba,
spoglie d'un naufragio,
in quell'odore vecchio di caserma
fuori città (nella garitta
si consumava adagio
la brace fioca e ferma
di una oscura sigaretta),

who offered you his arm and you trembled
from too much love; and led you, and was
pitiless; who's never returned,
like fogs, warm bears of fur and rubber and snow;

and with fingers and saliva and eyes and lunar smile
under his hat brim; and fur for the snow: oh, moon,
he's followed me far as here with the knife of his eyes,
he's wanted, moon, for me to call you
with an amorous flute of memories,

moon of these nights.

*

That unborn child of ours
who looked at us neglected,
silent with his airy eyes,
but who complains now often,
waving his small broken
arm, from his quenched
distant and solitary spring,

his crying like a bleat,
hesitant soft in the night
wind, look, it's reawakened
over us stretched out to smoke
in the meadow hardly breathing,
as from a sea choked with piles,
the unending bells, the sorry
voices of our defeats.

Forgotten on the grass,
remnants of a shipwreck,
in that old smell of barracks
beyond the city (the ember,
faint and firm, of a sombre
cigarette slowly consumed
within the sentry box),

la noia, l'ira, la fretta
amara e sonnolenta
del peccato: la circospetta
rinunzia che non ci tormenta;
gli anni passati, questa sorte
di non avere vissuto,
il loro sapore di morte:
tutto abbiamo riconosciuto

con la voce dolente
del nostro bimbo remoto,
nuda al vento del prato,
presente, assente, nel vuoto
arido ed innocente
d'un suo limbo diseredato.

*

Bastava in quei tempi questo, che tu mi mentissi:
remoti prati schiaravano l'inverno della stanza.
Delle inutili carezze, del lago dei nostri sudori m'avanza
solo questo, ed è bene: le tue bugie così tristi.

Ma care, oh, se frusciava la neve ai vetri! Non avevo
in me che neve, pioggia, fogliame morto, e in gola
un grido, da darti; e le braccia; e nessuna parola.
Da queste pieghe di carne ascoltarti: di più non sapevo.

Nei cavi delle ascelle tu mi mentivi, nella cera
del ventre, nelle mie povere coscie, sulle labbra.
Bastava che nel mio seno, riposo alla tua rabbia,
cieli immensi trovassi, oceani, isole... Però la sera,

ad occhi spenti nel buio, le tue fantasie sonnolente
sentivo dal nostro letto alzarsi in un funebre volo.
Bastava questo, allora, che tu ti sentissi un po' meno solo
quando ti veniva paura, lì dentro il niente, del tuo niente.

*

boredom, anger, bitter
and somnolent haste
of sin; the cautious
denial not tormenting us;
the years gone by, this fate
of having not lived,
their taste of death:
all of it we've recognized

with the aching voice
of our distant child,
naked in the meadow wind,
present, absent, in the arid
and innocent emptiness
of his dispossessed limbo.

*

This was enough in those times, that you lied to me:
distant meadows brightened winter in the room.
From our useless caresses, our lake of sweat, only this
is left me, and it's good: your so miserable lies.

But dears, oh, if snow brushed the panes! I have
nothing but snow, rain, dead leaves in me, and a cry
in the throat, to give you; and my arms; and not a word.
Listen to you from these folds of flesh: I knew no more.

In your armpits' caves you lied to me, in the wax
of your stomach, in my poor thighs, on the lips.
This was enough in my chest, rest from your anger,
I found immense skies, oceans, islands... But at evening,

eyes quenched in darkness, I heard your sleepy
fantasies rise from our bed in funereal flight.
This was enough, then, you felt faintly less alone
when fear came, there in the nothingness, your own.

*

Gli ineffabili autunni, le nebbie, i nevicati inverni,
i torpidi e polverosi ori delle alte estati;
abbandonarsi alla vecchia giostra delle stagioni, agli inferni
d'ogni ritorno inevitabile, spiando, come da un di là,

le sospirose labbra, le braccia, le lanugini bionde,
dolci, così dolci agli addii le mattine d'aprile;
addormentarsi; svegliarsi; sognare; alla fronte
battere il palmo; ridere; piangere; chamarsi vile

ed eroe; ma attendere, non aver fretta, marcissero
le cose in me, sospese, prossime a una caduta...
Per te, o poesia, così consumandomi vissi.
Così, vita, mia povera vita, mai t'ho vissuta.

I GIOCATORI

Si chiuda ogni finestra, ogni porta,
in questo tempo dell'anno il più amaro.
Dalla luna altro non c'è riparo.
Grande sta lassù, bianca, assorta.

Nelle case, dentro le stanze
quadrate, giocando, sospesi
sulle carte, i volti accesi
da indomabili speranze,

seduti ai tavoli, le candele
basteranno alla nostra vergogna,
ci offriremo alla piccola gogna
del loro fuoco fedele.

E pari ai morti che nelle tombe
ardono candidi nel sigillo
della calce, sognando lo squillo
che desterà coi galli tutte le trombe,

senza dormire, senza parlare,
veglieremo la luna, in ascolto

The ineffable autumns, the fogs, the snowy winters,
the torpid and dusty golds of high summers;
give yourself over to the seasons' carousel, to the hells
of each inevitable return, espying, as from a beyond,

the sighing lips, the arms, their blonde down,
soft, so soft to April mornings' farewells;
falling asleep; awaken; dream; on your forehead
beat your palm; laugh; cry; call yourself coward

and hero; but waiting, not hurrying, let the things fester
inside me, suspended, on the verge of a fall...
For you, o poetry, consuming me thus, I lived.
Thus, o life, poor life of mine, I never lived you.

THE PLAYERS

Close every window, every door,
in this bitterest time of year.
There's no other cover from the moon.
Large, white, absorbed, above.

In houses, inside the square
rooms, at play, poised
over the cards, our features
lit by untamable hopes,

sat at the tables, the candles
will suffice for our shame,
we'll offer them to the little gibbet
of their faithful flame.

And as the dead in their tombs
burn white in the seal
of the lime, dreaming the squeal
stirring every trumpet with the roosters,

without sleep, without speech,
we'll watch over the moon, aware

che sul nostro cuore sepolto
possa, non vista, tramontare.

CENA DI PASQUA

E quando nel giro del ballo oscuro che ci rimorchia,
dimenticate ombre nostalgiche a fingere la vita,
spirito della notte ci riavrai, dopo le ultime risa,
i baci sulle guance, gli auguri, gli addii sulla porta;

e là dalla soglia a scroscio, irrompendo, un vento crudele
disperderà le fioche ed esili voci come capelli
incanutiti, nel vuoto portico, di tra i cancelli,
cieco soffiando sulle deboli fiamme delle candele:

forse torneremo di sopra, in sala, seduti qua attorno al solito
tavolo, sotto la lampada, commensali distratti,
fermi, le labbra sigillate, pallidi di contro ai pallidi
ritratti dei nostri morti, morti anche noi, ma soli.

MASCHERATA

Qualcuno decideva per noi, accesa una sigaretta,
alzando il dito per gioco, ridendo tra un suo motto
e l'altro a un compagno affabile; né la sentenza fu detta,
per eleganza o fastidio non so. Gli spari, i fischi, le trombe,

fuori, oltre i vetri, languivano d'un carnevale puerile:
così remoto al riverbero del fuoco nel salotto!
La nostra vita fu tra le ombre, le foglie e il fango del viale,
indecifrabile, vile.

EMILIA

Per dove scende sereno
il Po tra l'erba rovente,
vien sul carro del fieno
un vecchio re indolente.

how on our buried hearts
it can, unseen, go down.

EASTER SUPPER

And when at the turn of the dark dance that gnaws us,
forgotten shades nostalgic to imitate life,
night's spirit you'll repossess us, after last laughter,
kisses on cheeks, best wishes, goodbyes at the door;

and there from the threshold irrupting in bursts a cruel
wind will disperse the thin and faint voices like white
hair, in the empty porch, from beyond the gates,
blowing out blindly the weak flames of candles:

perhaps we'll return upstairs, to the room, sitting round
the same table, under lamplight, distracted fellow diners,
still, lips sealed, pale against the pallid
portraits of our dead, we dead too, but alone.

MASQUERADE

Someone would decide for us, light a cigarette,
lifting a finger in play, laughing at an affable companion
between one jest and another; nor was the sentence said,
from smartness or upset, don't know. Shots, whistles, trumpets,

outside, beyond the panes, for a puerile carnival they pined:
how remote at the glare of the fire in the lounge!
Our life was through shadows, the avenue's leaves and mud,
indecipherable, evil.

EMILIA

By where through scorching grass
the calm Po goes its way,
an indolent old king has
come on a cart used for hay.

Sta con tristi parole
ebbre il regale ortolano,
il mento nella mano,
nel sole delle trebbie.

«Uomini», mormora, «rosse
bandiere della fame,
la mia corona è di sonno,
il nulla è il mio reame».

I CAMPI ELISI

E usciremo dal grigio labirinto delle dune gelide e alte
come bagnanti poveri a una spiaggia di polvere dove piano
rotolano gonfie sotto la bàttima piccole onde calde
tra pezzi di latta ruggine, fracidi sugheri, sterco umano.

Ci aspetta la capanna di frasche del pescatore emigrato,
il breve molo mozzo, la riga dell'orizzonte di stagno,
l'ansia in eterno di chi sorveglia il mare pietrificato
dal garbino, rimasto a terra, seduto sopra il calcagno.

IMITAZIONE DA ORAZIO

Quando alla cera del tuo volto, protervo alunno d'amore,
un'aspra piuma verrà, che ne contenda le rose;
quando i biondi capelli che ora al molle tepore
delle tue spalle fremono, cadranno, morte cose:

forse allora allo specchio mirandoti con triste orrore,
ispido e squallido: «Ahimè», dirai, «questo sono io?
Perché non torni bella, gota, al mio nuovo cuore?
È questo arduo conoscermi che offende il cieco iddio?»

EPITAFFIO PER UN TIPOGRAFO

No, non spezzare il sigillo
che ti nasconde il mio nome.

Here, with sad drunk words
the regal gardener stands,
his chin upon his hands,
in threshing-season sun.

"People", he murmurs, "crimson
banners of starvation,
sleep's my coronation,
nothingness my kingdom."

THE ELYSIAN FIELDS

And we'll go out from the grey maze of cold high dunes
like poor bathers to a dust beach where the warm
wavelets quietly swollen below the tideline roll
among rusty bits of tin, soaked cork, human faeces.

The migrant fisherman's wattle hut awaits us,
the short shattered pier, horizon line of pewter,
eternal fret of one watching sea turned to stone
by the south-west wind, onshore, sitting on his heels.

IMITATION OF HORACE

When a rough feather comes, daring pupil of love,
to the wax of your face, competing with the roses;
when your blonde hair now trembling on the soft
warmth of your shoulders, will fall, dead things:

then perhaps seeing yourself with sad horror, insipid
and squallid in the mirror: "Oh no," you'll say, "this is me?
Why can't you, cheek, turn fair once more to my new heart?
It's this hard self-knowing that offends the blind god?"

EPITAPH FOR A TYPOGRAPHER

No, don't break up the seal
hiding my name from you.

Vano è turbare col tuo lume
una notte di sillabe.

Se del mio sangue di pece
sparsi la pagina nuda,
la mia presenza non t'illuda,
se ti rispondo è senza voce.

Fuoco, acre fuoco delle mie vene,
che puoi dire mai di me stesso
se non che ira e disprezzo
han chiuso queste labbra di cenere?

E tu, cosa cerchi? Nei quieti
vesperi perché chini le palpebre
sulle candide carte
care agli ermi alfabeti?

Sui fogli aperti come abissi
non si specchierà che il tuo volto.
Odimi: io vivo, morto,
libero come vissi.

SALUTO A ROMA

Addio arena di calce, addio diamante,
il tuo cielo su me è un chiuso volto.
Lascia ch'io torni al mio paese sepolto
nell'erba come in un mare caldo e pesante.

Porte roventi nel cielo distante,
nero è il tuo sole, nera la tua luna.
Carne senza rimpianti, riso senza nessuna
memoria: addio città senza speranza.

Perché io so le tue vie, diritte spade, i suoni
delle tue piazze celesti; ma so il vento
che ti affila, il lamento
delle tue nascoste stazioni.

It's vain to trouble with your light
a night of syllables.

If with my blood of pitch
I spread the naked page,
don't be deceived by my presence,
if I reply it's without voice.

Fire, bitter fire in my veins
what can you ever say of me alone
except that anger and scorn
have closed these ashen lips?

And you, what do you seek?
Why do you lean in quiet sunsets
your eyelids onto white paper
dear to the lone alphabets?

On pages open like abysses
only your face will it reflect.
Hear me: me alive, dead,
free the way I lived.

SALUTE TO ROME

Goodbye limed arena, goodbye diamond,
your sky is a closed face above me.
Let me return to my hometown buried
in grass as in a warm and heavy sea.

Burning gates in the distant sky,
your sun is black, it's black your moon.
Flesh without regret, laughter without one
memory: hopeless city, goodbye.

For I know your streets, straight swords, and sounds
of your celestial squares; but I know the gales
that hone you, the wails
from your hidden stations.

No, la tua fronte non splende di grazia.
Chi ti raccoglierà, grido di giubilo?
L'iride che ti specchia è senza nubi.
Sei sola, dentro le tue mura di spazio.

I CARBONAI

Finito è il tempo delle decisioni solenni,
la stagione del gelo e del fuoco.
La foresta è d'intorno; è fioco,
come d'un sangue, l'urto delle bipenni.

Non parlatemi né di futuro né di passato,
uomini il cui riso mi è acerbo.
Tutti viviamo come nemici assediati
dentro un mastio di ferro.

Questo viottolo irto di sassi
ci tocca a tutti oramai percorrerlo.
Coraggio, dunque: curvi sui nostri passi,
sulle nostre lanterne, camminiamo.

NON PIANGERE

Non piangere, compagno,
se m'hai trovato qui steso.
Vedi, non ho più peso
in me di sangue. Mi lagno

di quest'ombra che mi sale
dal ventre pallido al cuore,
inaridito fiore
d'indifferenza mortale.

Portami fuori, amico,
al sole che scalda la piazza,
al vento celeste che spazza
il mio golfo infinito.

No, your brow doesn't shine with grace.
Who'll gather you, cry of jubilation?
The rainbow mirroring you is cloudless.
You're alone, within your walls of space.

THE COALMEN

Gone is the time for solemn decisions,
the season of the ice and fire.
The forest's all around; it's faint,
as of blood, the blow of axes.

Don't speak to me of the past or future,
men whose laughter is bitter to me.
Everyone lives like enemies besieged
within a bastion of iron.

This pathway bristling with stones,
it's up to us to follow it now.
Take heart, then: bent upon our steps,
upon our lanterns, let's continue.

DON'T WEEP

Don't weep, comrade,
if you find me lain here.
See, I've no more burden
of blood in me. I bemoan

this shade climbing me
from pale belly to heart,
parched flower
of mortal indifference.

Take me outside, friend,
into sun that warms the square,
celestial wind sweeping
my own infinite bay.

Concedimi la pace
dell'aria, fa' che io bruci
ostia candida, brace
persa nel sonno della luce.

Lascia così che dorma: fermento
piano, una mite cosa
sono, un calmo e lento
cielo in me si riposa.

RETROVIA

Non li vedi, tu, gli angeli tutelari
che compitano la tua croce.
Hanno come te gli occhi chiari,
quasi puerile la voce.

Li vedessi, forse sorrideresti.
Non portan clamidi, stole, o tocchi.
Polverosi, sono, rotti
di fatica. Hanno tute celesti.

Parlano. Li senti bisbigliare
di non sai che pace, che speranza:
in un paese di là dal mare
questa è sera di vacanza.

Nella sera il monte odora
oleandri da una tomba di sassi.
La vita non è più, ora,
per te che un dileguare di passi.

Allow me the peace
of the air, let me burn,
white host, embers
lost in the light's sleep.

Leave me to slumber: slowly
ferment, a mild thing
I am, in me a calm
and tardy sky is resting.

BEHIND THE LINES

Don't you see them, tutelary angels
who spell out your cross.
Like you, they have clear eyes,
and almost childish voices.

Perhaps, if you saw them, you'd smile.
They don't wear tunics, stoles, or toques.
Dusty, they are, overcome
with fatigue. They've blue overalls.

They speak. You hear them whisper
of what peace or hope you can't say:
in a country across the sea
this is an evening of holiday.

In the evening the hill is scented
from a stone tomb by oleanders.
Life is no more, now, for you
than footsteps fading away.

TE LUCIS ANTE / TE LUCIS ANTE

Cover of *Te lucis ante*, Rome: Ubaldini, 1947. (Fondazione Bassani, Ferrara)

I

VALLE DELL'ANIENE

Come suona, Aniene, il vento
che si torce fosco e lento
fra il tuo abisso e il monte! Pare
ora accento a me fraterno,
ora sibilo di biscia
che per erbe calde e amare
strisci in cerca di una vena,
desolata cantilena
suona sempre dalla sera,
finché a specchio d'una pura
aria, in fondo alla pianura,
sorgi tu, città straniera,
come un grande spettro rosa,
questo pianto che non posa
fuor che il giorno, lamentela
che ha ritorno con la vela
della notte, vento, tempo
che ogni forma e grido inghiotte,
che va, e mai non si riposa.

DAL CARCERE

Dalle torri di Ferrara
vola ormai la dolce luce,
ma a una grata nera, avara,
chi ti volge, chi ti induce
o carezza della sera?
Chi risponde a una preghiera,
ad un pianto abbandonato,
con questa esile fanfara?
Oh non cada sera, alcuna
notte mai se non vi porti
per lo spazio, per la bruma,
suoni deboli e distorti,
rari, trepidi segnali,
quando le ore son più eguali,
quando più lontano è il giorno
e ogni grido è sopra il mare.

VALLE DELL'ANIENE

How, Aniene, the wind sounds
writhing grim and slow
between your abyss and the hill! It seems
an accent brotherly to me now,
now a snake-like hiss that creeps
through warm and bitter grass
searching for a vein,
desolate lullaby
it always sounds at evening,
so long as mirrored in a pure
air, deep in the plain,
you rise up, foreign city,
like a great rose spectre,
this lament that doesn't rest
except by day, complaint
returning with the sail
of night, wind, weather
swallowing every form and cry,
how it goes, and never sleeps.

FROM PRISON

From the towers of Ferrara
by now the soft light flies,
but from a mean, black grating
who turns you, who leads you,
o caress of evening?
Who replies to a prayer,
to an abandoned keening,
with this slender fanfare?
Oh don't let dusk fall, nor night
ever, if it doesn't bring you
through space, through the mist,
sounds weak and distorted,
rare, anxious signals,
when hours are more of the same,
when the day is much further
and every cry over the sea.

II

Cover of *Un'altra libertà*, Milan: Mondadori, 1951. (Fondazione Bassani, Ferrara)

1

E riapprodi, ogni notte,
al mio carcere. Hai nere
risa rauche, rotte,
frasi alate, leggere.

Dormo, e ancora (oh mai,
mai si stanca!) il tuo rantolo:
«Cedimi, sì. Soltanto
così mi vincerai».

2

Dormo: o sei tu che pungi
il mio sonno quieto?
Tuo il grido che di lungi
cerca me, il mio segreto?

Se fosse questa veglia
perché tu sia! L'aceto,
tutto il fiele che al vino,
al forte vino tuo aggiungi,

chi non berrebbe, e lieto?

3

Dunque lascia il tuo regno
per me. Qui so, ad un chiuso
lume, aprirmi al tuo sdegno.
Qui no non mi ricuso.

Non mancare. T'aspetto.
Averti qui a convito
ogni notte fu il vecchio
mio vanto. Oggi è il mio vizio.

1

And you resurface, every night,
in my prison. You've black
hoarse laughter, broken,
winged phrases, light.

I sleep, and still (oh never,
it never tires!) your death-rattle:
"Give in to me, yes. Only thus
will you defeat me."

2

I sleep: oh is it you sting
my quiet repose?
Yours the cry that seeks me
from afar, my secret?

If only this vigil were
so you could be! The vinegar,
all the bile to the wine,
to the strong wine you add,

who'd not drink it, and gladly?

3

So then leave your reign
for me. Here I know, at a closed
light, how to open to your disdain.
Here, no, I don't refuse.

Don't miss it. I await you.
To have you here at table
every night was my old
pride. Today it is my vice.

4

«Chissà», tenti; «e se questo
nostro vivere è un sogno?
Un alibi, un pretesto
per una gioia che solo

a me, a te si darà?...»
Ma al fosco riso, agli sguardi,
sempre al bel viso atroce,
ti riconosco, oh, tardi.

5

Un ultimo segnale,
forse l'estremo avviso,
mi folgorò per nere
scale impresso in un viso.

O forse il giusto, il santo
angelo trafelato,
sorgeva a me, placato
per assolvermi, accanto.

Questa lingua che adoperi
così oscura è per me!
Mai l'intesi; fuorché
per averne paura.

6

Un fischio era (o mi parve
nel giorno che moriva),
a me, lingua furtiva,
che muovesse indolente?

Era un riso (o mi parve
nella sera imminente)
che salisse con tarde
ali a infiammarmi il viso?

4

"Who knows," you try; "and if
it's a dream, our life?
An alibi, a pretext
for a joy that's given

only to me, to you?..."
But by the dark laughter, the glances,
always by the fair dreadful face,
oh, late, I recognize you.

5

A very last signal,
final warning maybe,
by black stairs struck me
stamped on a face.

Or perhaps the just, saintly
out-of-breath angel
was looming, calmed
to absolve me, close by.

This tongue you use
is so obscure to me!
Never understood; beyond
being what I fear.

6

A whistle it was (or seemed
to me in the dying day),
for me, furtive tongue,
which would move lazily?

Was it a laugh (or seemed so
in imminent dusk to me)
climbing upon slow
wings to enflame my face?

E agli occhi ed alle vene
chi vi affollò, dirotte
voci d'amore, bocche
trafelate, e voi, tenebre?

7

Luce che i caldi tetti
della città saluti,
ombra che li tramuti...

(Un passo, solo un poco
più stanco; e soffi là,
dalla spia: «Sei libero,
non è che un gioco, va'...»).

Non hai pace. Prometti
cieco, ancora. Tu dài
sempre ciò che non hai:
luce, ombra, libertà.

8

Quando più ero solo,
forse tu m'assolvevi.
Al cieco aprivi prodigo
tu dunque i fulvi cieli

da cui torna ai roventi
maceri e all'erbe sera?
Febbre di ingiurie, lacrime
cocenti!... Alla preghiera

che si levò a or di notte
da un carcere, le chiare
già rispondean, le rotte
tue distanti fanfare.

And to the eyes and the veins
that crowded you, swarming
voices of love, breathless
mouths, and you, shades?

7

Light, you're saluting
the city's warm roofs,
shadow transmuting them...

(A step, only slightly
more tired; and you breathe
from the spyhole: "You're free,
it's just a game, leave...").

You have no peace. Promise
blind, still. You always give
what you don't have:
freedom, shadow, light.

8

When I was more alone,
maybe you absolved me.
Prodigal to the blind
you opened, did you, tawny skies

from where dusk returns
to burning ditches and grasses?
Fever of injustices, scalding
tears!... To the prayers

upraised in the night
from a prison, clear already
they responded, those your
broken distant fanfares.

9

Pur se m'eri vicino,
niente io seppi di te.
Fui ebbro del tuo vino
al primo sorso... Or se

dal mio nuovo, profondo
carcere, da questa notte,
a ignote, calde bocche
(ed è tardi) rispondo,

se, morto, ancor mi rende
al dolore, oh questa
io benedico tenera
luce che mi ridesta.

10

E sei tu che ove aggiorni,
povera, crivellata
ombra sempre ritorni?...

11

E voi, labbra ch'io volli
mute per sempre; palme
in eterno deluse;
e confidenti, illuse,

voi, palpebre consumate...

Degli anni e delle lacrime
d'oltre il vile, il pio Lete,
vecchie furie insaziate chi vi tenta,
chi ancora vi fomenta, quale sete,

fisse in me, a queste rive?

9

Though you were near me,
I knew nothing of you.
I was drunk on your wine
at the first sip... Now if

from my new, deepest
prison, from this night,
to unknown, warm mouths
I respond (and it's late),

if, dead, it returns me
still to sorrow, oh this
that I bless, tender
light bestirring me.

10

And it's you who where it dawns,
poor, riddled shadow,
you who for ever return?...

11

And you, lips I desired
silent for ever; palms
deceived for eternity;
and confident, deluded,

you, worn out eyelids...

Of the years and the tears
beyond the vile, pious Lethe,
old insatiable furies who tempt you,
stir you still, what thirst,

set in me, to these shores?

12

Da me, da me attendevi
il gesto interno, l'unica
parola? Avverso ai brevi
tuoi dubbi, ero io la sola,

l'unica, a caso eletta,
prova tra le infinite?
Forse fra tante vite,
questa, soltanto questa,

scelta avevi a vendetta.
Forse… O a segreto pegno
per aprirci il tuo regno,
la tua festa immortale?

13

Mi avessi da bambino
serbato alla tua legge!
Stato sarei del gregge
delle ombre a capo chino,

ombra anch'io, già pervasa
di buia infinità.
Tu solo, là, nella casa
della Ghiara vegliavi

dal tuo trono… Oh se agli avi
sommessi, cieco infante,
dedicato m'avessi
col tuo sguardo distante!

14

Stesa eri, sul prato,
una croce leggera.
Un sole innamorato
ti destava, una voce…

12

From me, from me you awaited
the inward gesture, the only
word? Opposed to your
faint doubts, I was the one,

the only, by chance elected,
test amongst the infinite?
Maybe among many lives,
this, and this alone,

you had chosen for vengeance.
Maybe... Or for a secret pledge
opening to us your reign,
your immortal feast?

13

If only when a child
I had kept to your Law!
I'd have been head bowed
among the flock of shadows,

a shadow too, already
filled with dark infinity.
There, in the Ghiara house,
you alone kept vigil

from your throne... Blind infant,
oh if to submissive ancestors
I'd devoted myself
with your distant gaze!

14

Lain you were, on the meadow,
a delicate cross.
A sun in love
awoke you, a voice...

15

D'oltre il passo del vento
chi ci risponderà?
Il tuo lamento, il mio,
chi mai raccoglierà?

Chiuso amore e restio,
oh distante pietà!
Scegliere: e chi vorrà,
se cade anche il brusio

del tempo nei pianori
dove non miete sguardo?
Ma i cieli, i cieli, se ardono
fra teneri vapori

di viola in rosse frange,
chi, escluso, con la gola
arida, li vedrà
spegnersi senza piangere?

16

Sei venuto alla porta.
Tossivi piano, lena
soffocata, ombra appena
appena scorta e già

sparita.

Come la verità,
come essa triste e bella,
proprio com'è la vita...

15

Beyond the wind's tread,
who'll reply to us?
Your own cry, mine,
who'll ever gather them?

Love closed and reluctant,
oh the faraway pity!
Choose: and who'd want to,
if the drone of time

in the plains also falls
where sight's not reaped?
But the skies, skies, if they glow
amid tender fumes

with violet in red fringes,
who, excluded, with dry
throat, will see them
be spent and not cry?

16

You came to the door.
Coughed lightly, choked
breath, shadow barely
caught and already

no more.

Like the truth,
sad and beautiful,
exacly as life is…

III

VIDE COR MEUM

Come lungo (chi chiama?) va stanotte un lamento!
Guada lento dal fiume per le erbe della riva,
sale a spire (chi cerca?), ed è qua, presso il lume,
di là, con le sue rotte voci, col suo spavento.

«Vide cor meum». Tu, chiami? Oh il cuore, il cuore, niente
altro di me (tu, cerchi?) ti specchia dal profondo.
Dunque toccami il cuore; gli occhi no, non la mente,
non il labbro insolente dietro cui mi nascondo.

VENUTO CON LA NOTTE

Venuto con la notte, che mi giova il tuo oblio?
Ecco la luce, e tu perché mormori «addio»?

Oh le rosse città cui, come a un viso
che si arrende febbrile, torna a volo la sera!

Di ogni cosa sei tu, solo tu il premio: vile
al tuo riso lontano risponde una preghiera.

DOVE SEI?

Dove sei? Donde chiami? Soltanto nelle cose,
solo ai vinti, agli arresi, sei presente? E le rose
per chi dagli orti umani hanno umane parole?
Solo ai morti le viole ridon spente e lontane?

IL VELO DI FIAMMA

Gloria che risponde a ogni cosa creata,
e in sé chiusa la serba, oh polvere infinita;
coltre immensa d'oblio entro cui, effusa,
si riposa ogni forma, torna buia ogni vita:

VIDE COR MEUM

How long (who calls?) does a cry go on tonight!
Slowly from the river through bank's grass it wades,
climbs in gusts (who searches?), and it's here, by the light,
over there, with its broken voices, with its fright.

"Vide cor meum." You, you call? Oh my heart, my heart,
nothing more of me (you, you search?) mirrors you deep below.
Then touch my heart; my eyes, no, nor my mind,
nor the insolent lip I hide myself behind.

COME WITH THE NIGHT

What good's your oblivion to me, come with the night?
And why do you murmur "farewell" now it's light?

Oh the red cities where, as in a face
surrendered to fever, back comes evening flying!

Of everything you are, only you the prize:
vile, to your distant grin a prayer replies.

WHERE ARE YOU?

Where are you? Calling from where? But only in things,
only to the beaten, surrendered, are you present? And roses
from human gardens, for whom do they have human words?
Only to the dead are the dull and distant violets smiling?

THE VEIL OF FLAME

Glory in response to each created thing,
and in itself enclosed retains it, oh endless dust;
vast pall of oblivion within which, flowing,
every form rests, every life returns to darkness:

lume, ombra, da te, ma più il pianto, più il riso,
che ribelle al tuo tempo (è dolcezza, è schianto!)
alza in me l'improvviso suo dolente diaframma,
questo è il velo di fiamma che da te mi separa.

PER UN QUADRO DI MORANDI

O tu cui lenta abbraccia la collina accaldata,
casa persa nel verde, esile volto e bianco,
solo tu durerai, muto, eroico pianto,
non resterai che tu, e la luce assonnata.

ARS POETICA

E non resti di me che un grido, un grido lento
senza parole. Nessuna mai parola: ché premio
m'eri, o frana celeste ed intima, tu sola.
Nel cielo senza tremito, quest'onda, questo accento...

CANZONE

Tu che a un profumo richiami per me
dal nulla tutti i fiori
che negli anni hai sommesse ombre distrutti,

distruggimi, purché
ogni sera, a un addio d'esuli cori,
io ritorni dal nulla per chi m'amò a rivivere.

Di nulla incoronato, fammi per sempre re
di chi mi ha amato.

PER IL PARCO DI NINFA

Perché dall'avvenire cui si assume esitante
ancora la mia vita verrà un riso? Oh distante

light, shadow, from you, but more the tears, the laughter,
rebelling against your time (it's sweetness, breathtaking!)
lifts in me its unforeseen, mournful diaphragm
dividing me from you, this is the veil of flame.

FOR A PICTURE BY MORANDI

O you slowly embraced by the hillside's heat,
house lost in the green, thin and white front,
only you'll endure, mute, heroic lament,
nothing will remain but you, and the bleary light.

ARS POETICA

And let nothing remain of me but a cry, no word
but a slow cry. Never a single word more: since reward
to me you were, o celestial and intimate flood, you alone.
In the sky without a tremor, this wave, this tone...

SONG

You who with a scent evoke for me
from nothing all the flowers,
subdued shadows, in the years you destroyed,

destroy me, so long
as each evening, at an exile choir's goodbye,
from nothing I return to live again for who loved me.

Crowned with nothing, let me be king forever
of those who have loved me.

FOR THE PARCO DI NINFA

Why from the future, where my life still hesitant
raises itself, will laughter come? Oh distant

isola del passato, là, che chiama, che invita!
Quel suo lume non è il tuo, morte, intriso e tremante?

VILLA GLORI

L'effimera creatura di luce incoronata
che dal ciglio del prato lentamente saluta,
non essa è che a un suo breve bisbiglio fa più acuta
(s'abbandona una musica...) la pietà che hai di te?

Ma l'altra che fra i tronchi, muta ombra assolata,
muove adagio col sole la rigida figura,
e schiena affardellata che si volge, paura,
noia ed ira rinnova, oh un miraggio non è!

SERA A MONTESACRO

Un vento umano, un alito, entra negli oleandri,
la sera nel giardino, il sonno nei tuoi pianti.

Di là da quante lacrime, luminosa e improvvisa,
ti apparirà una terra da dolci piogge intrisa?

ANGELUS

Bei colori del giorno, odiarvi, ora, che vale?
E te, se ormai dagli occhi fuggi senza ritorno,
luce estrema dell'angelus, che il mondo arreso adora?
Dunque addio e addio ancora, dolce squilla serale.

L'ALBA AI VETRI

L'alba ai vetri, e la musica d'un piffero e un tamburo
udivo, là, la sua opaca, un po' ebbra allegria.
Non eri tu che tornavi, vita, tu, vita mia,
tu che sopravvenivi, innocente futuro?

island of the past, there, calling, inviting!
Is it not yours, death, that dripping and tremulous light?

VILLA GLORI

The ephemeral creature crowned with light
at the edge of the meadow who slowly salutes,
does its brief whisper make more acute
(a music fades…) your own self-pity?

But the other between tree-trunks, mute sunny shadow,
the stiff figure moving slowly with the sun,
and burdened shoulders that turning renew
fear, boredom and anger – oh, a mirage it isn't!

MONTESACRO EVENING

A human breeze, a breath, enters through oleanders,
evening in the garden, sleep in your tears.

Beyond how much weeping, unforseen and shining,
to you will an earth drenched in tender rain appear?

ANGELUS

Fine colours of the day, to hate you, now, what gain?
And you, if by now you fly from the eyes with no return,
the angelus's last light, that the yielded world adores?
Then, sweet evening bell, farewell, farewell once more.

DAWN AT THE PANES

Dawn at the panes, and the music of a fife and drum
I heard, there, its opaque faintly tipsy mirth.
Wasn't it you that's returning, life, you, my life,
you appearing, innocent times to come?

«Empio evo venturo che premi dalle porte»,
dissi io allora con lacrime più soavi che amare,
«dimentica il mio nome!» Dicevo. E già, o morte,
già mi riassonnava l'esile inno tuo militare.

L'ORTO

Al vecchio, umano viso del mondo il sole torna,
muove muto tra i fiori. Signore, cieca mano
che rapisci, ed assumi, ed ignori... Ma qui,
qui, in questo orto perduto, qui è il mio paradiso.

I FIORI

Non va più dolce, più santo incenso,
grazie più umile al cielo immenso
del vostro, o fiori. Oh bocche miti!
Oh lieti, unanimi sguardi infiniti!

Va' dunque e perditi, negletta lode.
Ché se vien sera nei campi, e s'ode
parlar nell'erba calda d'amanti,
chi mai per l'aria bruna altri canti,

chi, pur se vecchio, se escluso, udrà?

Ma già li assonna, gli occhi sereni,
il lungo bacio d'addio dei treni.

LA CAMPANA

Come i primi ricordi (i più intensi!)
che la coltre degli anni sopiva,
al cader della notte dei sensi
tornan carne che incolume mordi:

"Wicked era coming, pressing at the doors,"
I then said with more sweet than bitter tears,
"forget my name!" I said. And already, o death,
already it sent me back to sleep, your thin martial hymn.

THE GARDEN

The sun returns to the world's old, human face,
it moves silent through the flowers. Lord, sightless
hand that ravishes, raises, overlooks... But here,
here, in this lost garden, here is my paradise.

THE FLOWERS

No sweeter, no more holy incense goes,
more humble gratitude towards the immense
sky than yours, o flowers. Oh mild mouths!
Oh joyful, unanimous, endless glances!

Go then, and fade, neglected praise.
For if dusk comes to fields, and you hear
talk in the grass warm with lovers:
who ever, through dark air, to other songs,

who, even if old, if outcast, will listen?

But already the trains' long-kissed goodbyes
send them to sleep, their clear eyes.

THE BELL

Like first memories (most intense!)
the years' pall soothed,
with nightfall of the senses
they return as unhurt flesh you gnaw:

la campana, così, la campana
che la febbre del giorno copriva,
io al tacer di ogni sera riudiva
la sua musica fedele e lontana.

SOGNO

Ho visto in sogno mio padre: «Tu qui?»
Timido e triste rideva: «Non vieni?»
O rive, o infanzia, o frangenti sereni,
voi tornavate, nel calante dì?

Tutto tornava. Eppure vano, oh fu,
al nembo che vi spense, onde fulgenti,
contendere e alla rena i lievi, argentei
suoi capelli, e all'oblio più che un sospiro.

A MIO PADRE

Se qui, nel petto, contro il vivo cuore,
s'entro me stesso seppellirti osai,
e offeso ora in me tremi, offesa mai
manchi alla vita che ancora mi resta,

lacrime a questa seppellita fonte
su cui, sospeso, con la fronte stai.

QUALCHE VOLTA

Qualche volta, come una fronte che si levi
lenta, esitando, a musiche meravigliose,
la cortina di brume non resiste più, le cose
ardono nel sereno, intatte e lievi.

La pietà che le assume è una cera lontana
che nessuna voce umana può incidere.

the bell, just so, the bell
day's fever concealed,
with each evening's quiet once more
I heard its music faithful and far.

DREAM

I saw my father in a dream: "You here?"
Timid and sad he laughed: "Not coming?"
O shores, o childhood, o calm breakers,
you were returning, in the waning day?

Everything returned. And yet, oh, it was vain
in the haze that quenched you, shining waves,
to contend with the sand his wispy, silvered
hair, and with oblivion more than a sigh.

TO MY FATHER

If here, in my breast, against the living heart,
if within me I dared to bury you,
and offended now in me you quiver, offence
never lacking to the life that's still left me,

tears to this buried source above which,
suspended, with your brow you remain.

SOMETIMES

Sometimes, like a brow being raised
slow, hesitant, at miraculous music,
the screen of mist resists no longer, things
burn in the clear day, intact and light.

The pity taking them up is a distant wax,
one no human voice can incise.

STELLA

Non tanto è fitta la nebbia
che tu non splenda dolcemente
sull'erba madida, sulle lente
mie lacrime, lontana stella.

COMMIATO

Scordami qui, disteso coi più vecchi, assopito
nel campo tutto arreso a uno sguardo infinito.

STAR

The fog is not so dense
that you can't sweetly shine
on moist grass, distant star,
on slow tears of mine.

LEAVE-TAKING

Forget me here, lying with the oldest, dazed
in the field surrendered to an endless gaze.

II
SENZA / WITHOUT

EPITAFFIO / EPITAPH

Cover of *Epitaffio*, Milan: Mondadori, 1974. (Fondazione Bassani, Ferrara)

FORO ITALICO GIUGNO '72

Lasciamiti vedere
piantala
di tirarti tutta indietro sulla sedia
di plastica
di mostrarmi soltanto la punta del nasino
di sotto in su
i bianchi degli occhi

NEGLI ANNI D'ORO

Negli anni d'oro della mia
gioventù
a quante sublimi auree cose credevo
con mica troppo ahimè
coraggio di crederci!

Adesso
quasi vecchio quasi
completamente incredulo
ne ho tanto però di
coraggio

ORMAI LO SO

Ormai lo so perché alla mia santa
gli occhi le si riempiono così spesso di lacrime
e dice che vorrebbe
morire

Lo so da quando le ho recitato
le tre terzine finali del decimo del Paradiso
spiegandole poi come
risulti chiaro che secondo Dante
la jouissance di lassù
non si diversifica minimamente
da questa di quaggiù

FORO ITALICO JUNE '72

Let me get a look at you
quit
that leaning right back on your
plastic chair
that showing me only your little nose tip
up from below
the whites of your eyes

IN THE GOLDEN YEARS

In the golden years
of my youth
how many sublime gilded things did I believe
with barely too much
courage alas to believe them!

Nowadays
almost aged almost
entirely unbelieving
I have plenty
courage though

BY NOW I KNOW

By now I know why for my saint
her eyes so often fill with tears
and she says she'd rather
die

I've known since I recited
the last three tercets of Paradiso ten for her
explaining to her then how
it grows clear that according to Dante
the jouissance up there
it doesn't differ in the slightest
from the one down here

tranne che per la durata
e che perciò l'eternità paradisiaca
altro non è in sostanza che un
unico
solo
interminato
venire

DA QUANDO

Da quando
ho deciso di non rispondere
mai più
a una tua lettera
nessun'altra lettera mai
ho più potuto
nemmeno aprirla

Lascio
che vengano
che mi cadano attorno
che giacciano laggiù ai miei piedi
capovolte e inevase
zitte
come me come ormai la mia
vita

GLI EX FASCISTONI DI FERRARA

Gli ex fascistoni di Ferrara
invecchiano
alcuni
di quelli che nel '39
mostravano di non più ravvisarmi
traversano mi buttano
come a Geo le braccia al collo
gaffeurs incontenibili
sospirano eh voi

except for its duration
and that's why eternity in paradise
in substance is none other than
one
single
endless
coming

FROM WHEN

From when
I decided not to reply
any longer
to one of your letters
not another letter ever
was I even able
to open

I let them
come
and fall around me
lying down there at my feet
topsy-turvy and unanswered
silent
like me like my own
life now

FERRARA'S EX-FASCISTS

Ferrara's ex-fascists
they grow old
some of those
who in '39
made a point of not acknowledging me
they cross over they greet me
as with Geo arms around the neck
irrepressible blunderers
they sigh ah you

propongono
dopo la dolorosa
pacca sulla spalla mancina
l'agape casalinga
che alfine consenta alla monumentale mummy cattolica
d'estrazione bolognese o rovigotta
ai brucanti in tinello strabiondi
teen-agers incontaminati
di incontrarlo una buona volta
il già compagno di scuola talmente
bravo
il bravo
romanziere
il presidente...

Hanno l'aria di insinuare
nel mentre dài piantala
non lo vedi che sei tu quoque
mezzo morto?
E poi scusa – continuano
uguali identici ormai
all'ingegner Marcello
Rimini
al rabbino dottor Viterbo –
in che altro modo senza di
noi
avresti potuto metterle insieme
le tue balle con relativo
appoggio di grana eccetera? Dopo tutto
cazzo
potresti ben cominciare
a considerarci anche noi quasi dei mezzi...

Corrazziali? Voi quoque? Dei quasi
mezzi cugini? No piano
Come cazzo si
fa?

Prima
cari
moriamo

they propose
after the painful
left-handed pat on the back
domestic agape
which in the end consents to the monumental catholic mummy
of Bolognese or Rovigo extraction
to the nibblers in the dining room super-blond
untainted teenagers
to meet him once and for all
the one-time schoolmate so
competent
the competent
storyteller
the president...

They have the air of insinuating
in the meantime come on cut it out
don't you see tu quoque
you're halfway dead?
And then sorry – they go on
by now looking just like
the engineer Marcello
Rimini
the rabbi doctor Viterbo –
in what other way without
us
would you have been able to put together
your bollocks with relative
liquid support etcetera? After all
fuck it
you could very well begin
to consider even us as almost half...

Co-racial? You quoque? Almost
half cousins? No not so fast
How the hell
can you?

First
my dears
we've got to die

A UN'AMICA

Mi dicevi
sdraiata lunga distesa
nel tuo immenso lettone Biedermeier
così decisamente
frocesco
– ed io in piedi dai piedi ti ascoltavo –

che sono un egoista egocentrico
che arrivo a fumare il sigaro nella camera di una dama
che con me non si può discutere
che una poesia o un racconto a me non li si può proprio
leggere
che faccio sempre sentire agli altri
me di qua gli altri di là
eccetera

Va bene cara ma come
scusa
potrebbe essere diversamente?

E senti
poi
chi
parla

INVETTIVA

Non essere
stupida sei già
porca
non ti basta?
Con quella zazzera genialoide pepe e
sale
con quello storto ammicco
tabagico
con quei jeans
di velluto

TO A LADY FRIEND

You told me
lying sprawled
in your huge Biedermeier bed
so definitely
faggoty
– and me on my feet at the foot I was listening –

that I'm an egocentric egotist
that I go as far as smoking a cigar in a lady's chamber
that one can't talk to me
that a poem or a story one simply cannot read
to me
that I always make others feel
I'm on one side the rest on the other
etcetera

Okay dear but how
excuse me
could it be otherwise?

And then
just look
who's
talking

INVECTIVE

Don't be
stupid you're already
a bitch
isn't it enough?
With that crazy-genius salt and pepper
mop of hair
that twisted tobacco
wink
those velvet
jeans

e il culo
dentro
sfasciato
non
ti
vergogni?
Pensa piuttosto a che
cosa
ci è sopra
alla putredine
di dopo

A UN PROFESSORE DI FILOSOFIA

È l'America ad averti
fatto male
gli U.S.A.

Partivi
tutto ex Pidàz stoica
ineffabilità dell'Io
tutto dover essere tutto
Capitini
Resistenza
eccetera
ed eccoti viceversa
di ritorno
con l'aria
di aver scoperto il cazzo la fica il culo
la droga
Love Story

Vecchia talpa accademica
fraterna talpa dammi retta
scòrdatele le nevi del Massachusetts
le pigre enormi
automobili
travalicanti inavvertite l'amaro
dormiveglia di Emily

and your flabby
ass
inside
aren't
you
ashamed?
Think rather of
what's
above us
of the putridity
to come

TO A PROFESSOR OF PHILOSOPHY

It's America that has
ruined you
the U.S. of A.

You'd leave
all ex-Partito d'Azione stoic
ineffability of the ego
all having to be all
Capitini
Resistance
etcetera
and here you are on the contrary
coming back
with the air
of having discovered cock ass pussy
drugs
Love Story

Old academic mole
fraternal mole I'm telling you
forget about the Massachusetts snows
the huge lazy
automobiles
crossing unnoticed the bitter
waking dream of Emily

cambia programma rinuncia
fin d'ora
il prossimo ferragosto a Cortina
d'Ampezzo
mandando lampi ottimistici
dalle spesse lenti dai denti dall'irta
canizie all'umberta
ad uscire alle nove del mattino all'attacco
dei Pelmi e dei Pomagagnòn
smettila
di tesaurizzare l'eventuale pelo biondiccio
ritto solo solo sul dorso
di una mano
no quaeso stop
basta di ricontare a ogni istante più ingordo che
avaro
i giorni le ore i minuti di questa minima
frangia di semivita che ancora ci
resta

CONVERSAZIONE LETTERARIA

Dimmi lo piglierai
nel caso che te lo
dessero?

Che intanto boh me lo
diano

Dopo al caso vedrò e
lo saprai

A UN CRITICO

Ben volentieri te lo darei
mio caro un calcio nel
culo

change program give up
right now
the next August holiday in Cortina
d'Ampezzo
sending optimistic flashes
from your thick lenses your teeth your bristly
Umberto-style grey hair
going out to attack at nine in the morning
the Pelmi and the Pomagagnòn
give up
hoarding a single blond hair
upright all alone on the back
of your hand
no I beg you stop
enough of recounting at each instant more greedy than
stingy
the days the hours the minutes of this minimal
fringe of a half-life that remains
to us still

LITERARY CONVERSATION

Tell me will you take it
if they give it
you?

Whatever let them
give it me

And then I'll see and
you will know

TO A CRITIC

Very gladly I'd give you
a kick in the ass
my dear

Ma ti farebbe
poi
male?

A UN ALTRO CRITICO

Se la poesia deve essere ormai – come tu dici –
considerata né più né meno d'un semplice
strumento di comunicazione
uguale a tantissimi altri ebbene
sia

Comunicare tramite l'arte del resto fu ognora
la mia ambizione suprema
pur se non giunsi mai e poi mai
a sperare di riuscirci persino con te
coglione

A FRANCO FORTINI

Incontrandoti
anni fa in bicicletta sulle pendici
tutte al sole di Monte Marcello
dove – spiegavi malinconico – vi siete fatti
la villetta del week-end e delle grandi
vacanze
ho invidiato tutto di te dalle polpe
di bronzo ai fenomenali
bigi cernecchi quasi neoclassici ma specialmente
il volto carnoso diventato
a forza di frequentare letterature nordiche
un po' da Nobel
svizzero

Che fatica lo so
anche io per esperienza
che fatica e che noia per dei fantasmi
dei semivivi del tuo e mio stampo

But would you
then
feel pain?

TO ANOTHER CRITIC

If poetry by now must be – as you say –
considered more or less a simple
communication tool
equal to a great many others so
be it

Communicating by means of art was after all
always my supreme ambition
even if I never ever went as far
as hoping to achieve it even with you
you pillock

TO FRANCO FORTINI

Coming upon you
years ago on a bike on the slopes
of Monte Marcello all in the sun
where – gloomily you explained – you'd got yourselves
a weekend and summer holiday
cottage
everything about you I envied
from the bronze calves to the amazing
near neoclassical grey quiff but most
of all the face become meaty
by dint of spending time with Nordic literature
a bit à la Swiss
Nobel

How tiring I know
me too from experience
how tiring and boring for the ghosts
the half-living of your and my kind

sentirsi sempre obbligati a far lavorare il
muscolo
a sfidare la vetta
essere quelli che siamo
e passare per dei Bassani e dei
Fortini

ANCHE TU

Anche tu
simile tu anche al misero
Edgardo
incapace di dire di sì
al mondo
altrimenti che salutandolo
facendogli ciao
tanto sono A.
B.

NUDO

Certe volte da che ho perduto
l'olfatto
mi dico per consolarmi
cieco non la vedrei

Ma poi ecco il mio giunco là la mia grande
bionda
e a guardarla non vedo che il
suo odore

4 MARZO '73

Oggi è il mio compleanno e la mia giovane
belva la mia
santissima
mi dice fra i singhiozzi che la sola

to feel we're forever obliged to make
the muscle work
to attempt the summit
to be who we are
and pass for a Bassani and for a
Fortini

YOU TOO

You too
you too just like poor
Edgardo
unable to say yes
to the world
other than by greeting it
saying hello
me being A.
B.

NAKED

Sometimes since I've lost
my sense of smell
I tell myself for consolation
blind I wouldn't see her

But then here she is my reed my great
blonde
and looking at her all I see is
her smell

4 MARCH '73

Today is my birthday and my young
animal my
saintliest
tells me between sobs that the only

cosa che lei rimpiange è che io non abbia
infiniti più anni di quelli che già
ho
che io non sia a tal punto decrepito insomma da trovarmi a un passo
dal termine dell'esistere
mio personale e
separato
perché l'amore – grida – quando è vero
non può essere che come il suo e cioè nemico
della vita

I DUE SANGUI

Fra i due sangui il rosso e il nero
che mi corrono arterie e vene
lei preferisce il rosso
naturalmente
il gioioso il pazzo l'ardente
il femminile

Ma non ammette che mi sia venuto
da mia madre nega
che da me sia poi passato
a mia figlia
dice che è la *sua* vita e che la vita
nasce e muore con me

ALL'AMATA

Prenderlo nel didietro – lo dico in tutti i
sensi – risulta sempre
proficuo o quanto meno
evento sublimante che può portare e contrario
dritti filati a Dio

Dunque perché vergognarmi dopo tanti anni di Te lucis
ante?
Perché non dovrei scriverle

thing she regrets is I'm not
infinitely older than I already
am
in short I'm so decrepit as to find myself one step away
from the end of my personal
and separate
existence
because – she cries – love when it's true
can be only like hers and therefore the enemy
of life

THE TWO BLOODS

Between the two bloods the red and the black
running through my arteries and veins
naturally she prefers
the red one
the joyful the mad the ardent
the feminine

But she won't admit it's come to me
from my mother she denies
it's passed from me
to my daughter
says that it's *her* life and life
is born and dies with me

TO THE LOVED ONE

Taking it from behind – I mean in all
senses – turns out always
profitable or at least
a sublimating event that can lead straight to and back
from God

So why be ashamed after so many years of Te Lucis
Ante?
Why shouldn't I write them

mio nuovo stolido dio distante anche per te
queste nuove parole?

NO NON AGGIUNGERÒ

No non aggiungerò nuova legna
al fuoco lasciamo
che la legna che già c'è si consumi
a poco a poco
che la vampa si trasformi a poco a
poco in brace
ed io e te zitti – seduti
uno a fianco dell'altro – dal fondo
buio della sala a guardare
spegnersi finalmente anche
quella

ALL'ADDIACCIO

Crois-tu qu'on en sortira?
ripetevi tremante e ogni tanto
baciandomi
la notte d'agosto e d'eclisse
di quasi due anni
fa
nudi entrambi e abbracciati sopra la nuda
pietraia di qua da Trècchina

Ma solo adesso lo so mia bella
mia assai
amata
che sempre ci se la cava sempre
in ogni caso e qualsiasi

e che dunque non ne usciremo
mai

my obtuse new distant god for even you
these new words?

NO I'LL NOT ADD

No I'll not add new wood
to the fire let
the wood already there burn through
bit by bit
let the blaze turn bit by
bit to embers
and you and I in silence – sitting
side by side – from the dark back
of the living room we watch it
go out finally
even that

IN THE OPEN

Crois-tu qu'on en sortira?
you repeated trembling and every now and then
kissing me
the night of August and eclipse
nearly two years
back
both naked and embracing over the naked
stone ground on this side of Trècchina

But only now I know it my beautiful
my very much
beloved
we always get through it always
in any case and every

and then how we won't get out of it
ever

DA HOFMANNSTHAL

Ride e dice no senti
chi mai se lo sognerebbe
di legarti?
Tu fedele? Lo so
lo so ben io cosa vali
anche tu a sentimenti

Giralo dunque il vasto mondo dài
cambia pur letto ogni notte se ci
tieni
piglia e lascia tutte quante le
belle tipe chic che vorrai

Stufi d'un vino lo si
pianta ma la mia bocca
la mia lingua eh com'erano?
Quel giorno che tu cominciassi
a scordartene vieni
torna

L'HO GIÀ DETTO

L'ho già detto sì nei miei libri
in prosa ma indirettamente
per vie traverse
simile anch'io a certi pittori di soffitti
d'una volta
– tutti più o meno di remotissima
ascendenza manierista –
costretti a lavorare al chiuso
per mesi e mesi magari per
anni
rimunerati a giornata come operai
qualsiasi dall'avaro
committente
da lui medesimo provvisti ad ore fisse del vitto
di casa lassù sui palchi

FROM HOFMANNSTHAL

She laughs and says no listen
who would ever dream of
tying you down?
You faithful? I know
I know very well what you're worth
when it comes to feelings even you

Then travel the wide world go on
even change bed every night if you
care to
take and leave all the
lovely chic girls you want

Sick of a wine we
give it up but my mouth
my tongue eh how were they?
The day you begin
to forget them come back
return

I'VE ALREADY SAID IT

I've already said it in my books
in prose but indirectly
at a slant
even me like certain ceiling painters
of days gone by
– all more or less of remotest
mannerist descent –
constrained to work indoors
for months on end perhaps for
years
paid by the day like any other workmen
by the skinflint
patron
provided at set times by him too with the household
meals up on the platform

non mai dimessi prima che fosse ben
notte
e nel frattempo soltanto a sognarsela
la trepida la cangiante l'instabile
luce di fuori
inventandosela
ricordandosene e
basta

MI CHIEDI PERCHÉ MAI E QUANDO

Mi chiedi perché mai e quando
ti rispondo che è stato così
accorgermi semplicemente in un tardo pomeriggio qualsiasi
poniamo – giacché non è nemmeno detto – d'ottobre
del modo come la luce del sole colpiva il roseo
impervio fianco sud-ovest di palazzo
Sacchetti
– colpiva e al tempo stesso bagnava la luce non so se mi
segui… –
accorgermi delle foglioline nere e aguzze del rampicante – l'aria era mossa
capisci? – percorse a tratti
su su per il tramite di oscuri rameggi da una specie di
reiterata scarica elettrica la quale contemporaneamente
fosse infusa chissà come d'autentico e liquido
oro
e aver voglia di schianto dopo anni infiniti
di ridere ridere e insieme del suo perfetto
contrario

LA CUGINETTA CATTOLICA

No non è affatto vero sono stato
molto felice da
ragazzo
però da bambino incomparabilmente
di più

        never released before it was good and
                    dark
        and in the meantime only dreaming it
        the hesitant the dazzling the unsteady
              light outside
               inventing it
            remembering it and
                that is all

YOU ASK ME WHYEVER AND WHEN

            You ask me whyever and when
             I reply that's how it was
       simply noticing in any late afternoon
let's say – given it's not necessarily so – in October
     how the sunlight struck the rosy
    impervious southwest side of Palazzo
                   Sacchetti
– the light struck and at the same time bathed I don't know if you
               follow me… –
noticing the sharp and little black leaves of the creeper – it was a breezy day
          you get it? – run through at times
       up above by means of dark twigs by a kind of
   repeated electrical discharge at the same time
   infused who knows how with authentic and liquid
                     gold
    and abruptly wanting after endless years
  to laugh and laugh and at the same time its precise
                  opposite

MY LITTLE CATHOLIC COUSIN

      No it's not at all true I've been
         very happy as a
             boy
     but incomparably more so
          as a child

La mia vita si svolgeva a quell'epoca
– l'epoca della guerra –
nella casa dei nonni in via
della Ghiara
col nonno Cesare che verso sera
tornava in bicicletta dall'ambulatorio o dall'ospedale
e che poi dritto in piedi dinanzi
ad una delle grandi finestre
di cucina
guardava verso Bologna l'oro delle nuvole a grado a
grado spegnersi
e intanto cantava a mezza bocca sogghignando e piangendo
Leonora addio

Sopraggiunse infine da Roma
una bella ardita
moretta
Bruna la cuginetta
cattolica

DAI GIORNALI

I furti di opere d'arte hanno ognuno uno
stile

Da una chiesa del sud della Francia nottetempo
risultano sottratti
ieri
un bassorilievo gotico a sei arazzi
del XVII secolo

Dalla vetrina blindata di un museo svedese
e per di più durante le ore
di visita
tre orologi del XVIII

In Nigeria tre statuette – non è detto
quando e dove –
le quali sarebbero a tutt'oggi in possesso

My life unfolded at that time
– in wartime –
in my grandparents' house on via
della Ghiara
with grandfather Cesare who towards evening
would come back by bike from the clinic or the hospital
and then standing up straight in front
of one of the large kitchen
windows
would look towards Bologna the gold of the clouds fading
away bit by bit
and meanwhile would sing beneath his breath grinning and crying
Leonora farewell

Finally arrived here from Rome
a beautiful fearless
brunette
Bruna my little Catholic
cousin

FROM THE NEWPAPERS

Work-of-art thefts have each their own
style

From a church at night-time in the south of France
there's been stolen
yesterday
a Gothic bas-relief with six 17th-century
tapestries

From the armored display case of a Swedish museum
and what's more during
opening hours
three 18th-century clocks

In Nigeria three statuettes – it doesn't say
when or where –
they're allegedly still in the possession

di anonimi
residenti uno a Parigi uno a New York e uno in
Olanda

Negli U.S.A. infine da due banditi
penetrati armi alla mano e di pieno giorno nella civica
pinacoteca di Worcester Mass.
quattro tele – un Rembrandt due Gauguin un Picasso – del valore di più di
un milione di dollari

AL TELEFONO

Mi racconta che stanotte al telefono
avevo parlandole una strana voce
molto calma e pacata che dicevo
cose affatto sensate e ragionevoli insomma ma con un tono un po' da
bambino

Non ne so nulla non mi ricordo
di niente
però mi chiedo vive dunque ancora
quel bambino medesimo che corrucciato abbraccia
la mamma nel minuscolo
quadretto fotografico che sta in salotto a Ferrara?
Possibile? Vivo e sepolto in me
così e da tanti anni?
Ma allora cosa gli accadrà che ne sarà di lui misero
tra poco?

ROLLS ROYCE

Subito dopo aver chiuso gli occhi per sempre
eccomi ancora una volta chissà come a riattraversare Ferrara in macchina
– una grossa berlina metallizzata di marca
straniera dai grandi
cupi cristalli forse una
Rolls –
a scendere ancora una volta dal castello Estense giù per corso

of anonymous
residents one in Paris one in New York and one in
Holland

In the U.S.A. finally by two thieves
got in weapons in hand and broad daylight to the civic
art gallery of Worcester Mass.
four paintings – one Rembrandt two Gauguin one Picasso – worth more than
one million dollars

ON THE PHONE

She tells me tonight on the phone
speaking to her I had a strange voice
very calm and peaceful in brief I was saying
utterly sensible and reasonable things but with a slightly
childish tone

I don't know anything about it don't remember
a thing
but wonder is he still alive
that same frowning child who embraces
his mother in the tiny
photo-picture from the parlour in Ferrara?
Is it possible? Alive and buried in me
just so and for how many years?
But then what will befall what will become of miserable him
in a little while?

ROLLS ROYCE

Straight after closing my eyes for ever
here I am who knows how crossing Ferrara by car once more
– a huge metalized foreign-made
sedan with great
dark windows perhaps
a Rolls –
descending once more from the Este castle down

Giovecca verso il roseo
ghirigoro terminale della Prospettiva che intanto piano
piano si faceva grande entro il concavo
rettangolo del parabrise

Lo chauffeur d'alta e dura collottola seduto a dritta davanti
certo lo sapeva molto bene da che parte dirigersi né io d'altronde
mi sognavo minimamente
di rammentarglielo
ansioso com'ero di riconoscere sulla sinistra la chiesa
di San Carlo più in là a destra
quella dei Teatini
a lei di contro già fermi così di buon'ora in crocchio sul marciapiede
dinanzi alla pasticceria
Folchini
gli amici di mio padre quando lui era giovane
i più con larghe lobbie bige in capo alcuni con tanto di mazza
dal pomo d'argento in pugno
ansioso anzi smanioso com'ero insomma di ripercorrere l'intera Main
Street della mia città in un giorno qualsiasi di maggio-giugno
attorno alla metà degli anni Venti un quarto d'ora avanti
le nove di mattina

Quasi sospinta dal suo stesso soffio lussuoso infine la Rolls svoltava
laggiù per via Madama e di lì a poco in via
Cisterna del Follo
e a questo punto ero io non più che decenne
le guance di fuoco per il timore d'arrivar tardi a scuola
a uscire in quel preciso istante coi libri sottobraccio
dal portone numero
uno
ero io che pur continuando a correre mi giravo indietro
verso la mamma spenzolata dalla finestra di sopra a raccomandarmi
qualcosa
ero io proprio io che un attimo prima di sparire
alla vista di lei ragazza dietro l'angolo
levavo il braccio sinistro in un gesto
d'insofferenza e insieme
d'addio

by Corso Giovecca towards
the Prospettiva's final rose-colored squiggle which was slowly
but surely growing big in the concave
rectangle of the windscreen

The chauffeur with high stiff collar sat on the right in front
he knew the way to take for sure nor did I
ever dream for a moment
of reminding him
anxious as I was to recognize the church
of San Carlo on the left
and the Teatini further to the right
already standing in a group on the pavement before it so early
in front of the pasticceria
Folchini
my father's friends when he was young
most with wide grey lobbia hats on their heads some even with silver-knobbed
canes in their fists
above all anxious desirous rather as I was to cross the entire Main
Street of my hometown in an anyday of May or June
around the middle of the Twenties at eight forty-five
in the morning

Almost driven along by its own luxurious breath the Rolls at last would turn
down by via Madama and a little way on into
via Cisterna del Follo
and by this point myself I was no more than ten
cheeks burning from the fear of being late for school
coming out at that precise instant books under my arm
from the front door
at number one
it was me who as I went on running would turn around
towards mother leaning out of the window above to remind me
of something
it was me really me who a moment before disappearing
round the corner seeing her girlish figure
would raise my left arm in a gesture
of impatience and at the same time
goodbye

Avrei voluto gridare alt al rigido
chauffeur e scendere ma la Rolls
sobbalzando mollemente già lungheggiava
il Montagnone anzi ormai fuori
Porta già volava per strade ampie deserte
prive affatto di tetti ai lati e affatto
sconosciute

PROMENADE DES ANGLAIS

C'è una cosa di lei di cui mi ricordo
ogni qualvolta penso che alla fine dovremo
pur lasciarci
lei già chiusa serrata dentro la stupida
nera scatola della
Morris
lei già immessa nolente nella ferrea
fiumara della Promenade
lei già non più in
lacrime anzi quasi
sorridente
girata un attimo indietro piena di buona
volontà
a dirmi ciao arrivederci a
tra poco
lei già mia proprio allora viceversa
per sempre

A LETTO

Ieri sera a letto mi ero messo
dalla parte destra quella che occupa
lei quando è qui
e stamani svegliandomi mi son ritrovato
a sinistra di dove nel buio ascolto insonne talora
il battito potente del suo
esserci

I'd have wanted to shout stop to the rigid
chauffeur and get down but the Rolls
bouncing softly already sidled
down the Montagnone actually by now
out of town already flying through wide empty streets
lacking roofs entirely to the sides and entirely
unknown

PROMENADE DES ANGLAIS

There's one thing about her I remember
whenever I think we'll eventually have to
leave one another
she already locked in her stupid
black box of a
Morris
she already unwittingly immersed in the iron-like
torrent of the Promenade
she already no longer in
tears if anything almost
smiling
turned around a moment full of good
will
to say ciao goodbye see
you later
instead she already mine forever
then and there

IN BED

Yesterday I went to bed
on the right side she occupies
when she's here
and this morning waking found myself
on the left where sleepless in the dark sometimes
I hear the mighty
beat of her being there

Cosa mi ha indotto dunque durante la notte
ad abbandonare lo spazio del suo grande
corpo assente
se non l'ansia d'essere anche io
niente?

INDOVINELLO

Cara non domandarmelo
chi sia mai la mia nuova segreta
ragazza
Bella? Oh sì stupendissima
grande con grandi occhi azzurri
come te

Come te possessiva rilutta
all'abbraccio anche lei forse frigida
ugualmente
Ma importa?
L'essenziale anche per lei è che non sia io
frigido
proprio niente

Giovane? Tale e quale
te col tuo stesso
piccolo viso appena un po' rugoso
agli angoli delle palpebre e della bocca
col tuo stesso sorriso sempre lì lì
sul punto di rompersi
in lacrime

Pazza? Né più né meno del più
pazzo giorno di questo aprile
romano
dura e molle esigente e
remissiva quasi altrettanto
quanto la tua
mano

What then had compelled me during the night
to abandon the space of her great
absent body
if it wasn't my angst at me being
nothing as well?

GUESSING GAME

Dear don't ask me
who might be my secret new
girlfriend
Beautiful? Oh yes quite stupendous
big with big blue eyes
like you

Like you possessive reluctant
to hug she too perhaps equally
frigid
But what matter?
The key thing for her too is I'm not
frigid
not at all

Young? Just like
you with the same
small face just a bit wrinkled
at the corners of the eyelids and mouth
with the same smile always
about to break
into tears

Crazy? No more and no less than
the craziest day of this Roman
April
hard and soft demanding and
almost as submissive
as your
hand

In ciò esclusivamente si differenzia
da te che giammai non mi lascia
un attimo al punto che è qui
perfino adesso
seduta a me vicina su questa medesima
panchina piena di vento

Il nome suo? Non mi va di dirtelo
Dirtelo non servirebbe
a nulla giacché fra l'altro rischierebbe
anima mia al contrario
di farti solo
ridere

Sappi ad ogni buon conto che pari al tuo
termina in *ie*

LETTERA

Carissima anche stanotte ho sognato mi trovavo
a Maratea figuràti però non a casa
su in paese bensì giù
al Porto e precisamente all'Hôtel
Fiorella
essendomi lasciato alle spalle un viaggio lunghissimo complicato
dalla neve caduta abbondante sull'autostrada
poco di qua dall'ultimo tunnel quello che sbocca in
vista di Lagonegro

Ci avevo dormito all'albergo occupando una delle solite
camerette col solito minimo
stambugio attiguo fornito d'una larva di doccia
del W.C. e d'un gramo
lavandino
e abitato puntualmente dalla solita metallica
quant'altre mai incarognita
povera mosca superstite magari là dalla scorsa
estate

In this alone she differs
from you as she never leaves me
for a moment so much so that she's here
even now
sitting next to me on this same
wind-blown bench

Her name? I don't feel like telling you
To tell you there'd be no point
given that among other things
my heart it would on the contrary
only make you
laugh

In any case take it from me like yours
it terminates in *ie*

LETTER

Dearest last night too I dreamed I was
in Maratea imagine though not at home
up in the town but down
at the harbor and to be precise at the Hotel
Fiorella
having left behind a very long journey complicated
by the abundant snow fallen on the autostrada
just before the last tunnel the one that opens up in
sight of Lagonegro

I had slept at the hotel staying in one of the usual
little bedrooms with its usual minimum
adjacent hovel equipped with a phantom shower
a WC and poor
sink
and punctually inhabited by the usual metallic
if ever there was one malignant
poor fly surviving there perhaps from the previous
summer

Adesso era mattina la mattina
susseguente al mio arrivo con un tempo di colpo
magnifico la spalla di Capo
Palinuro emergente nera sul mare la Colla perfetta
sgombra affatto di nuvole eccetera e il sottoscritto a girare
su e giù il naso all'aria
nei dintorni immediati della nostra avventizia
rosea villetta d'una volta così simile
come ben sai a quelle di Viserba o Bellaria
dei miei dieci anni

Rattristato e esaltato nel contempo dal fatto
di un imbattermi nel corso dei miei andirivieni in nessuno
per istrada e che ogni casa risultasse in aggiunta
con porte e imposte regolarmente
sprangare
non facevo che domandarmi se per avventura non fossero
tutti morti laggiù a marina e se anche io lì
nel quieto solicello fossi davvero
in vita

Più tardi nella vuota salle à manger del Fiorella pranzavo
accanto ad un signore brizzolato sulla cinquantacinquina
conversando con lui del più e del meno da tavolo a
tavolo assai
tranquillamente
abbastanza convinto in cuor mio nonostante
ogni opposta evidenza
d'averlo ben conosciuto altrove ed in altra
epoca non importa se ormai
lontana

Ma eccomi – ed era già quasi sera la sera
del medesimo giorno – eccomi stare ad un tratto nel mezzo
d'una candida cella – d'ospedale capivo – mentre lì innanzi supino
disteso completamente vestito sopra un lettuccio
di ferro
giaceva il signore brizzolato dai malinconici
occhi azzurri col quale dianzi avevo discorso
un poco d'ogni cosa inclusivi addirittura

Now it was morning the morning
after my arrival with weather suddenly
magnificent the shoulder of Capo
Palinuro emerging black on the sea the Colla perfect
quite free of clouds etcetera and yours truly going
up and down with nose in the air
in the immediate surroundings of our adventitious
period pink cottage so similar
as you well know to those of Viserba or Bellaria
from when I was ten years old

Saddened and elated at once by the fact
all through my comings and goings I'd not encountered anyone
on the street and every house turned out what's more
to have doors and shutters regularly
bolted
I couldn't help wondering if by chance they weren't all
dead down there at the marina and whether me too there
in the quiet sunshine I was really
alive

Later in the empty salle à manger at the Fiorella I had lunch
next to a grizzled gentleman in his fifties
conversing with him about this and that from table to
table very
quietly
quite convinced in my heart despite
all evidence against
to have known him very well somewhere else and in another
era no matter if now
far distant

But here I am – and already it was nearly the evening the evening
of that same day – here I am suddenly stood in the middle
of a white cell – a hospital's I realised – while there before me supine
lying fully clothed upon an iron
cot
lay the grizzled gentleman with melancholy
blue eyes with whom I had been talking earlier
a bit of everything including even

il governo Andreotti ed il centro
sinistra

Sapevo – oh lo sapevo molto bene! – che dopo esserci
levati su entrambi dai nostri
tavoli con largo sfoggio
dalle due parti di amabili forse un tantino
eccessive espressioni di simpatia reciproca
– e tuttavia trascurando di comunicarci l'un l'altro i rispettivi
nomi e cognomi –
lui era salito al Castello da solo
passo passo buttandosi
quindi giù a capofitto
nel sottostante
baratro

Della mia stessa età
come mi assomigliava – pensavo contemplandolo – come lo
ripetevo in tutto e per tutto con particolare
riguardo alle spalancate
chiare iridi talmente identiche
a quelle di mio padre!
Senonché mentre così ragionavo fra me e me rimirando
me stesso morto non eri dunque già tu
anima mia – mi dicevo anche – non eri dunque già tu
a ricordarmi?

NINFA RIVISITATA

La rara pianta orientale d'un bello e ricco
rosso focato all'agguato subito dietro la svolta
d'un sentiero là a Ninfa pari in tutto a una belva
non meno elegante che sanguinaria
ne ha fatta della strada durante gli ultimi
quindici anni dal minimo
cespo in vaso
che era!

È venuta su sviluppando al massimo il vello paludandosene
come d'un mantello di gran classe

the Andreotti government and the center
left

I knew – oh I knew very well! – that after getting up
both from our
tables with a large display
on both sides of lovable maybe slightly
excessive expressions of mutual sympathy
– and yet neglecting to communicate our respective names
and surnames to one another –
he had climbed up to the Castle on his own
step by step throwing himself
headlong then
into the abyss
below

At my same age
how he resembled me – contemplating him I thought – how I
would repeat him in each and every way with particular
regard to the clear wide open
irises so identical to those
of my father!
Except while I was reasoning thus to myself observing
my dead self wasn't it already you then
my dear – I wondered too – wasn't it already you then
who remembered me?

NINFA REVISITED

The rare oriental plant of a beautiful and rich reddish
colour lurking just behind the turn
of a path there at Ninfa equal in every way to a beast
no less elegant than bloodthirsty
it's come a long way over the last
fifteen years from the minimal
tuft in a vase
that it was!

It grew evolving its fleece to a maximum swamping it round
like a high-class mantle

che lascia appena intravedere
sotto
le sdutte nere membra attorte i bui
lunghi muscoli pronti
al balzo

Saresti cresciuta anche tu così tale e quale
immobile in un canto di questo mio vecchio orto
italiano
senza mai stabilire rapporto alcuno col dialettale contesto
abnorme e stupenda
silente e
minacciosa
per l'esclusiva gioia paurosa ogni tanto del mio
sguardo
per la cauta carezza soltanto
della mia mano

LE LEGGI RAZZIALI

La magnolia che sta giusto nel mezzo
del giardino di casa nostra a Ferrara è proprio lei
la stessa che ritorna in pressoché tutti
i miei libri

La piantammo nel '39
pochi mesi dopo la promulgazione
delle leggi razziali con cerimonia
che riuscì a metà solenne e a metà comica
tutti quanti abbastanza allegri se Dio
vuole
in barba al noioso ebraismo
metastorico

Costretta fra quattro impervie pareti
piuttosto prossime crebbe
nera luminosa invadente
puntando decisa verso l'imminente
cielo

which barely lets you glimpse
beneath
its lanky black twisted limbs its long
dark muscles prepared
for the leap

You'd have grown even you like so just the same
fixed in a corner of this old Italian
garden of mine
never ever forming any relations with the vernacular milieu
abnormal and stupendous
silent and
threatening
for the fearful exclusive joy every now and then of my
gaze
for the cautious caress alone
of my hand

THE RACIAL LAWS

The magnolia standing right in the middle
of the garden in our Ferrara house is exactly the one
the same as returns in very near all
of my books

We planted it in '39
a few months after the racial laws' enactment
with a ceremony
which turned out half-solemn and half-comical
everyone more or less happy God
willing
despite the tedious meta-historical
Judaism

Constrained between four impenetrable walls
rather close it grew
black luminous invasive
pointing surely towards the imminent
sky

piena giorno e notte di bigi
passeri di bruni merli
guatati senza riposo giù da pregne
gatte nonché da mia
madre
anche essa spiante indefessa da dietro
il davanzale traboccante ognora
delle sue briciole

Dritta dalla base al vertice come una spada
ormai fuoresce oltre i tetti circostanti ormai può guardare
la città da ogni parte e l'infinito
spazio verde che la circonda
ma adesso incerta lo so lo
vedo
d'un tratto espansa lassù sulla vetta d'un tratto debole
nel sole
come chi all'improvviso non sa raggiunto
che abbia il termine d'un viaggio lunghissimo
la strada da prendere che cosa
fare

ALLA PERIFERIA

Dunque addio anche a te alto e magro
ignoto quarantenne indugiante di qua dalla soglia
d'una saracinesca d'elettrauto o di carrozziere
mezzo calvo in blue-jeans ed in scura
maglietta con corte maniche
intento – sembra – a osservare perplesso
qualcosa di fronte che non scorgo
oppure semplicemente
a calcolare dentro se stesso i minuti
residui che lo separano dalla chiusura
serale

Sono quasi le diciannove d'una giornata
qualsiasi di mezzo maggio
e sto procedendo adagio attraverso uno qualsiasi

full day and night of grey
sparrows and brown blackbirds
restlessly stared down on by pregnant
cats as well as my
mother
even she tirelessly spying from behind
the windowsill overflowing always
with her crumbs

Upright from the base to the tip like a sword
now it flowers beyond surrounding roofs now it can see
every part of the town and the endless
green space that surrounds it
but uncertain now I know
I see it
suddenly expanded up there on the summit suddenly weak
in sunlight
as someone at the end
of a very long journey of a sudden doesn't know
what road to take what else
to do

ON THE OUTSKIRTS

Then goodbye to you too tall and thin
unknown forty-year-old lingering this side of the threshold
to an electrician's or body shop's shutter
half bald in blue jeans and dark
t-shirt with short sleeves
intent – it seems – on observing perplexed
something in front I don't see
or simply
calculating in himself the final few
minutes that keep him from the evening
closure

It's almost seven in the evening of any
day in the middle of May
and I'm slowly advancing across any

di questi nuovi quartieri periferici
che Carlo solo può frequentare senza sentirsi
anonimo
anonimo d'un tratto io viceversa tale e quale
l'individuo inquadrato non più d'un attimo fa
al centro del parabrise
il quale non domandava come me ormai
che d'essere dimenticato

DI PROFILO

A letto a tavola in macchina sempre
mi vuole a sinistra sostiene che il viso
che le offro da destra
risulta senza confronto più affascinante
più buono più quieto più virile e dunque
migliore

Capisco oh certo però francamente
che storia mostrarsi in eterno da un solo lato
ridotto uguale a un Cèroli
assecondando così fra l'altro il generale andazzo del secolo
ormai non più bramoso di niente tranne che di ritornare
antico!

E come poi non tifare al solito
pur se nell'intimo più segreto
per l'opposto del bello del fascinoso del
risplendente
per la parte cioè che grigia sente
soffre e ricorda?

ARRIVO MIA MADRE NON STA BENE

Arrivo mia madre non sta bene telefono al cugino
medico subito pronto a
dichiararsi in pigiama
prendo la macchina vado

of these new outer suburbs
which Carlo alone can frequent without feeling
anonymous
me suddenly anonymous au contraire exactly like
the individual framed no more than an instant ago
in the center of the windshield
who would ask like me nothing now
but to be forgot

IN PROFILE

In bed at the table in the car she always
wants me on her left side asserts that the face
I offer her from the right
is beyond compare more fascinating
more decent more tranquil more virile and therefore
the best

I understand oh sure though frankly
what a bother to forever show yourself from just the one side
reduced to the likes of a Cèroli
besides seconding thus the general trend of the century
no longer now desirous of anything but to return
antique!

And how can you not support as usual
even if in the most secret intimacy
the reverse of the beautiful fascinating
resplendent
the gray part I mean which feels
suffers and remembers?

I ARRIVE MY MOTHER'S NOT WELL

I arrive my mother's not well I phone my cousin
the doctor immediately ready to
declare himself in pajamas
I take the car I drive

ed eccolo là sotto giusto da basso che già m'aspetta
in cravatta dinanzi alla soglia del roseo tutto pimpante
suo vetusto palazzotto

Che cosa diavolo dirci dopo quasi trent'anni
che non si sta un po' assieme?
Nulla di impegnativo di troppo
intimo naturalmente
e così durante il breve
tragitto da casa a casa non ci diciamo
pressoché niente

Mi accorgo però guardandolo di sottecchi come in un quarto
di secolo ce l'abbia fatta a incredibilmente
assomigliare a mio padre anche lui medico
– ma a tempo perso – curante
Possiede gli stessi – mi dico – fragili zigomi
le stesse sottili stanche un po' viola
labbra nevrotiche le medesime
cartilagini gialline
adopera l'uguale identica paziente sommessa
ironia ebraica

Insiste frattanto a guidarmi di stradetta in stradetta
nel buio con la dolcezza un tantino beffarda
del cittadino trovatosi a pilotare per caso l'illustre
ospite forestiero
la dolcezza anche del vecchio che accoglie il quasi
vecchio altrettanto
o magari di chi defunto da assai più lungo
tempo l'appena

STORIA DI FAMIGLIA

Mi domando talora quale fra i miei parenti ed affini
meno ti sarebbe dispiaciuto e dopo averli
passati nuovamente in rassegna uno per uno
nella memoria
torno ogni volta a concludere che lo zio Giacomo

and he's right there downstairs already waiting
in a tie before the threshold of that rosy all fancied up
antiquated mansion of his

What the hell to tell each other after near thirty years
that we don't spend much time together?
Nothing too demanding
too intimate of course
and that way during the short
journey from home to home we say
barely a thing

I notice however looking at him from the corner of my eye
how in a quarter century he's come to look
incredibly like my father he too a doctor
– but in his spare time – a family one
He has the same – I tell myself – fragile cheekbones
the same thin tired faintly purple
neurotic lips the same
yellowish cartilage
uses just the same identical patient submissive
Jewish irony

In the meantime he insists on guiding me from lane to lane
in the dark with the slightly mocking sweetness
of a citizen piloting by chance the illustrious
foreign guest
the sweetness too of an old chap who welcomes the nearly
equally old
or maybe of one who dead a much longer time
does so for the recently

FAMILY HISTORY

I sometimes wonder which of my relatives and kindred
you would have disliked least and after
reviewing them once more one by one
in memory
every time I decide Uncle Giacomo

detto da me bambino zio Dedo
il quale a prescindere dal piccolo Max morto a quattro anni fu l'unico
fratello di mia madre quello no
quello forse non te la saresti
sentita di disapprovarlo

Sebbene nutrisse fin da ragazzo aspirazioni artistiche studiò da dottore
soprattutto per compiacere al padre il nonno
Cesare
ma col segreto rovello poi sempre di non aver mai trovato bastante
animo per rompere dandosi
alla pittura o magari
abbracciando la carriera
diplomatica
e ciò in ispecie dopo un semestre trascorso al Cairo – non appena ultimati
gli studi che aveva condotto innanzi nella Firenze
dei primi del secolo e quindi in Germania –
assunto pro tempore come personale suo medico dal Kedivè
d'Egitto

Al termine della prima guerra mondiale dove pare
si portasse da valoroso buscandosi
fra l'altro una lieve ferita al mento che gli lasciò
il bruno viso triangolare adorno d'una bianca
simpatica cicatrice
rieccolo a Ferrara nel '19 senza ad un tratto sapere
che cosa avrebbe fatto di se stesso ma in fondo già rassegnato
fin d'allora – lui che parlava
correntemente almeno tre lingue – all'esercizio
della professione se non in patria in qualche altro buco consimile
della provincia padana
previo tuttavia sposalizio
adatto nonché se possibile
conveniente

Si unì dunque in matrimonio nel '20 con una non bella né giovanissima
ereditiera concittadina che usciva da un clan ebraico-agrario assai chic genere
Finzi-Contini per intenderci la quale subito
gli dette un figlio maschio rivelatosi tuttavia a neanche
un anno dalla nascita minorato

who I called Uncle Dedo as a child
and apart from little Max who died at four was my mother's
only brother no him
maybe him you wouldn't have
felt like disapproving of

Though a boy with artistic aspirations he studied to be a doctor
specially to please his father
grandfather Cesare
but then always with the nagging secret thought of never finding enough
nerve to break away by giving
himself to painting or maybe
embracing a diplomatic
career
and this in particular after a semester spent in Cairo – soon as he completed
the studies he'd previously conducted in Florence
early in the century and then Germany –
was hired pro tem as his personal physician by the Khedive
of Egypt

At the close of the Great War where it seems
he bore himself bravely by getting
among other things a slight wound in the chin
that left his triangular brown face adorned with a nice
white scar
here he is again in Ferrara in '19 of a sudden not knowing
what he would do with himself but after all already resigned
even then – he who spoke
fluently at least three languages – to practice
as a doctor if not at home in some other similar hole
of the Po-plain province
upon suitable
as well as if possible
convenient marriage

He therefore married in '20 a girl neither beautiful nor all that young
a fellow citizen heiress who came from a very chic Jewish-agrarian clan
such as the Finzi-Continis to be plain who immediately
bore him a male child that not even one year
after his birth turned out to be mentally

mentale irrecuperabile
e tale perciò da rappresentare per lui durante
i residui dieci anni della sua corta
vita
una fonte perenne d'infinita
pur se nascosta amarezza

Troppo ricca e superba la moglie tremendamente
snob anche essa per riuscire
in qualche modo a consolarlo e difatti accadde
che menassero esistenze in pratica
separate
lui in una cittadina del Veneto in qualità di primario
d'ospedale ivi ognora assistito però e accudito da schiere
di buone e brave suore-infermiere adoranti
lei a Ferrara dedita al bambino affatto idiota – intestandosi
a rivolgerglisi per lo più in inglese – nella grande
dimora paterna di via
Montebello

Ma per restare un attimo ancora su di lui come mai nella solitudine
dei suoi anni ultimi
non gli capitasse più di produrre nessuno di quei curiosi disegni a penna
stile Simplicissimus ma d'argomento
in prevalenza famigliare
a cui si era fatto la mano all'epoca del perfezionamento
in Germania fra l'8 e il '10
– ne sarà rimasta sì e no una ventina poveri
ingialliti fogli d'album affissi a caso qua e là fra tinelli
e salottini nelle sparse tane del superstite
parentado –
non saprei dirlo con certezza
È probabile che badasse a tirare la carretta
giorno dopo giorno perseverando ciò nonostante dentro se stesso
a sperare così come per fortuna
succede spesso

Giacciono comunque tutti e tre assieme padre madre e figlio
sepolti da molti anni nel cimitero
israelitico di Ferrara

disabled irrecoverable
and therefore such as to represent for him during
the remaining ten years of his short
life
a perennial source of endless
though concealed bitterness

Too rich and proud tremendously snobbish
his wife she too to be able to succeed
somehow in consoling him and in fact it fell out
that they led practically separate
lives
he in a small town in the Veneto as a chief
hospital physician always assisted however and cared for by hosts
of adoring and virtuous good sister-nurses
she in Ferrara dedicated to the totally idiotic child – stubbornly
addressing him mostly in English – in the large
paternal residence in via
Montebello

But to stay a moment longer with him how come in the solitude
of his final years
he never happened to produce any more of those curious pen drawings
Simplicissimus-style but mainly
on family topics
that he got the knack of in his student years
in Germany between '08 and '10
– there'll have survived more or less some twenty poor yellowish
album sheets randomly stuck up here and there in dining rooms
and lounges the scattered dens of surviving
relatives –
I can't say for sure
It's likely he might have been plodding along
day after day continuing nevertheless inside himself
to hope the way fortunately
it often happens

Anyway they lie together all three of them father son and mother
buried years back now in the Jewish
cemetery at Ferrara

nel piccolo prato a sinistra che si stende giusto di là
dal cancello d'ingresso
tre snelle candide
lapidi sobriamente
iscritte
nel mezzo quella di Cesarino di poco premorto ventenne
alla madre vedova senza che
avesse potuto mai intendere non una sola
parola sia d'inglese sia d'italiano insomma niente
di niente

DAVVERO CARI NON SAPREI DIRVELO

Davvero cari non saprei dirvelo
attraverso quali
strade così di lontano
io sia riuscito dopo talmente
tanto tempo a tornare

Vi dirò soltanto che mi lasciai
pilotare nel buio
da qualcheduno che m'aveva
preso in silenzio per la
mano

LA BOCCA

Penetrata in punta di piedi nel tenebroso
stambugio della televisione
durerà dieci
minuti buoni seduta
a guardarmi da dietro mentre guardo
borbotto fra me e me tossisco
per colpa del sigaro impreco rido insomma sono
come normalmente
sono

in the small meadow on the left that stretches just beyond
the entrance gate
three slender candid
gravestones soberly
inscribed
in the middle Cesarino's he dead at twenty-years-old just before
his widowed mother without ever
being able to understand even a single
word of either English or Italian nothing in short
nothing at all

REALLY MY DEARS I WOULDN'T KNOW HOW

Really my dears I wouldn't know how
to tell you down which
roads so distant
after so much time I was
able to return

I'll only tell you how I let
myself be piloted through the dark
by someone who had
silently taken me by the
hand

MY MOUTH

Slipped in on tiptoe to the gloomy
hole-like television room
she'll last ten
good minutes sitting
and watching me from behind while I watch
mutter to myself and cough
because of the cigar swear laugh in short I'm
as I usually
am

È dunque così che sono quando sono
solo? – commenta poi tra mesta
delusa e divertita – Questa
lei assente la mia vita?
Ma soprattutto chi mai
sono io – accusa –
io realmente?

E non lo sa la mia santa bocca che l'ultimo
a saperlo è proprio colui
che appunto mentre lei parla la guarda
muoversi
e quindi prima di baciarla la tocca
col dito

SANTA SEVERA

Non fidarti troppo di te se a questo punto
della mia vita
ti appaio così somigliare
a questo quartiere di vecchie ville e villette
borghesi in riva ad un mare
che non è più
mare

Vòltati guarda il territorio selvaggio
che ci sta dietro completamente
disabitato
folto di nere foreste di lecci punteggiato
qua e là come sempre a maggio dai folli
capelli delle ginestre
e che va su su fino al blu
del cielo continuamente in
salita

ISOLA BISENTINA

Come è bella la vita e che peccato
dover lasciarla ho avuto la dabbenaggine

So that's how I am when I'm
by myself? – she comments then half glum
half disappointed and half amused – Is this
my life she absent?
But most of all who am I
ever – she reproaches me –
really?

And my blessed mouth doesn't it know that the last
to know is precisely the one
who exactly as she speaks watches her
moving
and then before kissing her touches her with
his finger

SANTA SEVERA

Don't trust yourself too much if at this point
in my life
I appear to you that similar
to this neighborhood of old bourgeois villas
and cottages beside a sea
that is no longer
sea

Turn round and look at the wilderness
lying behind us completely
uninhabited
thick with black forests of holm-oak dotted
here and there as always in May with the broom-plants'
crazy manes
and up it goes up to the blue
of the sky continuously
climbing

ISOLA BISENTINA

How beautiful life is and what a pity
we have to leave it I had the gullibility

di sospirare mentre la barca
nell'ora particolarmente ruffiana del tramonto lacustre
flottando leggerissima si approssimava
all'isola incantata

E subito l'acuto amico modernista a minacciarmi
con tanto d'indice alzato e corrugando
la fronte
pur se sollecito poi a convenire ghignando che sì
è vero benché a morire
c'è sempre tempo

Nulla a ciò ribattei durante tutto
il rimanente della traversata e nemmeno dopo
che fu toccata la riva boekliniana e dopo ancora
lungo la via del ritorno
Però – mi domando ora – c'è sul serio
sempre tempo?

E se davvero ce n'è
sempre
quanto allora ce
n'è?

MOLTO PACATAMENTE

Molto pacatamente
conviene alfine d'essere stata invidiosa
sia della gatta sia del cane così del pony
come dell'asinella
d'aver odiato per l'eternità le parole
bella mia mia dolcezza uniche
creature mie
ma alfine so di che cosa realmente
fosse gelosa
lo so dal freddo che oggi fa così dure
le mie vene

to sigh while the boat
at that particularly fawning lacustrine sunset hour
floating very lightly would approach
the enchanted isle

And immediately my acute modernist friend threatens me
raising his finger and wrinkling
his forehead
even if he's quick to agree with a grin that yes
it's true even though to die there's
always time

I'd nothing to say to that throughout
the rest of the crossing and not even after
we touched the Böcklin shore and again later
on our way back
But still – I ask myself now – is there really
always time?

And if there really
always is
how much is there
now?

VERY CALMLY

Very calmly
in the end she agrees to have envied
both the cat and dog as well as the pony
and donkey
to have hated for eternity words
my beautiful my sweetheart my
one and only creatures
but at last I know what she was really
jealous of
I know it from the cold today that makes
my veins so hard

DALLA SICILIA

È quasi sera percorro tutto solo la nuova fiammante
autostrada che ormai lungheggia un tantino più su dei binari
del treno la costiera delle zàgare
ritrovando l'odore ma senza riconoscere
dopo tre anni i luoghi singoli o non ravvisandone
che pochi
rari

Non lasciarmi andare randagio torna spesso rimanimi quanto
più puoi accanto non permettere
che mi dimentichi del tuo corpo che adagio
adagio lo
disimpari

DANSE MACABRE

Si avvicinano
pronto ognuno a occupare la propria seggiola
signori e signore appartenenti
– ovverosia appartenuti fra '30 e '40 – alla migliore
società
tutti quanti stasera resi un po' pazzi
all'idea della prossima
baldoria a base di boli
succulenti
e perciò esumando nelle more certi tremanti
loro lazzi decrepiti
ma ormai proni tutti assieme sul grande
piatto ovale d'entrée
alla ricerca chi della spigola
chi della sogliola
chi dell'ostrica
di roba tenera insomma la quale resta
sempre l'ottima per chiunque non ha
più denti

FROM SICILY

It's almost evening I travel all alone on the brand new
autostrada running now along the citrus coast
a little higher than the railway tracks
rediscovering the smell but without recognizing
after three years single places or recognizing only
a few
rare ones

Don't let me go straying come back often stay with me
as much as you can don't let me
forget your body so that slowly
slowly
I unlearn it

DANSE MACABRE

They're coming closer
everybody ready to take their own chair
gentlemen and ladies belonging
– having belonged that is in the '30s and '40s – to the highest
society
all slightly crazy tonight
at the thought of the next
spree based on succulent
boluses
and so exhuming from their repertoire some trembling
decrepit old jokes
but by now prone all together on the vast
oval plate of entrées
some looking for sea bass
some for the sole
some for the oyster
for tender stuff in short
that's always the best for whoever no longer
has any teeth

VILLINO TRICAMERE

Mi basta molto poco ormai un cancelletto
verniciato di rosso il cereo
lussureggiare d'una buganvillea ricascante giù da un bianco
intonaco falsamente rustico un asettico
praticello dinanzi
all'ingresso d'un villino tricamere arabizzante
col proprietario magari lì
mezzo pelato gli occhiali
da ipermetrope a metà naso
in canottiera pantaloncini corti mozzi
calzini bigi e sandali
di plastica
occupato a spendere quanto gli resta
di luce e di tempolibero
annaffiando...

Qualunque casa a questo
punto della mia vita mi piace qualsiasi
tana minimo-borghese è capace
di tentarmi di riempirmi
d'invidia e di gelosia

Dovunque ormai vorrei vivere
adesso tranne che a casa
mia

PER SCHERZO E PER GIOCO

Anche il tuo amore cominciò
non negarlo per scherzo fu per scherzo
che deliravi al principio promettendo ad ogni istante
di morire

Io queste poesie ho cominciato a farle
per puro gioco solo per me
ho messo insieme fin dall'inizio sillabe sempre ho giocato oramai distante
col mio sangue e col mio seme

THREE-BEDROOM COTTAGE

Very little's enough for me now
a red-painted gate a waxy
luxuriance of bougainvillea tumbling from white
falsely rustic plasterwork an aseptic
little lawn in front
of the entrance to an Arabianizing three-bedroom cottage
with owner maybe there
half bald his hypermetropic glasses
halfway up his nose
in undershirt cut-down shorts
grey socks and plastic
sandals
busy spending what's left to him
of light and free time
watering ...

At this point in life whatever
house I like any-old
minimal-bourgeois den is able
to tempt me to fill me
with envy and jealousy

By now I would live wherever
except at
home

AS A JOKE AND FOR FUN

Your love too began
don't deny it as a joke it was a joke
you being delirious from the start promising at every instant
to die

These poems I've begun to write
just for fun for me only
putting syllables together from the start always playing now distant
with my blood and with my seed

CARTA IGIENICA

Crespatina soffice va' là
che per stavolta te la sei cavata
splendidamente anonimo
confratello finito
nella Pubblicità!

Sfumato e realistico
insieme materico e
astratto
una volta tanto ci sei riuscito
ad assaporare anche tu per un giorno lo stordente orrore d'esistere
il diritto anche tu d'annunziare a gloria amore
giusto mezz'ora fa credo d'avere
fatto veramente
centro

SALTO DI FONDI

Perfino oggi tutto mi parla e tu perfino
ospite amico che marci zitto
nudi i piedi e gli stinchi chiuso nella canuta
tua magrezza nevrotica
un po' discosto da me lungo la clamorosa
immensità del mare
perfino oggi tutto mi parla non fosse che per dirmi
che non ci sto che non appartengo che la vita
è altrove che è un'altra
cosa

FORTE ANTENNE

Essere il ramo della foresta
la fogliolina di quel
ramo
tornare ancora come eri
allora a tre quattro anni

TOILET PAPER

Soft crêpe paper give over
this time you got away with it
beautifully anonymous
confrere who ended
up in Advertising!

Nuanced and realistic
both material and
abstract
for once you've succeeded
in savouring even you for one day the stunning horror of existence
the right even you to announce love to glory
exactly half an hour ago I think I've
really hit
the mark

SALTO DI FONDI

Even today everything speaks to me and even you
guest friend who tramps quiet
feet and shins bare closed in your
hoary neurotic thinness
not far from me along the clamorous
sea's immensity
even today everything speaks to me if only to tell me
I won't stand for it I don't belong life
is elsewhere it's something
else

FORTE ANTENNE

Being the branch in the forest
the little leaf of that
branch
returning the way you were
then at three or four years old

quando non conoscevi
nessuna femmina tranne la
mamma
nessun'altra città fuor che
la tua

BOCCA TRABARIA

Guardandomi ogni tanto nello specchietto retrovisore
con la stessa pietà e col medesimo senso
di rimorso
che sempre m'ispiravano lui già vecchio i fragili
zigomi di mio padre
son dovuto salire bene in su anziana
ginestra di quest'anno per ritrovarti
per bearmi l'ultima volta del tuo colore del tuo
odore!

Fra pochi giorni anche quassù vicino al passo
supremo dell'Appennino
non ci si ricorderà più di te
se non per commemorare invidiandola
l'eleganza silente
del tuo trapasso
se non per proporre come modello a noi stessi il finale
tuo sorridente ritrarti piano
piano in punta
di piedi presso il
cielo

TENNIS CLUB

So bene so che è assai poco importante
per gli altri per chiunque altro al mondo che il club
chiuso in vista dell'annuale disinfestazione mi appaia
oggi attraverso il cancello sprangato così distante
nel suo torrido silenzio assolato così stranamente
immortale

when you knew
no other female than your
mother
no other city beyond
your own

BOCCA TRABARIA

Looking at myself in the rear-view mirror every now and then
with the same piety and the same sense
of remorse
as inspired me always he already old my father's
frail cheekbones
antique broom-plant of this year I had to
climb far enough up to find you
to delight in your color your fragrance
one more time!

Up here too in a few days near the highest
Apennine pass
we'll remember you no more
except to commemorate and envy
the silent elegance
of your passing
except to propose as a model to ourselves your
final smiling withdrawal slowly
slowly on tiptoe
towards the
sky

TENNIS CLUB

Well I know I know it's really of little importance
for the others for anyone else in the world how the club
closed on account of the annual disinfestation appears to me
today through the bolted gate so remote
in its torrid sunny silence so strangely
immortal

Penso a noi due accanto per sempre penso ad un prato
echeggiato come questo dal feriale zip-zip soltanto
di invisibili irrigatori a pioggia automatici
e penso a un grande occhio celeste il quale da fuori
di tra le sbarre attonito per sempre
lo guardi

ODRADEK

Il filo bianco di refe sul pavimento
di lavagna bigia lui medesimo
quel minimo ghirigoro che la scopa
di domattina annullerà
può assumere lei assente il profilo
d'un canino
che domanda d'esserci che supplica
di durare solo un pochino
di più

PASSO VELOCE COME IL VENTO

Passo veloce come il vento lungo la riva
sinistra del Magra dove il vento scompiglia
le chiome dei salici dove le bianche
braccia dei pioppi gridano mutamente
nella luce
ovvii commedianti gli uni e gli altri effimeri
eterni guitti da niente

Di me e di te cos'altro rimarrà
negli occhi di chi ci avrà visti?
Un'immagine così
un flash e
basta
insomma niente

I think of us two beside each other forever I think of a meadow
echoed like this by the weekday zip-zip alone
of invisible automatic sprinklers
and I think of a great celestial eye which from outside
from between the bars forever astonished
watches

ODRADEK

The white thread on the grey
chalkboard floor itself
that minimum squiggle which tomorrow morning's
broom will sweep away
it can assume in its absence the profile
of a little dog
demanding to be there begging
to last just a little while
longer

I GO BY QUICKLY LIKE THE WIND

I go by quickly like the wind along the left
bank of the Magra where the wind ruffles
the willows' fringes where the white
arms of the poplars silently cry
in the light
obvious comedians the ones and the others ephemeral
eternal worthless ham-actors

Of you and me what else will remain
in the eyes of those who'll have seen us?
An image like this
a flash and
no more
all in all not a thing

LES ADIEUX

Piange ride grida sei molto
molto più giovane di me sei un'autentica
forza della natura
ma s'inganna non sa
in che misura
ad ogni istante io senta la mia
vita a grado a
grado lasciarmi
simile in tutto a lei
ogni qualvolta girata indietro ridendo
fra le lacrime se ne va
via

SUL POLLINO

Imbruna sugli alti pascoli la grande
vacca lattifera richiama a sé il vitellino
stolida mugghia alzando il muso attenzione
la carezza di quell'uomo là è menzognera
è ipocrita e poi tu sei
mio per l'eternità
mio per
sempre

Per sempre! Non più che per cinque o sei
mesi ancora finché il nato avrà voglia
della sua tetta fin quando lui
non preferirà mordere per conto proprio la foglia
dura del leccio l'irto
cardo selvatico oppure
non le sarà rapito come già fu di molti altri
prima

Senonché l'amore – non è vero amore? – l'amore
non sa cosa farsene della ragione
che calcola che misura che crede
l'istante più corto del secolo o perfino l'opposto

LES ADIEUX

She cries laughs yells you're much
much younger than me you're a true
force of nature
but she's mistaken she doesn't know
to what extent
at every moment I feel my
life step
by step leave me
similar in every way to her
whenever turning back and laughing
through her tears she makes
her way

ON THE POLLINO

It's getting darker on the high pastures the big
dairy cow draws the calf to itself
foolishly mooing raising its muzzle be careful
that man's caress it's deceitful
it's hypocritical and then you're
mine for eternity
mine for
ever

For ever! No more than for five or six
months still until the new-born wants
its nipple until
it prefers to bite on its own the hard leaf
of the holm oak the bristling
wild thistle or
it'll be kidnapped from her as with many another
before

Except that love – isn't it true love? – love
doesn't know what to do with reason
calculating measuring believing
the instant shorter than the century or even the precise

esatto
L'amore quando succede è sempre
un altro
fatto

LO SO QUEL CHE SIGNIFICA

Lo so quel che significa lo
indovino
questo frusciare qui vicino questa cosa che calma fluisce
calma e gioiosa
ed io per la prima volta immobile impietrito
nel mezzo della
corrente
io duro io gelido io assente io sbalordito
a guardare

DI RITORNO DA BUCAREST

Torno dopo dieci giorni appena e lei lieta
per la prima volta lei niente
affatto smarrita dall'altra
estremità del
filo

a raccontarmi subito dell'infinita
quantità di cose che ha fatto
durante il mio starmene
così lontano e zitto così
separato

Non era dunque questo che volevi? – mi dico intanto – Quando tra
breve tu riapparissi in un suo
sogno – se pure ciò
succederà mai – a toccarle timido una
mano

opposite
Love when it happens is always
one more
fact

I KNOW WHAT IT MEANS

I know what it means I can
guess it
this rustling nearby this calming thing flowing
calm and joyful
and me for the first time motionless petrified
in the middle of the
current
me stiff me chilly me absent me astounded
watching

RETURNING FROM BUCHAREST

I'm back after barely ten days and she happily
for the first time not at all
at a loss on the other
end of the
line

straight away she tells me about the number
of things she has done
during my remaining
so distant and silent so
detached

Wasn't this what you wanted then? – I tell myself in the meantime – When
you'd briefly reappear in one of her
dreams – if ever
that'll happen – shyly to touch her
hand

cos'altro potresti augurarti che lei pronunziasse sorridente
a fior di labbro – come un attimo
fa – se non questo suo calmo un po'
distratto ah
sei tu?

SATURNIA

Al centro esatto del fondovalle
mimetizzandola il verde limitrofo gli attigui fumacchi
della cascatella termale
modesta in tutto nelle proporzioni
nel lusso reticente nella sua stessa
prudente modernità
nessuno sa quale segreto
superbo calcolo l'abbia prodotta
la casetta da week-end d'artista la gentile
villetta quasi borghese nessuno sa quale intima
sfida

Soltanto il sole lo sa che splende alto nell'immacolato
cielo d'inverno ab aeterno conscio e
indifferente
e anch'io lo so trascorrente in auto lungo la provinciale
asfaltata a mezza costa
io sogguardante impavido laggiù la piccola
fronte morta io vivo
ancora

IN MEMORIA

Era alla Poesia che tiravi a quella
con tanto di P maiuscola ed a lei
soltanto

La tua vita? Quella là te la sei
anche tu bevuta

what else could you wish for but this in a whisper smiling
she pronounced – like a moment
ago – this calm of hers a bit
distracted ah
is it you?

SATURNIA

In the perfect centre of the valley floor
camouflaged by the neighbouring green the adjacent vapors
of the thermal waterfall
modest in all its proportions
its reserved luxury its own
prudent modernity
no one knows what secretive
proud calculation produced it
this weekend cottage for artists this gentle
almost bourgeois cottage no one knows what intimate
dare

Only the sun knows shining high in the immaculate
winter sky ab aeterno conscious and
indifferent
and me too I know passing by in the car on the blacktop
local road mid-hillside
me looking boldly down at the tiny
dead frontage and me
still alive

IN MEMORY

It was Poetry you were drawn to the one
with a capital P and only
to her

Your life? That one there you've
drunk it even you

PER UNA MACCHIOLINA

Per una macchiolina da niente sul candido
irreprensibile tuo polsino
di pizzo
tale quasi la viola d'Attilio ti lamenti ti
disperi

Sfòrzati d'essere un po' meno nitida
mia bella un po' meno pulita così in
generale
solo un tantino

Non te ne accorgerai
più

LA PORTA ROSA

Quando mi rimproveri di non occuparmi nei miei libri
che di Ferrara e del territorio immediatamente limitrofo
Reno e Po a sud e a nord non osando io varcarli che di rado e di strafòro
e l'Adriatico ad est non facendocela in pratica
a giammai raggiungerlo

dovresti ricordarti della nostra gita dell'estate scorsa alle rovine
di Velia
di come t'era piaciuto camminare accanto a me e al bravo
ospite Soprintendente
alta e bionda e straniera e di roseo sangue tu pura
fra noi due diversamente impuri
italioti
incantata in ascolto mentre salendo adagio verso la matematica
fulgida Porta parmenidea ritta sopra la cima
del colle giusto a
cavallo

venivamo noi uomini favoleggiando insieme degli aristocratici
coloni greci per secoli e secoli
lassù sopravvissuti in faccia al deserto del Tirreno incistata

FOR A LITTLE SPOT

For a little spot insignificant on your
blameless white lace
cuff
almost like Attilio's purple you complain you
despair

Do try to be a bit less limpid
my beautiful a bit less clean in
general
just a touch

You won't see it
any more

PORTA ROSA

When you reproach me for only dealing in my books
with Ferrara and its immediate surroundings
Reno and Po to the south and north only daring to cross them rarely and on the sly
and the Adriatic to the east never managing in practice
to reach it

you should remember our trip from last summer to the ruins
of the Velia
how you'd enjoyed walking near me and our good
host the Superintendent
you tall and blonde and foreign and with your pure rosy blood
between the two of us differently impure
Italiotes
you spellbound listening while climbing slowly towards the mathematical
refulgent Parmenidean Porta upright above the summit
of the hill exactly
straddling

we men were telling stories of the aristocratic
Greek settlers for century after century
surviving up there facing the Tyrrhenian desert encysted

asciutta stirpe carnivora di intellettuali sdegnosi d'intrattenere
rapporti con le plebi aborigene dell'entroterra
lucano
– tutti bassi costoro e di corte gambe nonché di grandi
deretani da divoratori d'amidacei e di
carboidrati –
che non fossero rigorosamente pratici e affatto
funzionali
superbamente beati essi dal primo all'ultimo della loro
perfetta solitudine

Come t'erano piaciuti i nostri discorsi come
ti sentivi tu pure greca partecipe in qualche modo e
depositaria
tu pure di un'aurea lingua particolare ed esclusiva
da adoperare esclusivamente fra rari eguali quasi divini dinanzi agli sbalorditi
umidi occhi nerissimi del semiservile
contadiname circostante
e come invidiosa anche e gelosa apparivi – così dichiarandomi
nel solito stile tuo che tuttora
m'ami –

del fatto che l'ellenica Porta suprema alla cui fresca ombra frattanto
nemmeno troppo affannato il trio nostro mirabile oramai ristava
l'eccellente archeologo l'avesse – non appena accadutogli
di restituirla intatta al bel sole e all'azzurro dell'antico privilegiato
straniamento ausonio –
battezzata Rosa – come spiegò – dal nome dell'ancor giovane sua
sposa conscia consorte negli studi congeniali e madre
dei suoi figli!

Non lasciarmi solo a scavare nella mia città a resuscitare
grado a grado alla luce
ciò che di lei sta sepolto là sotto il duro
spessore di ventimila e più giorni
È là Rosa mia mia Regina che io sono giovane e bello e puro
ancora
là l'esclusivo padrone e signore per sempre il solo
Re

dry carnivorous lineage of intellectuals who disdained to maintain
relations with the aboriginal rabble of the Lucanian
hinterland
– all of them short and short-legged too with large
starch and carbohydrate eaters'
posteriors –
which were not strictly practical and barely
functional
superbly blessed from first to last with their
perfect solitude

How much you'd enjoyed our conversation how
you too would feel yourself Greek a participant in some way and
repository
you too of an exclusive and particular golden language
to adopt exclusively amongst rare equals almost divine before the astonished
blackest wet eyes of the semi-servile
peasants surrounding
and how envious also and jealous you looked – declaring thus
in your usual style how you
still love me –

of the fact that the supreme Hellenic Porta to whose cool shade meanwhile
not even so out of breath our admirable trio would rest now
our excellent archaeologist – no sooner did he happen
to return it intact to the fine sun and the privileged ancient Ausonian
estrangement's blue –
he'd baptized it Rosa – as he explained – after the name of his still young
bride conscious consort in congenial studies and mother
of his children!

Don't leave me alone to dig in my city to restore
step by step to the light
what of it's buried there under the hard
thickness of twenty thousand and more days
It's there Rosa mine my Queen that I'm still young and handsome
and pure
there the exclusive master and lord forever the only
King

ARS DICTANDI

Grazie per essermi venuto incontro recando fra le dita
il bianco e bello pur se un po' osceno fiore dell'ellèboro il fiore
– m'hai ricordato – dei poeti
quello che fa
impazzire

Ma mi gioverà? Se c'è al mondo una cosa
capace di rendermi davvero
savio
questa è proprio l'attività diciamo poetica per cui io temo carissimo
io temo fortemente

che il tuo dono non mi riesca alla fine contro
producente

VALZER

Uscendo sul Lungotevere sotto la pioggia battente
che impegna al massimo il tergicristallo
scorgo in un lampo prima di immettermi
anch'io nel flusso della
corrente
una grande candida pagina aperta – forse la doppia
pagina centrale del giornale
d'oggi –
ballare gioiosa e disperata presa a mezz'aria nel vortice
di una ruota gommata
una specie di estremo valzer avanti di cedere
d'arrendersi a diventare informe e bigia
poltiglia
a ridursi a
niente

Eccolo dunque qua l'inverno un rapido
inverno ancora
così diverso dalla nera inclemente
stagione lunghissima

ARS DICTANDI

Thank you for coming to meet me bearing between your fingers
the white and beautiful only slightly obscene hellebore the flower
– you reminded me – of poets
the one that drives
them crazy

But will it do me any good? If there's one thing in the world
able to really make me
wise
it's precisely this call-it poetic activity for which I fear my dearest
I strongly fear

in the end your gift will be counter
productive

WALTZ

Going onto the Lungotevere in beating rain
which works the windshield-wiper to the full
I glimpse in a flash before immersing myself
me too in the flow of
traffic
a large white open page – perhaps the double
central spread of today's
newspaper –
dancing joyful and desperate caught in mid-air in the vortex
of a tyred wheel
a kind of extreme waltz before yielding
surrendering and turning to a shapeless and grey
pulp
in reducing itself to
nothing

So here then is winter another
quick winter
so different from the inclement black
extremely long season

capace ai tempi dei tempi di trasformare
il bambino in un ragazzo il ragazzo in un
uomo
la stagione interminabile piena di fiamme
e lacrime che a ricordarla
a ripensarci più tardi oramai dentro
la primavera
ti sussurrava ebbene no non temere se tanto hai
amato ebbene di nuovo e di più tra breve
amerai

IN CAPELLI

In capelli coi pantaloni a campana e col pellicciotto
corto al di sopra delle anche
sei venuta alle esequie di Momi
trafelata come a un appuntamento col
moroso

Hai fatto bene era così che piacevi
a lui vivo – e a me anche è così
che piaci proprio così
col tuo piccolo mento ardito sempre
in cerca d'un vero sposo

I GRANDI

Spesso – come se sognassi – ho innanzi agli occhi noi due fianco a fianco
stesi supini sopra un gran letto assai simile al nostro di Maratea
la camera risultando essa pure abbastanza uguale
nella candida mobilia ultramoderna nelle bianche
pareti tirate a gesso nell'alta finestra
verticale là a destra oltre l'opaco
profilo del tuo grande
corpo giacente
e perfino nella luce l'azzurra luce matissiana delle sette
del mattino che già si insinua attraverso le griglie a sconfiggere
la penombra tiepida

able to transform in the old days
a child into a boy a boy into
a man
the interminable season replete with flames
and tears which being remembered
being thought of later when it was now
already spring
whispered to you well then no don't fear if you've
loved a lot well soon you'll love
again and more

BAREHEADED

Bareheaded with bell-bottoms and a fur coat
short above your hips
you've come to Momi's funeral rites
out of breath as on a date
with a boyfriend

You've done right it was how he liked you
when alive – and that's how
I like you too just so
with your daring little chin for ever
in search of a genuine husband

THE GROWN-UPS

Often – as if I were dreaming – I've before my eyes the two of us side by side
stretched on our back on a large bed very like ours in Maratea
the room's also much the same
from white ultra-modern furniture to white
plastered walls to the high vertical
window there on the right beyond the matt
profile of your big
body stretched out
and even to the light the Matissean blue light of seven
in the morning already creeping through the shutters to defeat
the lukewarm penumbra

Senonché sarà sul serio a Maratea che ci troviamo? Proprio il blu della luce
più inquieta meno tersa e tranquilla come riflessa
quantunque in parte
mi induce presto a ritenere che no non siamo lassù
nella bianca casa eminente in cima al paese donde lo sguardo può dominare
ai dì sereni l'intero
golfo di Policastro
bensì chissà come in basso a livello della costa forse
a Filocaio o magari a
Cersuta
e a pochi metri in ogni caso dalla
riva del mare

Ma non ci troveremo per avventura a Conca – mi dico anche – da Sandro
o da Suni presso cui fummo tanto sovente in Santa
Liberata
o a Salto di Fondi da Lidia ospiti della rosea
casuccia mezzo nascosta in fondo al giardino un passo di qua
dalla spiaggia
ovvero su a Fiascherino da Mario messi a dormire anche lì
per ogni agio reciproco non già nella villa padronale ma nell'attigua ognora
disabitata
poetica baracca tutta vecchie assi all'esterno e dentro pietra scialbata
a picco sulla scogliera?

Il mare lui non si fa sentire è dunque una di quelle
meravigliose giornate d'accalmia assoluta quando alla vista laggiù
lungo la linea dell'orizzonte cielo ed acqua si confondono
si mescolano l'uno nell'altro col più
facile e più naturale dei consensi
mentre a riva la sua voce a colui che ristà
curvo sopra la bàttima ad ascoltarla
riesce ancor meno udibile d'un parlottio sussurrante e confidenziale
fra amico e amico fra amante e
amata

Tu dormi ma forse sogni di socchiudere come me le palpebre
e di vedere le stesse cose ch'io vedo
forse anche tu sognando ascolti come me o piuttosto
ti sforzi d'ascoltare
tu pure la conversazione che ferve sommessa nel vano adiacente giacché

But is it really at Maratea we find ourselves? Precisely the blue of the more
restless light less clear and calm as if reflected
albeit in part
it leads me soon to believe that no we're not up there
in the eminent white house at the top of the village overlooking
on clear days the whole
Policastro bay
but who knows how at the bottom on the level of the coast perhaps
at Filocaio or perhaps
Cersuta
and in any case a few meters from the
shore

But are we not by any chance at Conca – I also ask myself – guests of Sandro
or Suni with whom so often in Santa
Liberata
or at Salto di Fondi guests of Lidia's in the rosy
little house half hidden at the bottom of the garden a step
away from the beach
or up in Fiascherino at Mario's put to sleep there too
for every mutual comfort not in the main villa but in the adjacent always
uninhabited
poetic shack all old boards on the outside and dull stone inside
overlooking the cliff?

You can't hear the sea so it's one of those
wonderful days of absolute dead calm when visible down there
along the line of the horizon water and sky are blurred together
blent the one into the other with the easiest
and most natural of accords
while on the shore its voice to the one who lingers
curved above the shoreline to listen
is even less audible than a rustling and confidential murmur
between friend and friend between lover and
beloved

You sleep but maybe you dream of squinting like me
and seeing the same things I see
maybe dreaming you listen too like me or rather
you try to listen
you too to conversation softly humming in the next room as

dovunque adesso noi si sia nel sud
al di sotto di Napoli oppure al nord
sopra Orbetello
la stanza che ci accoglie risulta averne un'altra contigua
diversa di gran lunga più capace una sorta di salone
con mobili e arredi antiquati poltrone tavolinetti tappeti orientali sofà
ricurve bizzarre lampade in stile
floreale e via di seguito

A chiacchierare così bisbigliando a fior di labbro di là
dalla parete divisoria io quanto a me non ho dubbi su chi mai siano! Si tratta
del nostro rispettivo
parentado
di quello tuttavia maggiormente autorevole e responsabile non oltre
una ventina di persone nel complesso – inclusi
dieci almeno probabili
cugini e zii –
alcuni ancor oggi viventi e per fortuna in ottima
salute come ad esempio
la tua mamma e la mia nonché addirittura
Paolo mio fratello quattro anni
di me più giovane

altri al contrario – e prevalgono – scomparsi da svariati
decenni
quali i miei nonni Cesare e Davide e quali i due
ugualmente infelici nostri padri il mio ed il
tuo
e perfino da più d'un secolo e mezzo come nel caso
del baleniere e navigatore capitano Coffin tuo ascendente
materno
perdutosi in mare – m'hai raccontato – al largo della costa settentrionale
del Labrador verso gli inizi
dell'Ottocento

Intorno a quale argomento si aggiri la conversazione generale non so non riesco
in alcun modo a realizzarlo
può darsi che non si stia parlando che dello stato
del tempo odierno atmosferico o di qualche altra
amenità consimile
valida soprattutto a istituire contatti superficiali in attesa degli ulteriori

wherever we are now in the south
below Naples or to the north
above Orbetello
welcoming us the room appears to have another one contiguous
quite different far larger some sort of reception room
with antique furniture and furnishings armchairs coffee tables sofas oriental rugs
curved bizarre lamps in floral
style and so on

Chatting like that whispering under their breath beyond
the partition wall as for me I have no doubt who they are! They're
our respective
relatives
the nonetheless most authoritative and responsible ones no more
than twenty people in all – including
at least ten probable
cousins and uncles –
some still today living and luckily in excellent
health such as
your mom and mine as well as even
Paolo my brother four years
my junior

others on the contrary – and they prevalent – deceased for several
decades
like my grandfathers Cesare and Davide and like our two
equally unhappy fathers mine and
yours
and even for more than a century and a half as in the case
of the whaler and navigator Captain Coffin your maternal
ancestor
lost at sea – you told me – off the northern coast
of Labrador in the early
nineteenth century

Around what topic the general conversation revolves I don't know I can't
in any way make it out
it may be they're only speaking of the state
of today's weather or some other
similar pleasantry
valid above all for establishing superficial contacts while waiting for the other

indispensabili approfondimenti
Unica a emergere nel fioco contesto è se mai la voce cantante di mia
madre
riconosco all'improvviso la tipica
sua risata musicale
ed è comunque a partire da questo istante preciso che prendo anche a fisicamente
focalizzarli a distinguerli
ad uno ad uno in carne ed
ossa
i buoni i saggi i sempre molto pensierosi famigliari e consanguinei insomma quelli
che per chiunque si sia – da impubere – sono i
grandi

Mia madre con la bigia cagnetta acciambellata sulle ginocchia siede ilare accanto
a tua madre quest'ultima chiusa al solito nel rigido
suo perbenismo tutto anglosassone e
puritano
e altrettanto riservato sullo sfondo del salone in piedi
dietro la spalliera d'un divano – stupendamente
decorativo nel suo canuto e abbronzato mezzo
busto –
si mostra il capitano Coffin il quale reggendo con la sinistra il bicchierone
colmo per tre quarti di rum forse ora non sta
pensando che al momento
in cui – terminata che sia questa dannata
seduta fra intimi – lui potrà con l'aiuto di Dio svignarsela
riprendere l'interrotta
navigazione

Mio padre e il tuo così diversi a considerarli nella corporatura
nei tratti del viso nell'abito e ciò nonostante
fatti simili – quasi gemelli – dalla comune
sventura oltreché dai deboli
assurdi menti infantili levati su un po' di sbieco in chiara
espressione di sfida
pur tacendo occupano anch'essi due poltrone affiancate mentre invece
Paolo mio fratello spostandosi di frequente
da affine ad affine da parente a
parente
alacre come sempre ed ironico viene adoperandosi
al massimo per favorire

indispensable insights
The only one to emerge in the faint background if anything is my mother's
singing voice
suddenly I recognize her typical
musical laughter
and it's from this precise moment anyway that I also physically begin
to focus on them to distinguish them
one by one in flesh and
blood
the good the wise the always very pensive relatives and kinfolk in short those
who for anyone – still to reach puberty – are the
grown-ups

My mother with her little grey dog curled up on her lap sits amusingly next to
your mother the latter closed as usual in her rigid
Anglo-Saxon and puritan
respectability
and equally reserved in the background of the living room standing
behind the back of a sofa – beautifully
decorative in his hoary and tanned half-
torso –
Captain Coffin shows up holding in his left hand a big glass
three quarters full of rum perhaps now he's only
thinking about the moment
when – once this damned intimate
session is over – he'll be able to slip away with God's aid
to resume his interrupted
voyage

My father and yours so different if you consider them in their build
their facial features clothes and nonetheless
made similar – almost twins – by the common
misfortune as well as by their weak
absurd childish chins upraised a bit sideways in a clear
expression of defiance
though remaining silent they also occupy two armchairs side by side while instead
Paolo my brother frequently moving
from kin to kin from relative to
relative
zealous and ironic as always he does
his best to encourage

ad ogni costo possibile la comprensione in giro per alimentare
come sempre il dialogo

È di me e di te – ora sì ne son certo! – che fra un po' si verrà
a discorrere da parte di tutti gli intervenuti all'eccezionale
incontro delle famiglie
con l'opportunità ampiamente offerta a ciascuno di esprimere il suo particolare
punto di vista
circa quello che meglio converrebbe a entrambi fare e non fare
in una situazione complicata e difficile quale la
nostra presente
onde si eviti innanzi tutto per quel
piccolo margine d'anni che ancora ci resta da vivere qualsiasi superflua
dolorosa lacerazione qualsiasi inutile
scandalo eccetera eccetera

Quand'ecco – apparendo il tema sin qui eluso davvero prossimo
ad essere infine affrontato e sviscerato con ogni franchezza –
ecco tutte le volte proprio a questo punto nel mio tenace fantasticare il cuore
inondarmisi a un tratto di un'immensa
dolcezza le palpebre
di colpo farmisi
pesanti

non senza però che all'ultimo – nell'attimo in cui le palpebre sto per chiuderle
già arreso al sonno con la medesima
vorace nostalgia del buio che m'assaliva
ogni sera da bambino –
mi sia dato per un istante come al principio di riavere te nello sguardo e te soltanto
che respiri in pace lì
vicino

MARG

Non saprei dire se di giorno o di notte se calpestando
io l'opposto marciapiede oppure se rapido
una volta di più passando
via con la macchina
ricordo però assai bene d'aver letto qualche mese

understanding at any possible cost to fuel
as always dialogue

It's about you and me – now I'm sure of it! – that in a while
all those attending this exceptional
meeting of families will talk
with the chance amply offered for each to express their particular
point of view
about what would be better for us both to do and not do
in a tricky and difficult situation such as
our present one
so as to avoid first of all for that
small margin of years we have still to live any superfluous
painful rupture any useless
scandal etcetera etcetera

Lo and behold – the hitherto avoided topic looking really close
at last to being tackled and plumbed in all frankness –
there every time at just this point in my stubborn fantasizing the heart
is suddenly overwhelmed with an immense
sweetness my eyelids
quickly growing
heavy

not without though at the last – right when my eyelids are about to close
already given over to sleep with the same
greedy nostalgia for the dark that assailed me
every night as a child –
I have a chance for an instant as at the first to have you back in sight and only you
breathing in peace there
close by

MARG

I couldn't say whether by day or by night if trampling
the opposite sidewalk or if rapidly
passing yet another time
by car
I recall well enough though having read some months

fa giusto al principio
dell'inverno
scritto a caratteri maiuscoli e cubitali sopra un intonaco
dilavato di periferia con un pennello
intinto in una scura vernice color sangue
rappreso
– e facevano le lettere una specie d'arco in lieve un poco esitante
salita quasi ad esprimere
anch'esse nel loro incerto flettersi la tenerezza
commemorante d'ogni supremo
addio –
ciao dolcissima Marg proprio così
CIAO DOLCISSIMA MARG. e
nient'altro

Dove sei Marg – non faccio da allora che chiedermi – dove vivi in quale
anonimo quartierino del Salario del Tiburtino o del
Trionfale
dormi vegli parli mangi ridi sospiri gridi
piangi eccetera
trascini da una stanzuccia all'altra fino all'asfittico
balconcino la già molle
tua anca di imminente
Margherita
fai ondeggiare fra le magre scapole lunga
fino alla vita fino all'esile
giro dei blue
jeans
la fulva enorme
treccia
e dove mai sarà lui soprattutto – ignoto
completamente al comune lager metropolitano e forse persino
a te stessa –
lui l'ugualmente dolcissimo tuo
poeta?

back right at the start
of last winter
written in block capitals over washed-out suburban
plaster with a brush
dipped in a dark paint the colour of coagulated
blood
– and the letters made a kind of faint slightly hesitant rising arc
almost as if to express
even them in their uncertain curve the commemorative
tenderness of every last
goodbye –
hi sweetest Marge exactly thus
CIAO DOLCISSIMA MARG. and
nothing else

Marge where are you – I do nothing but wonder since then – where do you live
in what
anonymous little flat in Salario in Tiburtino or
in Trionfale
you sleep wake speak eat laugh sigh call out
cry etcetera
you drag from one poor room to the next far as the feeble
little balcony your already flabby
hip of impending
Margherita
you wiggle further down between thin shoulders
up to your waist up to the thin
band of the blue
jeans
your huge reddish-brown
plait
and above all wherever will he be – completely
unknown to the common urban gulag and maybe even
to yourself –
him that no less most sweet
poet of yours?

PARAFRASANDO ENGELS

Tutto ciò che esiste è *degno*
di perire recito anche io fra me e
me parafrasando
Engels

Ed ecco nel rosso deserto crepuscolo appena dopo
Bologna ecco quasi subito
volando io continuamente in discesa lungo il dritto asfalto laggiù
verso il buio il silenzio la
solitudine

eccola là già in vista la grande la tiepida
dimora
eccola ancora là la mia
gioventù

PARAPHRASING ENGELS

All that exists *deserves*
to die I recite to myself even I
paraphrasing
Engels

And there in the empty red dusk just beyond
Bologna there almost at once
my flying on and on downhill along the straight asphalt down
towards darkness silence
solitude

there it is already in sight the great the lukewarm
abode
there they are there still my own
young years

IN GRAN SEGRETO / IN GREAT SECRET

Cover of *In gran segreto*, Milan: Mondadori, 1978. (Fondazione Bassani, Ferrara)

I

ATTENTI!

Non lo si lasci andare da solo l'uomo vecchio attenti
che non s'allontani senza compagnia lungo un
viottolo fiancheggiato di qua e di là da giovani
alberi
non importa se per compiere – come potrebbe al caso garantire – due piccoli
passi e basta

Attenti a non permettere che lui affronti senza una mano
amica stretta nella propria il deserto
crocicchio urbano domenicale pur se verde il semaforo
lo inviti bonario a
traversare

Ma fate attenzione soprattutto che disinvolto non inalberi
un cappottino mezza stagione color
cammello oppure grigio
ferro spinato nonché un qualunque
cappello floscio
bigio o marrone o anche nero messo un tantino di traverso
in un certo modo impercettibilmente battagliero a sfida quasi d'ogni possibile
colpo di tramontano

E badate alle sue scarpe infine se non siano
troppo leggere e fragili – ma non obbligatoriamente per eccesso
d'uso e di consunzione – e al tempo stesso troppo
lucidate

VIGILIA DI FESTA

Come trasale all'improvviso come
si fa livida la città d'un tratto e pressoché
deserta

all'occhio di chi pari a me cammina da solo lungo
questa sua dritta via interminabile aperta a
campi e cielo

CAREFUL!

Don't let the old man go on alone be careful
he doesn't grow distant unaccompanied along
a path flanked here and there by young
trees
no matter if it's only to take – as he could perchance guarantee – two small
steps and no more

Careful not to let him confront without friendly
hand in his own the deserted
Sunday street crossing even if green the traffic light
kindly invites him to
walk over

But above all pay attention he doesn't casually adopt
a camel-colored or iron-gray herringbone
mid-season coat let alone any-old
floppy gray or brown or even
black hat
put on slightly askew
in a certain imperceptibly combative way to challenge almost all
possible north-wind gusts

And lastly take care his shoes aren't
too light and fragile – but not necessarily thanks to overuse
to wear – and at the same time far too
polished

HOLIDAY EVE

How suddenly it gives a start how
at a stroke the city turns livid and all but
deserted

to the eye of those who walk like me alone along
this endless straight street open onto
fields and sky

              anche io sospeso fra la
luce che si ritira e l'ombra che avanza anch'io diviso
                fra due età

                A MOMI

Gli anni – quaranta almeno dei tuoi sessanta – tutti una ritmica
      alternanza d'autunnali nebbie ineffabili di inverni
       del pari inesprimibili nelle opache loro o fulgenti
              nevi urbane e collinari d'estati
           anche esse da non dirsi nei loro padani
                   polverosi ori
                    supremi

   o nel frattempo tu sempre lì in attesa di un'improbabile
              inaudita primavera giammai
             avere tu fretta anzi marcissero
       in te cose ed eventi prossimi sempre a una mirabile
               epifania ad una imminente
                     caduta...

            Era alla Poesia che tiravi a quella
              con tanto di P maiuscola ed a lei
                      soltanto

            La tua vita? Quella là te la sei
                  anche tu bevuta

               TALE E QUALE

             Tale e quale come questo quaderno
       da me scordato iersera dentro il metallico
                armadietto del Circolo
    e là rimasto nel buio pesto e stantio fra la Dunlop
           l'accappatoio di spugna due paia
         di vecchie scarpe mezze rotte l'asciugamano
           non proprio di bucato quel decrepito
golf stile '38 che ti fa sempre un po' ridere e non so che altro...

me too suspended between
the light pulling back and advancing shadow me too torn
between two eras

TO MOMI

The years – forty of your sixty at least – all rhythmical
alternation of ineffable autumnal mists of winters
equally inexpressible in their opaque or bright
urban and hilly snows of summers
these too unbelievable in their supreme
Po-valley
dusty golds

and meanwhile you always there waiting for an unlikely
unheard-of spring you never in a hurry
rather you let them rot
within you things and events always near
to an admirable epiphany to an imminent
fall...

It was Poetry you were drawn to the one
with a capital P and only
to her

Your life? That one there you've
drunk it even you

EXACTLY LIKE

Exactly like this notebook
I forgot last night inside the metal
Tennis Club locker
and left there in the stale pitch black between the Dunlop
the towelling bathrobe two pairs
of old half-broken shoes a not quite freshly laundered
towel that decrepit
'38-style sweater that always makes you laugh a bit and I don't know what else...

Tu però non venirci ti supplico non cercarmi di
notte lascia
che riposi da solo fino a giorno pieno nel piccolo
mio letto

A NATALIA GINZBURG

Non ti piaccio eh? Figùrati la tristezza
gli sbadigli se ti
piacevo

ALLA STESSA

Anche a me piacciono cosa credi le periferie urbane le nebbie
che non appena esci dall'abitato parlano così fraterne
alla tua gioia e alla tua noia anch'io preferisco
i giorni qualsiasi delle settimane alla data memorabile
i colori vaghi al puro e squillante le sorti
di cui la Storia con la esse grande non si occuperà
non si curerà

anch'io cosa credi ho sempre nel cuore i poveri
morti
con questo di diverso però ricòrdati che io stesso vengo
proprio di là cioè da quei luoghi
donde – e so bene che lo
sai –
per solito non si ritorna respirando anzi mai e
poi mai

A UN LETTERATO

Non è ahimè che la bischeraggine generazionale
e lei soltanto
a farti ognora vagolare qua e là
alla ricerca ansiosa di chissà che
cosa

But don't you come here I beg you don't search me out
at night-time let
me rest alone until full daylight in my little
bed

TO NATALIA GINZBURG

I don't please you eh? Imagine the sorrow
the yawns if I were to
please you

TO THE SAME

Me too I like what d'you think the city outskirts the mists
which soon as you leave town so fraternally speak
to your joy and boredom I also prefer
the ordinary days of the week to the memorable date
the vague colors to the pure and sharp fates
with which History will not deal
it will not care

me too what d'you think I always have the poor dead
in my heart
with this difference however remember that me too I come
from there myself that's to say those places from
which – and I know very well that
you know it –
one doesn't usually come back breathing or rather never
ever

TO A LITERARY MAN

Alas it's only the generational idiocy
and this only
making you wander here and there every time
anxiously looking for who knows
what

Per cui anche se succede che talora succeda
una cosa – quantunque assai
di rado –

ecco pronta ciò nondimeno la bischeraggine ad arricciarti di bel
nuovo il bel
naso
a indurti subito a cercarne in giro un'altra
di cosa

ALLO STESSO

Volevo che l'ineffabile potesse diventare
eterno
dar voce all'inesprimibile far sì
che l'inesistente
esistesse

e che tu pure magari povero
vecchio semicanuto
bambino
persino tu – anche se
così indirettamente com'è appunto ora di
te proprio in quest'attimo medesimo –
in qualche modo per sempre ci
fossi

MUORE UN'EPOCA

Muore un'epoca l'altra è già qua
affatto nuova e
innocente
ma anche questa lo so non la
potrò vivere che girato
perennemente all'indietro a guardare
verso quella testé
finita
a tutto indifferente tranne a che
cosa davvero fosse la mia

So even if it happens that sometimes one thing
happens – albeit extremely
rarely –

nonetheless here's the idiocy ready once again to curl
your pretty
nose
to prompt you immediately to look around for something
else

TO THE SAME

I wanted the ineffable to become
eternal
give voice to the inexpressible allowing
the nonexistent
to exist

and how you too maybe poor
old half-clad
child
even you – although
as indirectly as it is indeed now really
about you in this precise moment –
somehow you forever
were

AN ERA DIES

An era dies the next is here already
entirely new and
innocent
but even this one I know
I'll only be able to live it perpetually
looking back towards
the one just
over
indifferent to all except to
what really was my

vita di prima
chi sia io mai
stato

ORLY

Da bambino siccome temevo
il grande fantasma bianco m'ero fatto
un rifugio dello sgabuzzino
del telefono

Il pensiero solo che fosse possibile
spedirmi giù sottoterra di notte alla ricerca
d'un altro ceppo per il
fuoco
bastava a riempirmi d'un incoercibile
spavento

E colma quasi altrettanto d'orrore era lassù
in cima in cima alla casa
la mansarda-granaio vasta
e vuota com'era e pervasa
tutta d'un fioco
semispento grigiore

Non sono cambiato non credere anche se mi dò
coraggio anche se ti
sembrai talvolta all'epoca così calmo e
saggio così
forte

Qualsiasi angolo o spigolo continua
ad allarmarmi qualsiasi promessa
di buio può farmi
ancor oggi tremare
qualsiasi viso

Vero è che il tuo soltanto o mia rara
o mia grande ed amara o mia
perduta

life of before
whoever I may have
been

ORLY

As a child because I was afraid of
the big white ghost I'd made
a shelter out of the telephone
cupboard

Even the thought it were possible
to send me down underground at night in search of
another log for
the fire
was enough to fill me with irrepressible
dread

And filled almost as much up there with horror
at the very top of the house
was the barn-like attic vast
and empty as was and quite pervaded
with a faint
near lifeless grey

I've not changed believe me even if I
give myself courage even if
back then I seemed to you so calm and
wise so
strong

Any angle or corner continues
to scare me any promise
of darkness can make me
shudder even today
any face

True it is yours alone o my rare
o my big and bitter o my
lost one

ogni qualvolta pensando lo riò
negli occhi di là dal cancelletto
d'uscita
mi fa oggi ancora sì trasalire
però di
vita

CONGEDO

Non li rivedremo assieme mai più garantito i ruffiani azzurrissimi
mari del nostro bel sud italico basta con le loro scogliere
corteggiate sempre più da presso da democristiani
sindaci docenti elementari da geometri
socialisti…

SANGUE E BUIO

Dio c'è asserisce
nel lampo dei
fari
il sangue là sul pilone di
cemento il mio
sangue

Dio *non* c'è asserisce
promette
garantisce
il solito grande buio di subito
dopo il buio di
sempre

DA VILLON

Esattamente come
Cristo Gesù
sei nata il giorno di
Natale

every whenever in thought it returns
before my eyes beyond the exit
gate
it makes me wince still
though with
life

FAREWELL

We'll never see them together again guaranteed the blue pandering
seas of our beautiful Italian south enough of their cliffs
increasingly courted by Christian Democrats
mayors elementary school teachers socialist
surveyors …

BLOOD AND DARK

God exists it asserts
in the flash of
headlights
the blood up there on the concrete
pylon my
blood

God does *not* exist it asserts
promises
guarantees
the usual vast darkness of now
after the darkness of
always

FROM VILLON

Exactly the same as
Jesus Christ
you're born on Christmas
Day

quel tal giorno – dovevi
pur saperlo anche tu! –
in cui ogni scherzo
vale

I CONGIURATI

Dite vi prego anime sante dov'è
che vi ritrovate
ogni qualvolta vi sia da apportare
qualche ritocco qualche divario anche minimo nell'ufficioso
nazional-cattolico-postermetico
organigramma letterario?

In quale sala segreta e
sotterranea in quale mai
tenebrosissimo insospettabile
scantinato
convenuti dal monte e dal
piano vi incontrate
vi date la
mano
vi scrutate negli
occhi vi annusate
sotto la coda l'un l'altro fate
lingua in bocca ed infine
parlate?

PIAZZA INDIPENDENZA

Nella quieta estasi mattutina e domenicale eccomi senza per niente
averlo premeditato a camminare da solo nei pressi
della stazione Termini

Saranno forse le undici seggono attorno ai tavolinetti
dei caffè del quartiere grandi baudelairiani
negri d'entrambi i
sessi
alcuni abbigliati all'occidentale i più no

that very day – you just had to
know it even you! –
where every practical joke
applies

THE CONSPIRATORS

Tell me I beg you holy souls where
do you meet
whenever you've got to make
some adjustment some minimum gap in the unofficial
National-Catholic-post-hermetic
literary organizational chart?

In which secret and
underground room in whichever
basement dark beyond
suspicion
gathered from mountains and from
plains do you meet
shake
hands
look into
each other's eyes sniff each other out
under the tail stick your tongue
down each other's throats and finally
speak?

PIAZZA INDIPENDENZA

In the quiet morning rapture of a Sunday here I'm without the least
forethought walking alone in the environs
of the Termini station

It's maybe eleven o'clock they're sitting round the little tables
of the neighborhood cafes tall Baudelairean
blacks of both
sexes
some clothed as in the west most not

simili a magre piante verdibrune ovvero a molli
sgargianti fiori lì lì
sul punto di
spampanarsi

È qua suppongo che usano darsi
convegno di sette in sette
giorni
qua che a ogni incontro – né mai senza il debito sfoggio
dell'ansietà più amabile –
ciascuno interroga con gli occhi gli occhi le labbra la dentatura
dell'altro
qua che reduci tutti da incolumi immense
aeree traversate
adagio con dolci risa incredule se le
raccontano

Non lungi ad un'ottantina
di metri di distanza come massimo dallo slargo d'asfalto
sul ciglio opposto del quale
sosto muto in attesa
una solida e bella vecchia villa cubica fine secolo con le rade
persiane chiuse serrate e con da tergo emergente un folto
di verzura che sa più assai di buie
selve africane che non di Roma
sta là offrendo al sole di questi primi di giugno il cereo volto silente la pura
fronte soltanto in alto – giusto al di sopra dell'orizzontale
riga della grondaia – un poco azzurra
d'ombra
e intanto attende anche essa anch'essa guarda
pensa rammemora

AL CRITICO D'UN ROTOCALCO

Grazie diamine grazie d'aver citato recensendo Epitaffio Catullo
grazie tante

Ma
e
Dante?

resembling lean green-brown plants or else like gaudy
soft flowers just
on the point of
fading

That's where I guess they tend
to convene every seventh
day in seven
here at every gathering – never without the proper display
of most lovable anxiety –
each one questions with their eyes the eyes lips teeth
of the other
here all returning unscathed from immense
air crossings
slowly with sweet incredulous laughter they tell
of them

Not more than eighty
meters at most distant from the asphalt's widening
on the opposite edge
where silent I stand waiting
a solid and beautiful old boxlike villa from the turn of the century
with bays closed-tight shutters and behind a thicket of greenery emerging
feeling so much more like gloomy
African woods than Rome
it stands there offering to these early June days' sun its waxy silent face its pure
frontage only up high – right above the horizontal
gutter line – shaded
slightly blue
and meanwhile it too waits it watches too
thoughtful it remembers

TO A MAGAZINE CRITIC

Goodness thanks thanks for the Catullus mention reviewing Epitaffio
thanks so much

But still
and
Dante?

QUARTIERE SALARIO

Via di Novella – dice – via di
Santa Priscilla
a me che guardo attonito la splendida
pianta gialla
rigogliosa nel primaverile
giardino tutto nuovo
via Ostriana – insiste con
la sua voce di vecchia
bambina –
e intanto io so che presto sarà
sera anche qui e dopo un lento
attimo notte

CAMPAGNA ROMANA

Uguale identico mi riconosco d'un tratto al cagnaccio biondastro
vecchio sì e non poco qua e là
spelacchiato ma ancora
abbastanza minaccioso a
vedersi
che chissà dove diretto e chissà da dove
proveniente
a testa bassa con le fauci grandi
mezze aperte a tirare il fiato e con neri occhi amari
furibondi e rassegnati batte
la scura campagna limitrofa alla più distante
periferia
e che allorquando appena dopo un bruno
piccolo ponte in muratura sterzo io rapido via
brucia per un lungo istante al fuoco
dei miei fari

DOVE VIVI?

Dove vivi? – mi chiede corrugando la
fronte e stringendo le palpebre – Dov'è
che diavolo stai?

QUARTIERE SALARIO

Via di Novella – she says – via di
Santa Priscilla
to me looking astonished at the splendid
yellow plant
luxuriant in the all-new
spring garden
via Ostriana – she insists
with her grown-up
baby voice –
and meanwhile I know it'll soon be
evening even here and after a slow
moment night

ROMAN COUNTRYSIDE

Exactly the same I recognize myself all at once in the blondish mongrel
old yes and here and there
not a little mangy but still
threatening enough to
look at
bound who knows where and come from
who knows where
head down with huge jaws
half open to catch its breath and with bitter black eyes
furious and resigned it pounds
the dark countryside bordering the furthest
outskirts
and when just after a little
brown masonry bridge I rapidly swerve away
it burns a long moment in the fire
of my headlights

WHERE DO YOU LIVE?

Where do you live? – frowning she asks me
and squeezing her eyelids – Where
the devil are you?

A Roma? A Ferrara? Laggiù a
Maratea? Oppure nuovamente
altrove?

Nessuno pensando a te saprebbe darti oggi il più
piccolo posto un po' tuo – conclude – proprio tu che fino
all'altro ieri soltanto
non ne hai abitato in fondo che
uno

IN COLLERA COL PIÙ GRANDE AMICO

Prosa robusta disse ai suoi dì di te
fra i denti il
Croce

Aveva anche quella volta là più che
ragione ragione da
vendere

Era il cervello ed è
– così come il cuore –
di' pure un po' andante e qualsiasi
insomma debole

A FRANCO FORTINI

Se li riconto gli ex infiniti della tua carriera-ghirigoro compreso l'ex
traparlamentare odierno…

Ma adesso basta stop all'inferno ovvero come tu stesso assai
più soavemente mi
scrivi
perdoniamoci

In Rome? In Ferrara? Down there in
Maratea? Or somewhere else
entirely?

Nobody thinking of you would know how today to grant you the least
little place of your own – she concludes – really you who
till just the day before yesterday
lived after all in only
the one

ANGRY WITH HIS BEST FRIEND

Robust prose in his day said Croce
under his breath
about you

Even that time he was more than
right he was right
as rain

It was your brain and it is
– just like your heart –
you could say a bit on the cheap and whatever
in short weak

TO FRANCO FORTINI

If I recount the infinite exes of your scrawling-career including the ex
tra-parliamentary of today ...

But enough now stop this inferno or as you yourself much
more sweetly
write me
let's forgive ourselves

LO SO PERCHÉ

Da ragazzo e da giovane prediligevo
il mare tanto il suo blu
pacifico
quanto le bianco
azzurre sue tempeste

Ora – e lo so perché – sono le montagne
ad attirarmi e quelle soltanto che di
là dalle foreste salgono
più su nude
tacite

SE HO CAMBIATO!

Da ragazzo e da giovane ero sempre lì a storicizzare
goccia a goccia me stesso

Del poi non mi curavo bastava
quella specie di fiammeo risucchio di folle vortice fatale
a cui m'abbandonavo giorno dopo
giorno a garantirmene
l'avvento ineluttabile

Se ho cambiato! Non faccio adesso che pensare
a domani al mese venturo al prossimo anno
pronto a giurare su tutti i sarà possibili come se fossero bell'e
accaduti
storico del mio futuro non meno avaro e indefesso di quanto
già fui del mio passato

Di niente o quasi più mi ricordo i mari in cui mi bagnai
non sono ormai per me che d'un solo blu le erbe che via
via calpestai d'un verde
solo
i cari innumeri sguardi della mia vita un unico
grande occhio distante e imperscrutabile

I KNOW WHY

As a boy and young man I would prefer
    the sea its peaceful
    blue
    as well as its white
    blue storms

Now – and I know why – it's the mountains
    attract me and them only
    if beyond the forests they rise
    higher naked
    silent

IF I HAVE CHANGED!

As a boy and young man I was always historicizing myself
    drop by drop

For tomorrow I didn't care it was enough
that type of blazing suction of mad fatal vortex
to which I'd abandon myself day after
    day to guarantee
    its inevitable arrival

If I have changed! Now I do nothing but think
of tomorrow of next month of next year
ready to swear on every possible will-be as if they had already
    happened
historian of my future no less stingy and tireless than
    I already was with my past

I remember nothing or barely a thing the seas where I bathed
are no more to me now than one single blue the grass
    I walked on in time a single
    green
the dear innumerable looks of my life a single
    great distant inscrutable eye

DOMENICA MATTINA

È buffo e strano l'ho sfiorata
sottocasa iersera simile in tutto
a un piccolo silenzioso grumo di buia
vita

ed ecco là stamattina mentre la guardo
dall'alto del balcone
illuminati e scaldati entrambi dal tenero solicello
delle nove

morta apparirmi d'un tratto niente da fare minima
sbiadita capottina bige gracili
gommette
mezze fuori di sbieco dagli ammaccati
parafanghi anteriori

assolutamente finita insomma buona non più che
per lo sfasciacarrozze

SUNDAY MORNING

It's funny and strange I brushed against her
last night in the street entirely like
a small silent lump of dark
life

and there she goes this morning while I look at her
from the top of the balcony
both lit up and warmed by the tender sun
of nine o'clock

appearing to me suddenly dead with nothing to be done
minimal faded hood grey fragile
tires
sloping half out the bruised
front mudguards

absolutely finished then good for nothing
but the wrecker's yard

II

RACCONTO

Mentre scendeva in macchina giù dalle brulle
montagne dell'interno mentre guidava
verso il mare e la luce di
Fonteblanda

sentì a un tratto d'assomigliare a quell'esile scuro
albero là ritto da solo sull'ultimo
crinale proprio a quel vecchio
pino

di stare aprendosi come lui adagio
adagio per un'altra volta
ancora al tenero
mattino

15 GIUGNO 1975

Guardami ti prego esclusivo Iddio dei più vecchi dall'amaro
e deliziato sport d'abbandonarmi
– giusto come toccò a mio padre a partire circa dal '30 fino ad almeno
il '38 e le leggi della Razza –

nelle braccia del ceto moderato italiano eternamente
traditore incolpevole da sempre
fascista e innocente

scampami te ne supplico – tu che puoi! – dalle sue dolci
femmine dalle promesse dei loro intatti quasi infiniti
cari gerghi cattolico-agricoli da tutto quanto
so che di esse
forse più amo e più abomino al mondo più adoro ed
esecro

STORY

While driving down the bare
mountains inland while going
towards the sea and light of
Fonteblanda

of a sudden he felt himself resemble that thin dark
tree stood there alone on the final
ridge exactly that old
pine

to be opening up really
slowly like him yet one more
time to the tender
morning

15 JUNE 1975

Protect me please exclusive God of the eldest from the bitter
and delighted sport of giving myself over
– just as happened to my father from about 1930 till at least
'38 and the Racial Laws –

into the arms of the moderate Italian middle class eternally
betraying blameless forever
fascist and innocent

save me I beg you – you who can! – from its sweet
females from the promises of their intact almost infinite
dear catholic-agricultural parlance from everything
I know how of them
I love more and abhor more perhaps in the world adore more and
condemn

MODENA NORD

Lasciala finalmente dimenticala l'atroce fiumara di sangue e di metallo esci
a sinistra nella intimidita verde quiete
improvvisa

passa oltre qualcuno laggiù a Ferrara forse t'aspetta però non scordatene mai
più fin quando avrai vita fino a che
respirerai

dell'esile stradone a perpendicolo fiancheggiato da pioppi altissimi appena appena
serpeggiante che hai scorto a un tratto a lato della vecchia
provinciale delle lucciole

e in fondo al quale al termine del suo deserto della sua bigia tiepida
polvere era già
sera

A CASA

Qualche chilometro appena fuori Ferrara dalla
parte delle Valli e del Po
d'estate non meno che d'inverno subito il verde dirada si
va
lungo la provinciale che lenta fra le brune
piatte terre serpeggia
librati quasi a mezz'aria o addirittura come con sotto
il più perfetto dei vuoti

Andavamo avanti assai piano senza affatto
guardarci eppure taciti
tranquillissimi
neanche se entrambi alfine lo sapessimo
dove fossimo diretti e perciò appunto sentendoci
entrambi molto buoni tutti e due
pieni di pace

Lo vedi? L'inverno qua – mormorò a un tratto io sì e no
traudendola – è tale e

MODENA NORD

Finally leave it forget it the atrocious torrent of blood and metal exit
left to the cowed sudden green
peace

move on perhaps someone awaits you down there in Ferrara but never forget
long as you'll have life far as
you will breathe

the narrow perpendicular road flanked by the tallest poplars only barely
twisting you suddenly caught sight of alongside the old
main road with the fireflies

and down there at the end of its desert of its warm gray
dust it was already
evening

AT HOME

Some kilometers just beyond Ferrara on the
side of the Valli and the Po
in summer no less than in winter the green soon thins you
go
down the main road that slowly twists through
the flat brown lands
soaring almost in mid-air or for that matter with below
the most perfect of voids

We were going on ahead very slowly without really
looking at each other yet silent
completely calm
as if both of us didn't in the end even know
where we were heading and hence really feeling
both of us very good us two
completely at peace

You see? Winter here – she suddenly murmured I more or less
catching her – it's quite the same

quale come la primavera uguale
identico all'estate

Non pensare dunque all'inverno ti prego non
pensarci d'ora innanzi mai più da'
retta
Amami sempre stammi dentro per
sempre come adesso per l'eterno
così

IN VACANZA

Dici per sottintesi
– copiando tutta compunta N. G. perfino nella famosa
gnàgnera e intanto fissando
il mare –

la tua gioia non è
gioia ma pura esibizione vanitosa la
tua gioia è soltanto fatuità
soddisfazione

E sia però anche tu da che sommità da quale
Everest di dolore credi di
parlare?

Ricòrdati che chi davvero soffre non si
annoia mai
bada anche tu che il tedio non è che
tedio
squallore

AL TELEFONO

Sbuffa smettila su dài lo so fammi un po' prendere il mio
tè

– lo dice è chiaro perché io *non* le dica quello che lei *non* sa
di me –

as spring exactly
the image of summer

So don't think of winter I beg you don't
think of it from now on never again
listen
Love me always be inside me for
always as now everlastingly
so

ON HOLIDAY

Implicitly you say
– copying in all contriteness N. G. even in her famous
rigmarole and meanwhile staring at
the sea –

your joy is not
joy but pure conceited performance your
joy is just fatuitous
satisfaction

And yet you too from what height from what
Everest of pain do you believe
you speak?

Remember whoever truly suffers is
never bored
take heed you too that tedium's only
tedium
wretchedness

ON THE PHONE

She huffs and puffs stop it give over I know let me just have my
tea

– says it plainly so I *don't* tell her what she *doesn't* know
about me –

senza neanche supporlo lei la filosofa – così
sbuffando e dicendo e poi subito
riagganciando – che d'ora innanzi forse
forse non le succederà mai più assolutamente
di sapere niente che è niente non
dico tanto di me quanto soprattutto
di sé

DA ORAZIO

Spaghetti – enumera e ride – alla carbonara
paillard con verdura cotta
ananas
vino rosso
sei felice?

L'anima avara ma giusta è però lì subito
a sussurrarmi a parte per così
poco?

Talché riandando io a un'ora fa non posso
che dire muto di sì che darle
– a lei l'anima mia – come quasi sempre
del tutto ragione

IN UN ORECCHIO

Ero molto lontano non sai
quanto

Ti ho stretto forte la mano per restarti
accanto
per non tornarci mai più
là

without even assuming it she the philosopher – so
huffing and puffing and speaking and then straight away
hanging up – that from now on perhaps
perhaps it won't happen absolutely ever again
that she knows not one single thing
I don't so much mean about me as most of all
about herself

AT ORAZIO'S

Spaghetti – she reads off and laughs – carbonara
paillard with steamed vegetables
pineapple
red wine
you're happy?

My stingy but fair soul's nonetheless suddenly there
whispering aside to me for so
little?

So much so that going back an hour I can only
silently say yes she got it
– my own soul – as almost always
she's entirely right

IN ONE EAR

I was very distant you don't know
how far

Tightly I squeezed your hand to remain
near you
to never ever go back
there

CIAMPINO

Lassù appena più in basso a destra della vetta del colle
l'azzurra cima ventilata dove fummo insieme l'altro
ieri mattina

vedo a tratti risplendere remotamente una qualche
lastra – vetro o metallo – un labile
minimo lampeggio d'oro dentro il grande oro del
crepuscolo

Ma tu a che pro guarderesti? Lascia farlo a me solo e soprattutto
non domandare
che cosa ancora abbia mai da cercare di là dalla dolce
curva della tua spalla bambina il vecchio
mio occhio l'azzurra insaziata mia folle
iride

DA ALCEO

Non so che cosa cerca in me che cosa diavolo
a me vecchio domanda alla mia vecchia
vita

– lo so ma cerco di non saperlo di neanche
domandarmelo –

lei giovane lei tenera lei piccola lei quasi
come figlia lei perfino in
braccio timida
intimidita

PER CARTOLINA

Ah lungo il filo il tuo ciao
il tuo piccolo fioco miao
d'ogni mattina che è una...

CIAMPINO

Up there just below to the right of the hilltop
the breezy blue peak where we were together the day
before yesterday morning

at intervals I see some sheet remotely
shining – glass or metal – a fleeting
minimal gold flash inside the great gold of the
dusk

But you to what end would you watch? Leave it to me alone and most of all
don't ask
what else has it still to seek for beyond the sweet
curve of your childlike shoulder my old
eye my mad blue insatiable
iris

FROM ALCAEUS

Don't know what she's looking for in me what the hell
she's asking of old me of my old
life

– I know what it is but try not to know not even
ask myself –

she young she sweet she small she almost
like a daughter even
in my arms she timidly
intimidated

BY POSTCARD

Ah down the line your ciao
your little faint meow
each and every morning ...

E tuttavia come è buono il silenzio di Vienna
di Vienna asburgica e socialista!
Non sai come fu tenero o mia tenera dormirci
dentro scordarcisi
scordare

UT PICTURA

...in primo luogo per informarti – facendo seguito alla cartolina da Vienna ma
[adesso scrivendoti
con ogni tranquillità oramai da qui
da casa –
che la sera di quel giorno stesso subito dopo il mio arrivo a Graz
mi son trovato d'un tratto dinanzi a un'ampia tela rettangolare
ascrivibile a ignoto – «unbekannt» – pittore austriaco dell'800
la quale tela – l'unica o quasi rimasta appesa alle pareti fin troppo bianche
[d'uno Stadt
Museum in evidente
via di disarmo o di radicale
trasformazione e di ciò m'ero accorto di primo acchito non appena
avevo raggiunto la sommità
del ricurvo barocco scalone interno d'ingresso –
la quale tela ripeteva punto per punto cominciando in alto dal malinconico
enorme cielo crepuscolare
a sinistra dorato com'era a destra un tantino più bruno
più cupo...

...Graz-città voglio dire una Graz incredibilmente uguale
a quella apparsami mezz'ora avanti inquadrata tutta intera nel largo
parabrise della placida
220 D che mi trasportava
con la sua brava Mur a scorrere turchina e argentea nel mezzo e solitario
da un lato e dominante
però velando i bigi intonachi degli spalti e delle torri per una sorta
d'anticipo di buio di vaga
premonizione...

...come partenza il solito vecchio Altdorfer s'intende e il Canaletto e magari
Turner magari Friedrich e negli opachi

And yet how good Vienna's silence is
Habsburg and socialist Vienna's!
You don't know how sweet it was my sweety to sleep
within it to forget about us
to forget

UT PICTURA

...first of all to inform you – following the postcard from Vienna but writing
[to you now
in complete peace of mind from here
from home –
that the evening of that same day straight after arriving in Graz
I found myself suddenly in front of a large rectangular canvas
ascribable to an unknown – "unbekannt" – 19th-century Austrian painter
whose canvas – the only one or almost left hanging on the all-too-white walls
[of a Stadt
Museum in evident
process of being dismantled or radically
altered and I'd realized this at first glance as soon as
I reached the top
of the baroque curved inner entrance staircase –
whose canvas repeated point by point beginning at the top with the melancholy
huge twilit sky
golden on the left as it was on the right a little darker
deeper...

...Graz-city I mean a Graz incredibly like
the one appearing to me half an hour before completely framed in the broad
windshield of the placid
220 D carrying me
with its good Mur flowing deep blue and silver in the middle and lonely
on the one hand and dominant
nonetheless veiling the gray plaster of the bastions and towers
kind of anticipating the dark in a vague
premonition...

...to start with the usual old Altdorfer of course and Canaletto and maybe
Turner maybe Friedrich and in the opaque

vortici di verzura in primissimo piano forse il ricordo
dell'école de...

...ma lascia intanto che ti racconti del blu sempre diverso degli infiniti
tetti della città – per ogni tetto un blu – nonché di quello
affatto particolare – un blu di palese
derivazione impressionista –
delle ombre che le chiome di certi splendidi platani in doppia schiera resi
[piccoli piccoli
dalla distanza mettevano
giusto al centro del
quadro
sulla compatta cenere d'un obliquo in discesa
stradale sottostante
un blu che da solo – anche a voler trascurare
la minima figuretta
di un nero prete in
bicicletta
a fatica discernibile laggiù sullo sfondo del verde tenerissimo
d'un gran prato dall'aria d'essere
pressoché contiguo –
sarebbe bastato d'avanzo per datare con sufficiente approssimazione
[d'esattezza...

...e poi d'un edificio singolo assai dissimile dagli altri prova di nuovo a
[pensare a qualcosa
d'isolato e di prominente immagina insomma una specie
di torracchio d'epoca vagamente feudale un poco
arretrato sulla sinistra ed un poco
esso pure da
parte
che sebbene infiammato a gloria dai lunghi
raggi del sole occiduo tuttavia risultava
esso pure chissà mai perché livido
in qualche modo intirizzito tremante...

...e infine del senso di dolcezza suprema che penetrava adagio in me
[riguardante
la vasta così perdutamente gremita immagine dipinta
una dolcezza quasi...

eddies of greenery in the near foreground perhaps the memory
of the école de...

...but meanwhile let me tell you about the ever-changing blue of the endless
city roofs – a blue for each roof – as well as of that
quite particular – blue of a blatant
impressionist derivation –
of the shadows that certain splendid plane trees' quiffs in a double row made
[really tiny
by the distance would put
right in the middle of the
painting
on the compact ash of an oblique downhill
road below
a blue that alone – even if you overlooked
the slightest little figure
of a black priest on a
bicycle
barely discernible down there against the background of a large meadow's
tender green with the air of being
almost contiguous –
it would have been more than enough to date it with sufficient approximation
[of precision...

...and then of a single building quite different from the others try thinking
[again of something
isolated and prominent imagine in short a
kind of vaguely feudal tower slightly
set back on the left and slightly
to one side
as well
that though inflamed to glory by the declining
sun's long rays appeared however
it too who knows why
livid in some way numb and trembling...

...and at last the sense of supreme sweetness that would slowly penetrate me
[concerning
the vast so desperately crowded image depicted
a sweetness almost...

COMPLEANNO

A schiera
di là dal bel verde estatico del Central Park
che altro stasera ti dicono tutti rosa e in gloria i
grattacieli

se non che basta da' retta ascoltaci senza più arte
né parte né senso ormai devi
chiuderla una buona volta con l'unica
cosa che c'è?

CAMPUS

Richiamandosi imperterriti alla qui ormai universalmente riconosciuta
opportunità dei confronti infra ed extra senza più la minima
remora insomma a ruota
libera
– né sto a descriverti le musare Mario mio che quelle puoi di sicuro
immaginartele –

si considera più affine al Manzoni – interrogano dolcemente – oppure al
[ferrarese
Antonioni?
Opta per la linea Bernini-Borromini-Fellini diciamo o per quella Giovanni
Verga-Rossellini?
E Verdi? Non sembra a lei che Giuseppe
Verdi ricordi come fenomeno un po'
il nostro Gershwin?
E quel particolare cattolicesimo post-tridentino che solum è
lombardo
opera secondo lei più in Vincenzo
Monti o più in Luchino
Visconti?
E va bene Lotto
e Bellotto
e persino Giotto
ma
e

BIRTHDAY

Terraced
there beyond the fine ecstatic green of Central Park
what else do they tell you tonight the skyscrapers
all pink and in glory

if not that it's enough pay attention listen to us with neither skills
nor talents nor sense by now you have
to stop it once and for all with the only
thing there is?

CAMPUS

Referring undaunted to the here now universally accepted
opportunity for infra and extra comparisons without the slightest
hesitation in short
freewheeling
– nor am I going to describe you their faces Mario mio for sure you can
picture them –

do you consider yourself more akin to Manzoni – they tenderly ask – or to the
[Ferrarese
Antonioni?
Do you opt for the Bernini-Borromini-Fellini line let's say or for the Giovanni
Verga-Rossellini?
And Verdi? Doesn't it appear to you that Giuseppe
Verdi as a phenomenon recalls a little bit
our Gershwin?
And that post-Tridentine Catholicism which alone is
Lombard
according to you is it more productive in Vincenzo
Monti or in Luchino
Visconti?
And fair enough Lotto
Bellotto
and even Giotto
but then
and

Zanzotto?
E lei medesimo infine in che rapporto si sente
col Boccaccio?

Questo è all'incirca ciò che mi chiedono non pochi importanti
cervelli in giro come se niente
fosse
talché più morto che vivo delle due l'una o di
botto li abbraccio oppure spezzato
giusto a metà da una gran
tosse
fronte ai ginocchi ho cura di coprirmi ben bene
con entrambe le mani il
viso

Ecco quanto carissimo però per dirla
col vecchio Griso è
dura

VISITANDO L'INDIANA

Credevi d'esserci riuscito confessalo meticoloso tu storico
di scandali a non darne a non viverne
tu stesso
mai

vivente scandalo anche tu viceversa – come ben sai! – tu stesso fin da
                                                                                                       [principio
fin dal tuo primo
trovartici
scandaloso innocente

PER LETTERA

Come è sempre bravo il cuore nini come non sbaglia mai stamattina
in Detroit di ferro lungo la così chiamata Cass mentre arrancavo
via controvento in fretta nella dura gelida
luce di qua

Zanzotto?
And you yourself finally what relation do you feel
with Boccaccio?

This is roughly what they ask me these not a few important
brains around as if really nothing
had happened
so that more dead than alive one of the two I either
suddenly hug them or broken
in half by a great
cough
forehead to knees with both of my hands I carefully
thoroughly cover
my face

That's how it is my dearest but to put it
in old Griso's terms it's
hard

VISITING INDIANA

You thought you'd succeeded confess it you meticulous historian
of scandals not to provide any not to live any
you yourself
ever

living scandal conversely you too – as you well know! – you yourself from the
[start
ever since your first
finding yourself
scandalously innocent

BY LETTER

How it's always good the heart darling how it's never wrong this morning
in iron Detroit along the so-called Cass while I trudged
off against the wind in a hurry in the hard icy
light hereabouts

lui m'è sfuggito a un tratto a sinistra dentro un vicolo
laterale ma che dico un vicolo! dentro una pura
fessura da sorci e da micie e da cicche mezza al buio
fra due nere muraglie a strapiombo – e di laggiù
proprio di laggiù dal fondo d'una qualsiasi
povera penombra senza nome alfine ce l'ha pur fatta
a ritrovarti

A UN GIOVANE GIORNALISTA INDISCRETO

Tu mi hai inquadrato vedo sebbene con qualche
residuo margine d'incertezza cosicché non fai male
come per vero abbastanza
ostensibilmente fai
a puntare forte e deciso sull'obbligatoria
mia pazienza sulla mia più che doverosa e quindi più che obsoleta onni
comprensività

Comunque sia se per sentirti esistere se per esserci se per essere sul serio te
hai bisogno di sapere proprio da
me
in che modo io ce la faccia a «sbarcare
il lunario» a
«guadagnare»

va' prima di là spéttolati
smóccolati
piscia
sgrava diligentemente il
pancione
fa' il bidè làvati
la bigia zazzera bisunta
i dentacci marrone d'un marron
cioccolata
néttati
le dure ungule hippy inalberante ognuna la sua mezza
luna color carbone o color
cacca

how it suddenly escaped to the left into an alley
to the side but what am I saying an alley! into a pure
crack for mice and cats and butts half in darkness
between two black overhanging walls – and from down there
right down there from the bottom of some
nameless poor penumbra it was even able
to find you at last

TO AN INDISCREET YOUNG JOURNALIST

You've situated me I see though with some
residual margin of uncertainty so that you're not wrong
as ostensibly enough
you truly do
to bet strongly and decisively on my mandatory
patience on my more than dutiful and therefore more than obsolete ubiquitous
understanding

In any case if to feel you exist if to be here if to be really you
you need to know precisely from
me
how I manage to "make ends
meet" to
"make a living"

first go and blow your nose
pick your snot
take a piss
diligently relieve your
big belly
have a bidet wash
your greasy gray mane
your ugly brown teeth of a chocolate
brown
clean
your hard hippy claws each one with its hovering
charcoal or shit-colored
half-moon

dopodiché se ancora
ci tieni allora su
dài
vieni
torna di qua e domanda
domanda pure

DA MACHADO

Dimmi che con tuo marito non lo fai
nemmeno col
dito

Dimmi che a partire dall'attimo che mi vedrai
morto non lo farai
mai più

Giurami che subito dopo morirai
anche tu

SHATTUCK HOTEL

Chi l'avrebbe mai detto pensa il sigaro
dopocena dinanzi
alla tele

e te lì accanto una mano
nell'altra mia
mano
nemmeno più tanto in cuor tuo deplorando
toscano e tele

IN GRAN SEGRETO

A parte la circostanza del resto persino un po' comica che top secretly
vi si decedesse senza mai soste e che sempre non appena evocata al telefono
la dura vociaccia nazista del portiere giovane sbottasse pronta dentro il ricevitore

after which if you still
care come on
come on
come back
back here and ask
by all means ask

FROM MACHADO

Tell me you don't do it with your husband
not even with a
finger

Tell me from the moment that you'll see me
dead you'll never do it
again

Promise me immediately after you'll die
you too

SHATTUCK HOTEL

Who'd ever have said imagine a cigar
after dinner in front
of the TV

and you there by me one hand
in my other
hand
not even much regretting in your heart
Toscano and TV

IN GREAT SECRET

Aside from the circumstance after all a bit comic even how top secretly
there you died with never a pause and always as soon as summoned to the phone
the young doorman's harsh Nazi voice blurted straight into the receiver

in un desk somigliante assaissimo a un dusk
non era poi così male a ripensarci quello Shattuck Hotel di dove
durante il mio primo mese di permanenza in orbita non una volta
come ben sai e ben so m'è venuto fatto di scriverti
né di significarti per qualche via differente che ancora c'ero che tuttora
esistevo

Certo si è per es. che l'enorme candido parallelepipedo del fabbricato soltanto
a considerarlo da fuori con le sue mille
grandi calme finestre verticali prospicienti lo
stradone omonimo da una parte e dall'altra la curva
soleggiata della baia ed il
mare
avrebbe potuto dare a chiunque stesse arrivando coi suoi piedi metti da
Telegraph Ave. o con la
macchina da San
Francisco
– e si riconoscesse anche lui vecchio ad un tratto molto moltissimo
vecchio o magari sognasse
ad occhi aperti se stesso
tale –
il desiderio immediato d'approdarci
l'illusione di poter cominciarci subito il più
dolce e lungo dei sonni
possibili

Tu però non pensarmi giammai a letto così di buon'ora
o mia rondine pensami viceversa
seduto a un tavolino – le più volte il medesimo – del bar giusto di fronte un bar
underground dall'aspetto
ovviamente semi
clandestino
vedimi là a covare solo solo dentro
il biondo cuore alcoolico l'immenso
vascello all'ancora dal lato opposto della via soprastante sul ciglio
della notte e dell'oceano e di nessun altro più in attesa prima
di salpare e di dileguare tranne
che di me

in a desk very much like a dusk
it wasn't so bad on second thoughts that Shattuck Hotel from where
during my first month's stay in orbit not once
as you well know and I'm well aware did I write you
nor inform you in some other way I was still alive I still
existed

It's certain for instance the huge white parallelepiped of the building only
to consider it from outside with its thousand
large calm vertical windows facing the
homonymous main road on one side and on the other the sunlit curve
of bay and
sea
could have given anyone who was coming by foot as it might be from
Telegraph Ave. or by
car from San
Francisco
– and recognized himself as old too of a sudden really extremely
old or perhaps dreamed
eyes open of himself
as such –
the immediate desire to make landfall there
the illusion of being able straight away to start the sweetest
and longest
possible sleep

But don't ever think of me in bed so early
o my swallow think of me rather
sitting at a table – most times the same one – in the bar opposite
an underground bar looking
obviously semi
clandestine
picture me all alone there brooding inside
the blond alcoholic heart the immense
vessel at anchor on the opposite side of the road above on the edge
of night and ocean and no one else waiting before
setting sail and vanishing except
for me

IN MAREMMA

Dice che vende
fieno

Grida che ne potrebbe dar tanto
da farne fare a chiunque il
pieno

Spiega quindi a parlargli che col suo fieno
uno andrebbe più forte del
treno
del baleno
e addirittura della
morte

PARLA IL DEPRESSO

Superata Palidoro sta' attento
non girare a sinistra
bada bene a quello che
fai

D'un bel blu la straduccia è però subito
minutissimamente rugosa – chiaro? – da
farti di continuo un po' tremare
andando

Turpe a tratti d'un cieco quasi ferino
rigoglio di neri ciuffi di bui
ricci e pressoché senza
tetti frammezzo od altro qualsiasi
avviso umano

la vegetazione che intanto
ti circonderà
con qua e là emergenti soltanto i grandi
tralicci dell'alta
tensione

IN MAREMMA

He says he sells
hay

Shouts he could give quite enough
to fill anyone's
tank

Then explains should you talk to him with his hay
one could go faster than the
train
than lightning
and even than
death

THE DEPRESSED MAN SPEAKS

Once you've passed Palidoro be careful
don't turn to the left
mind what you
do

The little road's a nice blue though right away
minutely wrinkled – d'you see? – to
make you constantly tremble a bit
as you go

Repugnant at times of a blind almost feral
luxuriance of black strands of dark
curls and almost without
roofs in between or any other
human sign

the vegetation in the meantime
surrounding you
with only here and there emerging the huge
high voltage
pylons

Rossi poi – d'un rosso impossibile! – i papaveri nei
campi
e gialle come lampi
d'afa nei rari prati immensi le chiome
dell'eucalipto

Non prendere dunque a manca appena
oltre Palidoro
Séguita ti prego – anzi t'imploro! – va'
dritto

PADRE E FIGLIO

Parla di là dal muro il vecchio bimbo non so
con chi e senza s'intende
nemmeno sognarselo lui che il suo ancora
troppo giovane padre sia qui
che ascolta

Sta dicendo dimmi com'è
che la libellula non ce la fa
a vivere più d'un giorno
solo
capisci bene un'unica
giornata e
basta?

E perché – continua – perché
mai
tutte le strade – le belle e grandi ma anche le più
piccole le più
nascoste e in ombra sai tipo quelle
minime piste di sabbia che attraversano
la Feniglia metti o l'Uccellina –
tutte le strade insomma che abbiano come traguardo
ultimo il
mare

Red – an impossible red! – poppies in the
fields
and yellow like flashes
of heat in immense rare meadows the eucalyptus'
tufts

Don't turn to the left then just
past Palidoro
Continue I beg you – indeed I implore you! – keep
straight on

FATHER AND SON

The old child speaks beyond the wall I don't know
with whom and without even
him dreaming of course that his still
too young father is here
listening

He's saying tell me how is it
the dragonfly can't
live more than one single
day
d'you understand a solitary
day and
that's it?

And why – he goes on – why
on earth
do all roads – the fine and great but also the tiniest
the most
concealed and in shadow you know like those
minimal sand tracks running through
the Feniglia for instance or the Uccellina –
in short all roads that have as their final
goal the
sea

debbono ogni volta darmi così
tanto desiderio d'andarci
subito anch'io proprio laggiù dove vanno
a terminare dove si
pèrdono?

LA CAPANNA DELL'ORTOLANO

Non ci sono che io lungo la stradetta parte in asfalto e parte
sabbia battuta
zigzagante adagio con la grande
pineta quasi nera da un lato e dall'altro l'acqua
supremamente calma e azzurra della
laguna
io qui venuto ad un appuntamento inutile e incerto
datomi non so nemmeno da chi stamattina presto sulla più nitida
delle terrazze a mare di Santa
Liberata

Ho fermato la macchina appena oltre pressoché di contro al cancello
che separa l'intatta selva demaniale dai condominii
dell'Argentario
e guardo ora davanti a me ad una trentina
di metri di distanza senza ricavarne
nessun senso d'invidia anzi con tutta
l'oggettiva carità di cui ancora sono capace la magra
capannuccia d'assi dell'ortolano affatto isolata là e come sospesa nella sua
pace

Da sotto il biondo frascame che la mimetizza stanno uscendo lievi
suoni di radio
un cagnetto bastardo bianco e nero abbaia – l'ho veduto
un attimo fa infilarsi a coda ritta per entro le canne
palustri che circondano folte in giro il piccolo
tetto anche suo –
una voce di ragazza si leva ogni poco a chiamarlo
a sgridarlo
ma ilare in fondo come se stesse
cantando

why do they every time have to give me such
a desire to go there
right then me too exactly there where they
end where they're
fading away?

THE MARKET-GARDENER'S SHED

There's no one but me on the back road part asphalt part
beaten-down sand
zigzagging slowly with the great
almost black pine-tree to one side and the other the lagoon's
supremely calm and blue
water
me come here for a useless and uncertain appointment
made by whom I don't even know this early morning on the sharper
of the seaside terraces at Santa
Liberata

I stopped the car just beyond almost against the gate
separating the untouched state-owned wood from the Argentario's
condominiums
and now before me I look some thirty metres
away without extracting from it
any feeling at all of envy but rather with such
objective charity as I'm still able
at the greengrocer's little narrow shed of slats isolated there as if suspended in its own
peace

Underneath the blond fronds that camouflage it there come issuing faint
radio sounds
a little black and white mongrel is barking – I saw it
a moment ago tail upright slip between the marsh
reeds thickly circling all about his own
little roof as well –
every now and then a girl's voice rises to call him
to tell him off
but delighted at heart as she was
singing

scherzando fra sé e
sé
oppure come rivolta sognandone a un suo
bambino

Quand'ecco dietro lungo la costa giusto di fronte
tra la riga blu dell'Aurelia e il margine verde-sfumato del
litorale
un treno che scivola fioco e parallelo
interminabile
va piano del resto assai piano ha l'aria
d'un accelerato di quelli di prima dell'ultima guerra sul grigio
la tinta dei vagoni i vetri
dei finestrini e degli sportelli a quando a
quando lustranti nel sole
dolcemente

Passa s'allontana scompare in direzione di Roma e questo è tutto
non c'è proprio più niente né da vedere né da udire né da sentire niente
d'altro

and joking to
herself
or as if dreaming of it she were addressing her own
child

When behind along the coast exactly ahead
between the Aurelia's blue line and seashore's
shaded green
a train faint and parallel
interminably slides
goes slowly ever so slowly what's more has the air
of one of those stopping trains from before the last war in the grey
the color of its coaches the panes
of its windows and doors now and then
softly glinting
in the sun

It passes by grows distant disappears in the direction of Rome and that's all
there's really nothing more to see or hear or feel not one thing
more

III

BRINDISI PER L'ANNO NUOVO

Da oggi in poi le mie poesie voglio farle
giuro
sulla prima cosa che mi verrà in
mente sul
niente
di tutti i minuti d'ogni mia
ora d'adesso sul nulla
del mio
futuro

AMORI IMPOSSIBILI

A cosa sei mai ridotto a che
punto arrivato!

Sette otto pomeriggi fa a Orbetello un solo attimo avanti
d'uscire dal W.C. di un baretto
qualsiasi
te la sei trovata a un tratto lì di fronte sul muro una spanna a
destra dello specchio
tenere labbra semichiuse e tremanti un tantino in su dolce
fragile bocca di profilo appena appena
offerta

precario ma come sempre immortale
zimbello
frutto una volta più del puro caso complice ignaro un magro
intonaco azzurrino prossimo a diventare
grigio e subito dopo grigia
briciola

e da quell'attimo non fai che pensare a lei che hai
mancata
smarrita
al po' che ti resta di
vita e senza di
lei

TOAST FOR THE NEW YEAR

From here on I want to write my poems
I swear
on the first thing that comes to
mind on the
nothing
of every minute of my
every hour of right now on the nothing
of my
future

IMPOSSIBLE LOVES

To what have you reduced yourself what's
become of you!

Seven eight afternoons ago in Orbetello just one moment before
leaving the toilet in whatever little
bar
you found her suddenly right there in front on the wall a hand's span
right of the mirror
tender half-closed and trembling lips slightly lifted sweet
fragile mouth in profile just barely
offered

precarious but as always immortal
laughingstock
fruit once again of chance unknowing accomplice a thin
bluish plasterwork about to grow
grey and right after grey
scrap

and from that instant you've done nothing but think about her who you
missed
lost
about the little you've left
of life and without
her

RACCORDO ANULARE

Sta là
nell'erba vasta e deserta di fianco alla superstrada
la
poltroncina

Viola dentro l'immenso
azzurro con la lustra
seta vieux-jeu – specie dello schienale – un po' strappata
lisa

sola
spaesata
in
bilico
proprio come la
mamma

DA BALLARE

Bastò che sterzassi a sinistra – perché l'ho fatto
non lo so – e tutto d'improvviso fu
differente
il rosso dei papaveri nei campi era mio quello del mio
sangue
quanta amarezza quanto dolore provavo guardando il giallo d'un ciuffo
di ginestre
in esilio laggiù sul margine d'un
prato
e che enormi che paurosi i tralicci della corrente
nel cielo già un po'
oscurato

È da allora da quell'istante che non t'ho più
amato

RACCORDO ANULARE

It's there
in the vast and deserted grass next to the superstrada
the
armchair

Violet inside the immense
blue with shining
vieux-jeu silk – especially the backrest – slightly
torn

alone
displaced
on
the edge
exactly like my
mother

FOR DANCING

It was enough for me to swerve to the left – why I did
I don't know – and of a sudden everything
was different
the red of the poppies in the fields was mine that of my
own blood
how much bitterness how much pain I felt in looking at the yellow of a tuft
of broom-plants
in exile down there on the edge of a
meadow
and how vast and frightening the electricity pylons
in the sky already slightly
darkened

It's from then from that instant I've no longer
loved you

NEGLI SPOGLIATOI DEL TENNIS

Quest'oggi – borbotta invisibile – è meglio di
no mi
riposo

Ma domani gioco però e
con
coso

A MIA FIGLIA PER IL SUO COMPLEANNO

Proprio stamani pensa uno settembre lungo uno stradello del centro di cui
non mi ricordo mai il nome
ho visto sopra un intonaco questo TI AMO
PAOLA
che ti compiego fotografato a
colori

Bello no? Guarda quel bianco delle maiuscole come viene fuori...

Però malandrina non me lo avevi mica detto
che avevi uno che ti fila un
ragazzetto
dalle parti di Largo
Argentina!

GLI SPETTRI
(frammento)

Non trovi mica anche tu d'un qualche significato che persino P.P.P. figùrati
tornasse ogni poco a meravigliarsi
del mio interesse anzi di' pure della mia tenace infatuazione
nei riguardi del parentado mio israelitico e
ferrarese?
Pier Paolo medesimo dopo tutto simile in questo a P.
C.
fu se non propriamente marchese per lo meno

IN THE TENNIS CHANGING ROOM

Today – he mutters invisible – I'd better
    not I'll take it
        easy

But tomorrow I play though and
    with
    what's his name

TO MY DAUGHTER FOR HER BIRTHDAY

Right this morning guess what September First in a side street downtown whose
    name I never remember
    I saw on some plaster this TI AMO
    PAOLA
    which I snapped for you in color
    and include here

Nice eh? Look how that white of the capitals comes out…

    Still you rascal you hadn't even told me
    there was someone after you
    a little boyfriend
    from round Largo
    Argentina way!

THE GHOSTS
(fragment)

Don't you find it you too of some significance that even P.P.P. imagine
    would every so often be amazed
    by my interest or rather my tenacious infatuation
    with regard to my Jewish and Ferrarese
    kinship?
    Pier Paolo himself after all similar in this to P.
    C.
    was if not actually a marquis at least

conte
e questo – con l'aggravio per lui del duplice
quarto materno agricolo e dialettale –
questo fa chiare un mucchio di cose quando noi due viceversa se Dio
vuole
pur se divisi all'origine dall'azzurra
minima roggia per metà pensile e per metà quasi
ctonia che ben
conosciamo
nonché ab aeterno dai nostri due sangui – il tuo
dolce e luminoso così diverso dal mio
grigio ed amaro –
noi in fondo non siamo che quelli che siamo
sempre e dovunque uno
dinanzi all'altro
sempre e per sempre io e
te

È a te dunque e soltanto a te che prima che sia troppo tardi
prima che gli anni via via più
rapidi
sottraggano alla mia memoria troppi particolari
del suo fisico
– fu uomo alto atticciato senza alcun
dubbio fra i più appariscenti e robusti dell'intera
Comunità
con un volto che da giovane doveva mostrarsi addirittura bello
a giudicare dagli occhi chiari chiari chiari e dal ciuffo
di capelli bianchi argentei ancora folto in cima alla cupola
robusta insieme e delicata d'un cranio
d'oramai più che
sessantacinquenne –
è a te dunque e soltanto a te che voglio oggi cantare
la storia del cugino
Arrigo

Papà mio non l'amava anzi di' pure che lo tollerava a stento non fosse altro che
[perché
si riteneva da più e non esclusivamente
sul piano delle famiglie – noi stavamo di casa
dove sai e cioè nella parte più chiara e bella e simpatica

a count
and this – with the burden for him of
the agricultural and dialectal maternal double quarter –
this makes a pile of stuff clear when the two of us rather God
willing
even if divided from the start by the minimal
blue stream half upraised and half almost
submerged that we well
know
let alone ab aeterno by our two bloods – yours
sweet and bright so different from mine
grey and bitter –
us deep down we're none other than what we are
always and everywhere one
in front of the other
always and forever you and
I

It's to you then and only you that before it's too late
before the years gradually faster
and faster
subtract from my memory too many particulars
of his physique
– he was a tall man without any
doubt among the most striking and robust of the entire
Community
with a face that as a young man must have even been handsome
judging by his very clear eyes and forelock
of silvery white hair still thick at the top of the robust
yet delicate dome of a skull
now more than
sixty-five years of age –
it's to you then and only to you that today I want to sing of
my cousin Arrigo's
story

My father didn't love him on the contrary could barely tolerate him if only
[because
he believed himself superior and not only
on the level of our families – we lived
where you know and that's in the clearest and most beautiful and nicest

della città
«quelli là» invece formicolavano a decine in un vecchio
stabile sito a pochissimi
passi dall'ex
ghetto –
ma anche sul piano dei modi dei gusti di tutto
essendo in fondo lui medico sebbene
quasi giammai esercitante e in ogni caso affatto
gratis
mentre l'altro cos'era in fondo ad onta delle sue ridicole
pretese intellettuali se non un piccolo pressoché inesistente
assicuratore-avventizio impegnato in suoi perpetui maneggi da vicolo a
vicolo da porta a
porta
nel tentativo non sempre riuscito di mettere insieme ogni dannato giorno quel po'
che consentisse a sé e alla «razza» di
sopravvivere?

Non so esattamente da quando ma penso che a cominciare circa dal '10
fosse entrato a far parte della locale
Loggia massonica
e che poi subito dopo la guerra del '15 che aveva combattuto da alpino
dalle parti del Carso per un paio d'anni e quindi sul Piave
avesse un tantino subìto anch'egli l'appeal manesco d'Italo Balbo e di Olao
Gaggioli
limitandosi però nella pratica ad assistere a qualche riunione delle meno
[importanti
in casa di questo e di
quello
o a sedersi talvolta un po' in disparte verso sera all'esterno del Caffè
Folchini
quasi sempre zitto comunque di null'altro pareva desideroso
che di guardare e d'ascoltare...

IN SOGNO

È venuta qui mi ha detto sussurrando prima
che di nuovo sparisse scusa
abbi

part of the city
"that lot" on the other hand swarmed by the dozen in an old
building located a very few
steps from the ex
ghetto –
but also on the level of their ways their tastes of everything
his being after all a doctor though
hardly ever practicing and in any case completely
for free
while the other what was he after all in spite of his ridiculous
intellectual claims but a little almost non-existent
adventitious insurer engaged in his perpetual scheming from alley to
alley from door to
door
in a not always successful attempt to put together every damn day that little
allowing him and the "race" to
survive?

I don't know exactly from when but think that starting around 1910
he'd joined the local
Masonic Lodge
and straight after the Great War where he fought with the Alpini
around the Carso for a couple of years and then on the Piave
he too succumbed a little to Italo Balbo and Olao Gaggioli's
roughneck appeal
confining himself however to the practice of attending some less important
[meetings
in the house of this one and
that
or sometimes towards evening sitting a little apart outside the Caffè
Folchini
at any rate almost always silent apparently unwilling to do a thing
but watch and listen…

IN DREAM

She came here she told me whispering before
disappearing once more I'm sorry
be

pazienza
non prendertela se ti capito a casa a un'ora
simile sul finire
del mondo e dunque di...

patient
don't take it out on me if I find you at home
at such an hour at the end of
the world and then of...

Cover of *L'alba ai vetri*. Poesia 1942-'50, Turin: Einaudi, 1963. (Fondazione Bassani, Ferrara)

Postscript

["Postscript" ("Poscritto") is the afterword to Bassani's collection of poems *L'alba ai vetri* (Dawn at the Panes) (Milan: Mondadori, 1963), originally written for RAI, the Italian State Television, in 1952, and published in the magazine *Paragone-Letteratura* in 1956 (a. VII, n. 76, April). For this translation, we have used the final revision both of the text and the poems, as they appear in Giorgio Bassani, *Opere* (Milan: Mondadori, 1998, 1162-1168). The nine poems included in "Postcript" are: "Towards Ferrara," "Evening at Porta Reno," "Variation on the Preceding Theme," "Angelus," "Dawn at the Panes," "Te Lucis Ante" II (5), "Villa Glori," "Te Lucis Ante" II (7), and (13).]

Critics are born: poets emerge – Roberto Longhi said. In the spring of '42, the first impulse to write verses came to me from art, from culture, more than from life and reality. For some time I had been struck by the poetry of two old university classmates: Francesco Arcangeli and Antonio Rinaldi; and that of Pompeo Bettini, which Benedetto Croce had reprinted the preceding winter, from Laterza. I also followed my history of art friends – the same Francesco Arcangeli, Giuseppe Raimondi, Carlo Ludovico Ragghianti, Cesare Gnudi, Giancarlo Cavalli – on the tracks of the Ferrarese and Bolognese painters of the sixteenth and seventeenth centuries: in this way, the countryside between Ferrara and Bologna, which my train would cross almost every day, showed itself to me by way of the colors, soaked with light as if veiled, in those old-time paintings. The spring of '42! Stalingrad, El Alamein, and the future uncertain, dark… Even so, despite everything, life has never again appeared so beautiful to me, so beautiful and tender as it did then. I was coming out of youth, I could feel it: but without regrets, looking at my past mistakes (I had never been able to pardon myself for them) with a sort of benign condescension. For the first time, I felt as if I were an indulgent spectator of myself. And thus, in the train that would carry me back each evening to Ferrara, from Bologna where I had completed my university studies and where, even after, I had continued to go with the same regularity as before, the occurrence of student love-affairs, from which I saw myself suddenly excluded, unfolded, enchanting but remote, forever remote, before my eyes. One of the first poems I wrote is about that evening train. Well then, what you could see through the third-class carriage windows is my landscape, yes; but rendered with my mind on canvases that in those very months my friends were showing me, distant and pathetic as it appears behind those rustic provincial madonnas, those huge saints with red and sweaty limbs.

> It's at this hour through endless warm grasses
> towards Ferrara the last trains run, with slow
> whistles they greet the evening, indolently drown
> in sleep slowly snuffing red, turreted churches.
>
> From open windows the meadow's ferment
> faintly enters to veil the shine of poor benches.
> It loosens weary fingers of poor lovers in singlets,
> renders the parched lips empty of kisses.

All the poems of that spring and summer (I wrote some one hundred, most of them lost) were, more or less, along these lines. The same pathetic sense of exclusion, the same bright landscapes. In the summer, I remember, I would go everyday by bicycle to have a swim in the Po, near Pontelagoscuro. The light had become too intense. For this reason, to rediscover the golden light of the previous spring and the paintings that, first, had revealed the Ferrara countryside to me, I would pedal under the baking August sun balancing smoked glasses on my nose. Only evening pleased me, only the light of dusk.

Later – but it really was evening by then –, we would meet up for dinner at the *Voltini*, a small *trattoria* in sight of the large metallic hangars of the airport, that would soon be destroyed.

> This side of the old arches I'm alone numbering
> rapt wretched tablecloths. But down there gentle
> gypsies set their fire, from childish mouths go
> warm songs, from the still blue aerodromes
>
> the shadow slowly rises, night falls, and a soft wind
> carries off the engines, in the firmament disperses them.

Later still there were the great nights of the Po valley summer: with its enormous moon and stars glittering on the sleeping fields. The sonnet that follows I wrote in the autumn of '43, in Florence, with extreme ease: a rare occurrence for me. But by now distant, and forever, from the places where I was born and grew up, hidden as I was, in that terrible time after the 8th of September, under a false name, the landscapes of my plain returned to me with the same calm the images of the familial dead sometimes know how to instill in us.

> If a high horn-moon crosses the serene streets
> and with its faint glow heats the glaucous stones
> out come mantled horsemen through sleep
> to warm roads that drown amongst the hay.
>
> The night's calm and clear, wavering in slight
> wind-gusts a pale milk rises from the meadows,
> you hear at intervals the far trains' blind fright
> as headlong towards packed markets they descend.
>
> But you, god who smiles at the loss and the gain,
> enchant your black flock along their path,
> along the sweet path skirting fields already green!
>
> The hostess's window half-open, call servant girls
> back to the door from their odorous beds,
> shine in the wine, sparkle loved eyes in the shadow!

Eugenio Montale, generously reviewing, in 1945, the little volume collecting these first exercises of mine, hoped that I wouldn't lose, with the years, "that fresh sense of poetry which these already suggest in part" (they were more or less his words), and in the future to employ my "admirable craft" in a "more ample and more assiduous struggle" for the possession of my "poetic truth."

I don't really know if I reached to this possession in the two books, *Te Lucis Ante* and *Un'altra libertà*, I wrote and published over the next five years, and in any case it's not for me to say if, from a critic, I became a poet. The truth is that, nevertheless, my work developed in a fundamentally opposed direction to my first book. There had been the war – I thought – and imprisonment, in between. If I wanted to accommodate, in the verses I was writing, *all* the new reality of myself and the world, then I had to fight without mercy, without the slightest condescension towards my own nature, against the carved paradise of taste and culture, against the easy paradise of primordial affections painted, inevitably!, on an idyllic background. To tear a delicate weft, to hate what I most loved: it was a necessary risk.

> Fine colours of the day, to hate you, now, what gain?
> And you, if by now you fly from the eyes with no return,
> the angelus's last light, that the yielded world adores?
> Then, sweet evening bell, farewell, farewell once more.

Only if I felt life abandon me, only in such a case could I allow myself to turn about, upon the world's scene, the one-time calm gaze *of an artist*.

> Dawn at the panes, and the music of a fife and drum
> I heard, there, its opaque faintly tipsy mirth.
> Wasn't it you that's returning, life, you, my life,
> you appearing, innocent times to come?
>
> "Wicked era coming, pressing at the doors,"
> I then said with more sweet than bitter tears,
> "forget my name!" I said. And already, o death,
> already it sent me back to sleep, your thin martial hymn.

Otherwise, reality would not have tolerated hesitations at its being represented. Its lightning messengers attacked me at every moment, when least expected. There was, for example, one wounded in the neck, a horrendously disabled war veteran who, along the stairs of a ministry building, came up to me suddenly to ask with a sort of death rattle, what was it?, the time, the location of an office...

> A very last signal,
> final warning maybe,
> by black stairs struck me
> stamped on a face.
>
> Or perhaps the just, saintly
> out-of-breath angel
> was looming, calmed
> to absolve me, close by.

> This tongue you use
> is so obscure to me!
> Never understood; beyond
> being what I fear.

From the window of a tall block, where the office in which I worked during those years was located, I could see the grove of pines covering the curved back of the little hill of Villa Glori. Between eleven and twelve every morning a ray of sun, slanting down between branches and trunks, evoked to my eyes the most definite image, that I yet vainly attempted to show to one colleague or other, of a soldier with his backpack and bayonet attached to a long nineteenth-century rifle, seen from behind. And such an image, pregnant with silence and upset (and real, oh how real!), seemed to me to appear, down there through the trees, only to distract me from another image (that one purely mental, purely dreamed) which, in those same days, a consoling fantasy conjured up for me.

> The ephemeral creature crowned with light
> at the edge of the meadow who slowly salutes,
> does its brief whisper make more acute
> (a music fades…) your own self-pity?
>
> But the other between tree-trunks, mute sunny shadow,
> the stiff figure moving slowly with the sun,
> and burdened shoulders that turning renew
> fear, boredom and anger – oh, a mirage it isn't!

It could also have been the memory, equally sudden, of another messenger, a prison guard, who during the months I spent in prison, in the spring of '43, would come at night to speak to me and propose through the peephole absurd plans of escape.

> Light, you're saluting
> the city's warm roofs,
> shadow transmuting them…
>
> (A step, only slightly
> more tired; and you breathe

> from the spyhole: "You're free,
> it's just a game, leave…").
>
> You have no peace. Promise
> blind, still. You always give
> what you don't have:
> freedom, shadow, light.

And thus, even the old print of the law-giving Moses, hanging above my bed when I was a child, and I believed, as a child, represented the Lord God, came back in memory then like the sign of a judgment, which I had not taken part in, of a destiny that had decided otherwise about me.

> If only when a child
> I had kept to your Law!
> I'd have been head bowed
> among the flock of shadows,
>
> a shadow too, already
> filled with dark infinity.
> There, in the Ghiara house,
> you alone kept vigil
>
> from your throne… Blind infant,
> oh if to submissive ancestors
> I'd devoted myself
> with your distant gaze!

Notes

IN RIMA / IN RHYME

The titles for two of the three sections to *In Rhyme* are *Poor Lovers' Stories* and *Te Lucis Ante* derived from Bassani's first two collections: *Storie dei poveri amanti e altri versi* (Rome: Astrolabio, 1945; 2nd edition 1946) and *Te lucis ante (1946-47)* (Rome: Ubaldini Editore, 1947).

Storie dei poveri amanti / Poor Lovers' Stories
Preludio / Prelude
Collecting his poems in 1982 for *In rima e senza* (In Rhyme and Without), Bassani declared in an interview that this poem "is the prelude to the complete gathering of my poems" (Dolfi 2021: 422).

Sera sul Po / Evening on the Po
The Po River, in Northern Italy, is the longest of Italy's rivers. It laps the city of Ferrara and marks the border between the regions of Lombardy and Emilia-Romagna, and Emilia-Romagna and the Veneto.

Pontelagoscuro / Pontelagoscuro
Pontelagoscuro is a township in the Lower Po Valley seven kilometers from the center of Ferrara, on the right bank of the river. In "Postscript" Bassani remembers how as a young man he would swim near Pontelagoscuro (p. 296).

Piazza d'Armi / Piazza d'Armi
In the area of the ancient Piazza d'Armi, the fortress of Pope Paul V was built in 1608, and an aqueduct and park were constructed during the fascist period. As Dolfi notes in her commentary, the "invisible walls" with which the poem begins could allude to the walls of the ancient fortress (Dolfi 2021: 429).

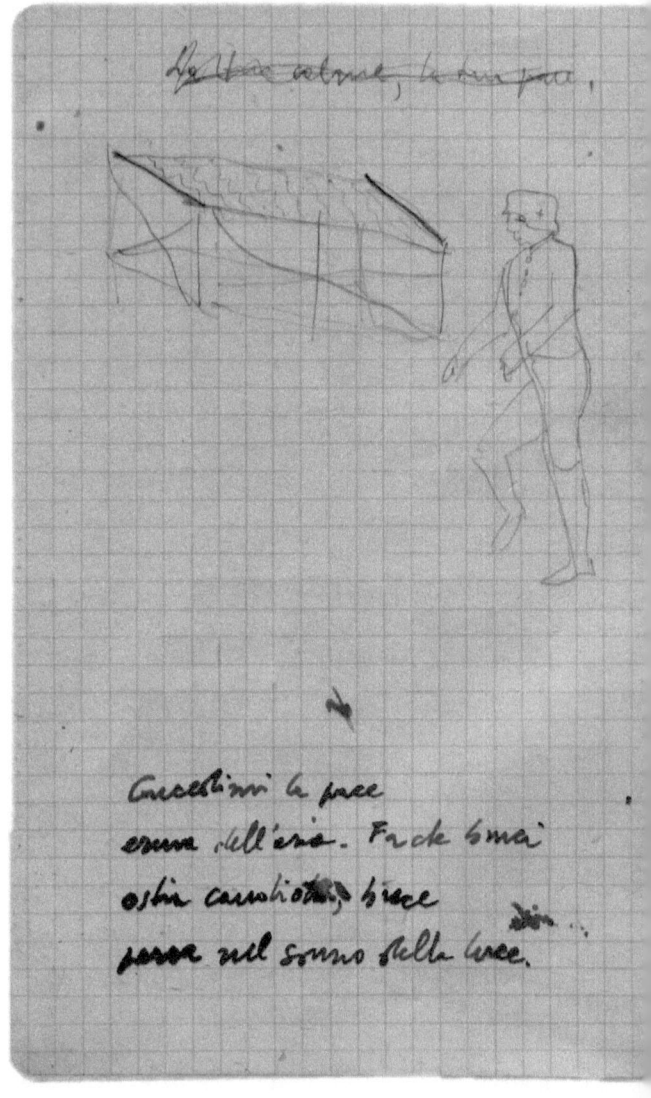

Manuscript version of "Non piangere" ("Don't Weep") in *Storie dei poveri amanti*. From a handwritten early notebook with diary entries, reflections on political meetings, drawings, and numerous poems. On the left is a sketch of a parallelepiped with a German soldier (Dolfi 2021: 464). (Fondo manoscritti Eredi Paola e Enrico Bassani)

Non piangere, compagno
se non hai trovato qui disteso.
Vedi, non ho più peso
in me di sangue. Mi bagno

di quest'ombra che mi sale
dal ventre pallido al cuore,
inaridito fiore
d'indifferenza mortale.

Portami fuori, amico,
al sole che scalda la piazza,
al vento celeste che spazza
il mio golfo infinito.

Concedimi la pace
dell'aria. Fa che brucî
~~oltre ogni limite,~~
~~ogni confine,~~ ~~ogni~~ ~~domanda~~
~~questa appassita età dell'uomo~~
~~questa mia disperata voce~~
~~amara della vita.~~

Dai bastioni orientali / From the Eastern Bastions

The Mura degli Angeli, the part of Ferrara's city walls at the end of Corso Ercole I d'Este – the "cardo" of the Renaissance area, one of its most famous streets and a UNESCO World Heritage Site – are at the heart of Bassani's work, in particular in his most famous novel, *The Garden of the Finzi-Continis*. To the East, right behind the Mura degli Angeli, is the Jewish cemetery.

Di settembre a San Giorgio / In September at San Giorgio

San Giorgio is the patron saint of Ferrara, celebrated on 23 April, the day when a traditional fair is held. Dolfi writes that Bassani was called Giorgio because it was on the day of this anniversary in 1916 that his parents became engaged: Giorgio Davide (like his paternal grandfather) Mameli (from Goffredo Mameli, poet and patriot of the Risorgimento, author of the Italian anthem). (Dolfi 2021: 436.)

Verso Ferrara / Towards Ferrara

A large proportion of what Bassani wrote is set in Ferrara, the small town in Emilia-Romagna where the writer grew up. Even though the place has already made its appearance in the collection (in "From the Eastern Bastions" and, above all, in the previous poem, "In September at San Giorgio," where the city is described as of "stone," "implacable, gloomy" and invoked as "my closed city"), this is the first time its name appears in any of Bassani's works (Scarpa 2018: 224). The Ferrara-Bologna train also plays an important role in two of his novels, *The Gold-Rimmed Spectacles* and *The Garden of the Finzi-Continis*. For this poem, see "Postscript" (p. 296).

Sera a Porta Reno / Evening at Porta Reno

Corso di Porta Reno is one of the main streets in Ferrara. The "rapt wretched tablecloths" belong to the trattoria Voltini, which also appears in *The Garden of the Finzi-Continis*: "the Voltini, a trattoria outside Porta Reno" (*The Novel of Ferrara*: 423). Also, in "Postscript", "the *Voltini*, a small *trattoria* in sight of the large metallic hangars of the airport" (p. 296). Bassani's geography is always "true," places and times are described with great precision: "because my poems happen, they have a temporal and spatial position exactly like my fiction" (in the interview "Meritare il tempo," [Deserving the Time], in Dolfi 2003: 177). In another interview, Bassani declared: "if I have always talked about Ferrara it was because I'm convinced it's necessary to point a lens, excavate a microcosm and go into it vertically until everything there comes to the surface" (Bassani 2019:

94-95 and see also the end of "Porta Rosa" in *Without*, where the poet writes of digging in his city for "twenty thousand and more days" – in 1974, when *Epitaffio* was published, Bassani was 58, that's to say approximately 21,170 days old).

Marina d'ottobre / Seaside in October

In her commentary to the next poem, "Punta Marina," Dolfi writes that some August 1943 photographs portray Bassani and his wife Valeria during their honeymoon at Marina di Ravenna, a seaside resort on the Romagna Riviera, northeast of the city center (Dolfi 2021: 442). Bassani himself evokes it in one of the pieces from *The Smell of Hay* (*The Novel of Ferrara*: 703). The English translation for the titles to both poems is problematic. In the title "Marina d'ottobre," *Marina* is a noun, and because of its initial position, it could be the proper name for the resort or simply mean "seashore." In the next poem, "Punta marina," *marina* is in lowercase, and therefore an adjective. There is a longer version of this poem whose title, "Marina presso Ravenna" (Dolfi 2021: 441), literally "Marina by Ravenna," clearly refers to the resort. The ambiguity of the Italian titles is lost in English, so we have translated the first but kept the second in the original as "Punta Marina."

Variazione sul tema precedente / Variation on the Preceding Theme

For this poem, see "Postscript" (p. 297).

Monselice / Monselice

Monselice is a town near Padua in the Veneto. There is a mention of Monselice in one of the prose pieces in *The Smell of Hay* (*The Novel of Ferrara*: 706).

Storie dei poveri amanti / Poor Lovers' Stories

A series of four poems that gives its title both to Bassani's first collection, its first edition published in 1945, and to the first part of the *In rima* section to *In rima e senza*. The young man with the fur coat and the woman addressed in the first poem closely resemble the two main characters of "Lida Mantovani," opening story from *Inside the Walls*, the first book in *The Novel of Ferrara*.

Cena di Pasqua / Easter Supper

The tragic farewell taking place in this poem is the same as described in *The Garden of the Finzi-Continis* (*The Novel of Ferrara*: 375-376) – told in almost the same words. As Bassani reported, some crucial elements of the novel were

Manuscript version of "Retrovia" ("Behind the Lines") in *Storie dei poveri amanti*. From a handwritten early notebook with diary entries, reflections on political meetings, drawings, and numerous poems. (Fondo manoscritti Eredi Paola e Enrico Bassani)

Nella sera il monte odora
oleandri
~~pioveva mi~~ che una tenda di passi.
La vita non è più, ora,
per te che un abbigliare di vene.

— . —

Gli angeli tutelari
che proteggevano la tua voce,
come ti hanno gli occhi chiusi
quasi puerile la voce.

Li vedevi provvisoriamente.
Non portano tuniche ma camicioni.
Polverosi sono volti
di fatica, appena vesti.

Parlano. Li senti bisbigliare,
Cosi remota è la guerra!   traverso un velo di terra
Ridono anche. Han voglia d'amare,
di vivere ~~anche di vivere~~

Nella sera il monte odora
oleandri che una tenda di passi.
La vita non è più, ora,
per te che un abbigliare di vene.

already in his poetry (Bassani 2019: 73 and 95). See also "The Ghosts (Fragment)" in *Without*.

Emilia / Emilia
The city of Ferrara is in Emilia. Emilia and Romagna are now part of the same region, Emilia-Romagna, with the first located to the north-east and the second to the south-west. The main difference between these regions is historical: from the fall of the Roman Empire to the unification of Italy, Emilia and Romagna were always divided. Emilian cities were organized into largely independent municipalities and duchies, whereas Romagna was first under the Byzantine Empire and then part of the Papal States.

Saluto a Roma /Salute to Rome
Bassani lived in Rome from 1943 until his death in 2000. The "hometown buried" is, of course, Ferrara.

Non piangere / Don't Weep
In a note to the 1945-'46 edition of the *Poor Lovers' Stories* collection, Bassani wrote that this poem and the following, "Behind the Lines," were dedicated to those who died in the Second World War. These two are among the few Italian poems on the Resistance, and Eugenio Montale valued them highly in his review of Bassani's first book (Dolfi 2021: 466; and see "Postscript": p. 297). A fragmentary rendering of this poem is probably the first English translation of any text by Bassani (see Introduction: p. 32).

Te lucis ante / Te Lucis Ante
This second section bears the title of Bassani's second published collection of poems (1947). Of the 22 original lyrics, without a title and numbered, 16 remain in the definitive version. According to Dolfi, this entire section is influenced by the first cantos of Dante's *Purgatorio*, and by the passage from one world to another (Dolfi 2021: 476). They recount a dream or hallucinated vigil repeating itself every night during Bassani's imprisonment for antifascist activity in 1943 (*ivi*: 478).

Valle dell'Aniene / Valle dell'Aniene
The Aniene is a river in Lazio. The "foreign city" could be Rome where, as noted, Bassani moved after the war and where he spent most of his adult life.

Dal carcere / From Prison
Bassani participated in the anti-fascist resistance and was arrested in May 1943, spending three months in prison. He then fled to Florence, where he hid under the false name of Giacomo Marchi (Marchi was his Catholic maternal grandmother's surname). This poem was written in the Ferrara prison.

5 Un ultimo segnale / A very last signal
For this poem, see "Postscript" (p. 298-299).

7 Luce che i caldi tetti / Light, you're saluting
When Bassani was in prison, he had the recurring dream of being freed by a guard, which he talks about in a 1993 interview (Bassani 2019: 353). Also, in "Postscript," Bassani remembers "a prison guard, who during the months I spent in prison, in the spring of '43, would come at night to speak to me and propose through the peephole absurd plans of escape" (p. 299; and see Dolfi 2021: 482-483).

8 Quando più ero solo / When I was more alone
The "ditches" in the second line of the second stanza, *maceri* in Italian, are water basins that were used for processing hemp. They have a rectangular shape and a variable depth, although generally no more than two meters.

13 Mi avessi da bambino / If only when a child
The house of the Ghiara is Bassani's maternal grandparents' home in Ferrara, which was situated in Via Ghiara. As a child during the First World War, Bassani spent the years 1915-1918 there. His grandfather Cesare Minerbi was a famous clinician, head physician of the Ferrara hospital. For this poem, see "Postscript" (p. 300). A few poems in the *Without* section, either directly or indirectly mention Cesare Minerbi.

16 Sei venuto alla porta / You came to the door
The first two lines of the second stanza of this poem appear in the final part of *The Garden of the Finzi-Continis* (*The Novel of Ferrara*: 416).

Vide cor meum / Vide Cor Meum
According to Dolfi, the title and quote "Vide cor meum" are probably a variation on the opening to Dante's *Vita Nova*'s "Vide cor tuum," although she also sug-

gests Manzoni as a likely source (Dolfi 2021: 492; Litrico 2020: 250-251). The epigraph to *The Novel of Ferrara* is a quotation from Chapter VIII in Manzoni's *The Betrothed*: "Of course, for whoever pays heed to it, the heart always has something to say about what's to come. But what does the heart know? Just the least bit about what has happened already" (*The Novel of Ferrara*: vii). With others from the third and last section of *In Rhyme*, this poem appeared in *Botteghe Oscure* (July-December 1948, II, 191-93; January-June 1950, V, 90-91).

Per un quadro di Morandi / For A Picture by Morandi
Giorgio Morandi (1890-1964) was a painter and printmaker who specialized in still lives, depicting notably bottles, vases, pitchers, fruit dishes, and other everyday objects. Bassani deeply admired Morandi and considered him the greatest painter of his time (Bassani 1998: 957).

Per il parco di Ninfa / For the Parco di Ninfa
William Weaver, the great American translator of Italian literature, wrote a long and passionate article about this enchanting park near Rome, one of the most beautiful in Europe ("A Legendary Garden," *New York Times*, March 30, 1997, available online). The immense property had belonged to the Caetani family since the Middle Ages, and when Weaver was in Rome, he was often a guest of Marguerite Chapin Caetani, wife of Roffredo, the last Caetani prince (see comment on "Don't Weep"). Marguerite Caetani was the founder and director of the literary journals *Commerce*, in France, and *Botteghe Oscure* in Italy (see Introduction: p. 32 and Chronology). Weaver met Bassani when he worked at *Botteghe Oscure* as an editor. He became the poet's first English translator (see comment on "Valle dell'Aniene"); except for the *Gold-Rimmed Spectacles*, Weaver translated all of Bassani's narrative works (see Translators' Note). Since 2000, the entire Ninfa area, run by the Roffredo Caetani Foundation and open to the public, has been declared a natural monument. Bassani often mentioned how the garden envisioned in *The Garden of the Finzi-Continis* was inspired by Ninfa, along with Rome's Botanical Garden and other gardens in Ferrara (Dolfi 2021: 500).

Villa Glori / Villa Glori
Villa Glori Park is in Rome in the Parioli district. Opened to the public in 1924, it is immersed in a Mediterranean greenery of pines, holm oaks, laurels, cedars, and olive trees, lined in rows. As its name "Parco della Rimembranza" suggests,

Manuscript version of "Villa Glori" (in *Te lucis ante*) written on the letterhead of the Prime Minister's Office when in the immediate post-war period Bassani was employed at the Ministry of Labor in the War Veterans Office. (Fondo manoscritti Eredi Paola e Enrico Bassani)

it was created to remember those who died during the First World War, and subsequently, to all Romans who died for their homeland. See "Postscript" (p. 299) for Bassani's comment on this poem.

Sera a Montesacro / Montesacro Evening
Montesacro is a Roman neighborhood where Bassani and his family lived during the fifties. The name comes from the hill, which rises on the right bank of the Aniene river just before it flows into the Tiber.

Angelus / Angelus
For this poem, see "Postscript" (p. 298).

L'alba ai vetri / Dawn at the Panes
This poem gives the title to the collection published in 1963, of which "Postscript" is the afterword (p. 298). Dolfi described it as expressing "a moment of transition towards a future that shows itself both innocent and ungodly, insofar as it concerns the blameless poet, who can only ask history to forget him, and the massacres that have soaked Europe in blood" (Dolfi 2021: 505).

Sogno / Dream
Bassani often insisted on the importance of his relationship with his father. In the last chapters of *The Garden of the Finzi-Continis*, he creates a moving portrait of the narrator's father (*The Novel of Ferrara*: 439-446; and see Dolfi 2021: 508-509). The image of the father's *silvered hair* returns both here and in the novel.

A mio padre / To My Father
Bassani's father died in 1948, the same year this poem was published in *Botteghe Oscure* (July-December 1948, II, 193).

SENZA / WITHOUT

The titles for two of the three sections in *Without* are those of Bassani's last two collections, *Epitaffio* (Milan: Mondadori, 1974) and *In gran segreto* (Milan: Mondadori, 1978). The third section, without a title, contains eight poems written after the publication of *In gran segreto*, integrated in the 1982 collected edition, *In rima e senza* (Bassani 1982).

Epitaffio / Epitaph

Foro Italico giugno '72 / Foro Italico June '72
Bassani was a great tennis fan and player, and the sport is a recurring theme in many of his works. In particular, tennis plays an important role in *The Garden of The Finzi-Continis*. In the poems, the setting is either Tennis Parioli or Foro Italico in Rome, hence the title of this poem. See also "Tennis Club" in *Epitaph*, and "Exactly Like" and "In the Tennis Changing Room" in *In Great Secret*.

Gli ex fascistoni di Ferrara / Ferrara's Ex-Fascists
This is one of the few poems in which Bassani, as he often does in his novels, refers to historical facts and political events, in this case the racial laws of 1938, and their consequences in Italian society (see Dolfi 2021: 527). The "Geo" mentioned is Geo Josz, the main character in one of Bassani's most famous short stories, "A Memorial Tablet in Via Mazzini" (*The Novel of Ferrara*: 60-89) who returns to Ferrara after surviving the Holocaust, "the character in whose hands I have entrusted my message" as Bassani said in an interview (Kertesz-Viali 2011: 278). Bassani not only adopts the role of storyteller but appears as the president of Italia Nostra, an organization for the protection of Italy's historical, artistic, and environmental patrimony, of which he was one of the co-founders and president (1965-1980; see Chronology). Marcello Rimini and Rabbi Viterbo are real people whose names Bassani has slightly changed (Kertesz-Viali 2011: 278). He often experienced criticism when people of Ferrara claimed to recognize themselves in his characters. "Tu quoque" is a Latin expression commonly used in Italian to mean "even you" and derived from words allegedly spoken by Julius Caesar to Brutus: "Tu quoque, Brute, fili mi?" (Even you, Brutus, my son?).

A un professore di filosofia / To a Professor of Philosophy
We don't know who the "professor of philosophy" is, a visiting professor in a Massachusetts institution returning to Italy. The interpretation of "ex Pidàz" provides a fascinating window into Bassani's way of working, with his poems deeply interwoven with the prose. The word "pidàz" is Ferrarese dialect for a large and ungainly foot and, by extension, a bad soccer player. It can also be used as a general insult. Bassani had indeed been a fan of Spal in his youth, the Ferrara soccer team, of which his father had been president in the 1920s. However, "Pidàz" also appears in one of the pieces for the 1972 first edition of *L'odore*

Bassani in 1957 in Castiglioncello (province of Grosseto), with Pier Paolo Pasolini and Natalia Ginzburg. (Archivio Eredi Paola e Enrico Bassani)

Bassani in the late 1950s-early 1960s in Tivoli at the Sorgenti Acque Albule, the so-called "thermal baths" of Rome. He is with Mario Soldati in front of a cabin used for changing. (Archivio Eredi Paola e Enrico Bassani)

del fieno (*The Smell of Hay*). Writing about his friend Borelli (possibly the philosophy professor), Bassani says that among other things they had in common, such as university and Naples Littoriali, they "belonged to the so-called Pidàz." In the 1980 edition of *Il romanzo di Ferrara* (of which *L'odore del fieno* is now the sixth and last chapter), Bassani replaced "Pidàz" with "partito" (party), and Borelli became B: "Between me and B there were many things in common: university [...], the Naples Littoriali, and finally, now, we both belonged to the same Party" (*The Novel of Ferrara*: 729). Read in the context of *The Smell of Hay*, "Pidàz" is almost certainly an acronym for Partito d'Azione, *Pi d'Az*, an anti-fascist party founded in 1942 that played an important role in the Resistance and to which Bassani belonged until 1946. William Weaver, working from the 1974 edition of *L'odore del fieno*, translated "Pidàz" as "Action Party" (Weaver 1975: 78), not only confirming our supposition, but also providing us with a translation.

The poem is an ironic cultural excursus taking place between Italy and the United States: Aldo Capitini, philosopher and politician, theorist of non-violence; *Love Story*, the best-selling 1970s novel by Erich Segal; "Emily" is Emily Dickinson; ferragosto, the mid-August holiday celebrated on 15 August throughout the entire country; Cortina d'Ampezzo, the famous jet-set tourist resort in the Veneto Dolomites; "Umberto-style" hair was cut very short to the same length and combed back, as worn by King Umberto I of Savoy (1844-1900); Pelmi and Pomagagnòn are mountains in the Dolomites.

A Franco Fortini / To Franco Fortini

Franco Fortini (1917-1994), poet, writer, essayist, translator, and polemicist. Bassani and Fortini were friends for almost thirty years. Monte Marcello is a village in Liguria, between Lerici and Bocca di Magra. It's on top of Monte Caprione, a promontory, at 266 meters above sea level. There is another poem addressed to Fortini with the same title in *In Great Secret*.

Anche tu / You Too

A.B. stands for the writer Anna Banti (1895-1985) who was Roberto Longhi's wife. Bassani and Banti both worked for the literary magazine *Paragone-Letteratura*. Roberto Longhi (1890-1970), the famous Italian art historian was close to Bassani, who had been his student at the University of Bologna. Bassani remembered Longhi in one of his most beautiful prose pieces in the non-fiction collection *Di là dal cuore*, "Un vero maestro" (A True Mentor) (Bassani 1998:

Bassani in the late 1950s-early 1960s at the Lido di Venezia, with Aldo Palazzeschi and Arnoldo Mondadori. (Archivi Mondadori)

1073). "Edgardo" is Edgardo Limentani, the main character in Bassani's last novel, *The Heron*, published in 1968, the fifth book of *The Novel of Ferrara*. At the end of the book, Edgardo commits suicide.

All'amata / To the Loved One
Te Lucis Ante is the title of Bassani's second book of poems, published in 1947 in Rome, by the small press Ubaldini (see above: p. 24, 301 and 308).

All'addiaccio / In the Open
The first line in French means "You believe we'll get out of it." Trècchina is a small town in Basilicata, close to Maratea where Bassani and Anne-Marie Stehlin had a summer house (see comment on "Letter") where they spent many summers (Paola Bassani 2016: 87). In her memoir, Mimma Mondadori, the

publisher's daughter, recalls: "We spent many summers together, in Maratea, the legendary Maratea whose wonders and secrets Bassani would recount and reveal [...] Maratea was the venue for one of his great, long, difficult loves, with a beautiful and tyrannical woman. For her, he had built that house and built his image of Maratea. Then something changed, the story thinned out; maybe it was over, I don't know. He was alone in Maratea; she no longer came. He suffered a lot." (Mondadori 1985: 193-194). Anne-Marie was the muse for many of the *Epitaph* poems. Like other women associated with the Italian poetic tradition, we don't know much about her, except, for the most part, what Bassani himself says. In the poem "In Bed," he tells us that she had a "great body." In "Porta Rosa," that she was "tall and blonde and foreign." In "The Grown-Ups" we learn a few things about her family. We know that her birthday was on Christmas Day from "From Villon" (*In Great Secret*). Paola Bassani writes that they had a relationship which, beginning in 1969 immediately after the publication of *The Heron*, lasted until the end of the seventies (Paola Bassani 2016: 87). Dolfi describes her as "refined and snobbish" (Dolfi 2021: 556). A petition found online – which Anne-Marie filed in 1960 with the US Senate to retain her American citizenship while abroad with her husband (a petition that was granted) – adds a few details to her biography. She was born in 1926 in France to an American mother, Marjorie Stralem, and a French father, Maurice Schwob (a Free French government agent who died in a plane crash in 1944). In 1939, the family returned to the States, where they remained until 1949. During that period Anne-Marie applied for American naturalization. In 1951, she married the general and politician Paul Stehlin, who died in 1975 after being hit by a bus in Paris. Stehlin was a member of the French National Assembly and just hours before his death "it was revealed that he was on the payroll of Northrop Corp., maker of the F-17," when a year before he "had caused a sensation by insisting that the U.S. F-16 and F17 aircraft were superior to their French competitor, the Mirage Fl." (*Time* obituary, 7 July 1975). At the Hôpital Cochin where Stehlin was admitted after the accident, Anne-Marie denied that her husband could have committed suicide, because of the possible subsequent scandal: "My husband is very religious. It can't then be a suicide attempt. It's just a dramatic new incident in our lives" (*Le Monde*, 10 June 1975). Anne-Marie died recently in Paris on 29 April 2021, followed by her only sibling, her sister Diane Strong Schwob, who died in Houston one year later. Anne-Marie and her husband had a son, Marc Pierre Stehlin (born 1954). Of Anne-Marie there are a few Getty images that portray her together with Baron Guy de Rothschild.

Bassani described this poem as "small and narrow, therefore very lyrical" as opposed to "Rolls Royce," "long and wide, with narrative elements inside, so to speak" (as quoted in Dolfi 2021: 535). The flexible nature of these epitaphs allows the poems to adopt different shapes, adapting themselves thus to different moods.

Mi chiedi perché mai e quando / You Ask Me Whyever and When
Palazzo Sacchetti is a late Renaissance, centrally located palazzo, one of the most beautiful buildings in Rome. Its construction began in 1542 to a plan by the architect Antonio da Sangallo, the same architect of the Palazzo Farnese and assistant to Raphael in the construction of the Saint Peter's Basilica.

La cuginetta cattolica / My Little Catholic Cousin
"Nonno Cesare" Minerbi (1856-1954) was Bassani's maternal grandfather. See comment on "If only when a child," no. 13 in *Te Lucis Ante* from the *In Rhyme* section. "Addio, addio, Leonora, addio!" is an aria in Verdi's Opera *Il Trovatore*.

Rolls Royce / Rolls Royce
The Este Castle, Corso Giovecca, Prospettiva, the church of San Carlo, the church of the Teatini, the pasticceria Folchini, via Madama, via Cisterna del Follo, the Montagnone: the phantom motor car travels through streets and places linked to Bassani's youth in Ferrara. He might well have got a suggestion for the poem from the Rolls Royce Phantom, the name the company used for its luxury cars from 1925 to the present day. The Bassani family home was in via Cisterna del Follo where he lived until 1943. The pasticceria Folchini, in corso Giovecca, one of Ferrara's main streets, is among its historical cafés. It appears again in the second-to-last poem of this book, "The Ghosts (Fragment)." The Prospettiva is an arch located at the end of Corso Giovecca. The Montagnone is a mound of earth created with material from the construction of the city's beautiful walls. Ferrara's walls were built at the end of the sixteenth century but were never used for the defense of the city. They are among the few still intact in Italy. About nine kilometers in length, they entirely surround the historical center. Now, the walls are a large ring-shaped garden, with meadows, tree-lined roads, and wooded areas.

Promenade des Anglais / Promenade des Anglais
In Nice, the Promenade des Anglais is a seven-kilometer walk along the seafront.

Lettera / Letter

In October 1967, Bassani bought a house in Maratea, a seaside village in Basilicata along the beautiful Cilento coast. There, at the top of the village, he spent his summers until 1980. Lagonegro and Colla are places near Maratea (see comment on "In the Open"). Capo Palinuro is a promontory on the Cilento Coast, north of the village. Viserba and Bellaria are seaside villages on the Adriatic coast in Emilia-Romagna, where Bassani grew up. A Fiorella bed & breakfast still exists in Maratea, but is not near the castle, and so probably only named after the hotel mentioned in the poem. The ruins of the castle of Castrocucco are located 200 meters above sea level. Giulio Andreotti (1919-2013) was a leader of the Christian Democrats, the ruling party in Italian political life for most of the second half of the twentieth century. Andreotti was prime minister seven times. Bassani's use of the expression "center left" refers to the Italian political phase that ran from 1962 to 1976.

This is "a poem of exceptional importance in the context of my things" Bassani declared in the interview "Meritare il tempo" (Deserving Time): "It's a distant self, remote in time, in space" which "is brought back to life, that is to identity, at the very moment when the poet imagines himself dead" (Dolfi 2003: 178). The source is a letter the Roman poet Gioacchino Belli (1791-1863) wrote from Genoa to his wife Maria Conti, on 26 August 1829, where he describes a situation similar to the one told by Bassani in this poem: "In Pisa [...] I had lunch with a very clean and very nice man [...] about 50 years old [...] After lunch he saluted me with the greatest cordiality and then threw himself from the top of the leaning tower" (as quoted in Dolfi 2021: 542).

Indovinello / Guessing Game

In the final verse, the syllable *ie* doubtless hints at the name Anne-Marie Stehlin.

Ninfa rivisitata / Ninfa Revisited

For this park near Rome, see the comment on "For the Parco di Ninfa" in the *In Rhyme* section.

Le leggi razziali / The Racial Laws

The racial laws were a series of directives issued by the fascist government regulating the exclusion of Jews from all sectors of public and private life. Drafted and initially enforced between September and December 1938, they dramatically changed the lives of Italy's Jews and prepared the way for their wartime inclusion in the Nazis' final solution, as narrated in *The Garden of the Finzi-Continis*.

Alla periferia / On the Outskirts
The "Carlo" mentioned in this poem could be the writer and painter Carlo Levi (1902-1975), a friend of Bassani's who painted his portrait in 1953.

Di profilo / In Profile
Mario Cèroli (1938-) a sculptor and theater set designer whom Bassani greatly admired began his career in Rome in the 1960s and was fascinated by American pop artists (Paola Bassani 2012: 32; 2021: 9-12 for her father's interest in their art). Cèroli participated in the Italian "Arte Povera" movement. Bassani seems to be referring to the silhouettes of human figures in wood, for which the artist is famous.

Arrivo mia madre non sta bene / I Arrive my Mother's Not Well
Bassani's mother, Dora Minerbi (1893-1987) was the daughter of the head physician of the Ferrara hospital, Cesare Minerbi (see comment on "If only as a child I had", no. 13 in *Te Lucis Ante* from the *In Rhyme* section). After she married, she lived in the paternal home of her husband, Angelo Enrico Bassani (1885-1948), in via Cisterna del Follo 1 in Ferrara. Angelo Enrico's father, as Bassani writes here, was a gynecologist but never practiced. The Bassanis lived on the proceeds of their lands, like many other Ferrara Jews who were "almost all bourgeois, merchants, landowners, etc...." (Bassani 1998: 1345).

Storia di famiglia / Family History
We first encountered "nonno Cesare," Bassani's maternal grandfather in the poem "If only as a child I had" (no. 13 in *Te Lucis Ante* from the *In Rhyme* section, see comment), and he appears frequently in the *Without* section. The Finzi-Continis are, of course, the family of his novel, *The Garden of the Finzi-Continis*. Via Montebello is a central street in Ferrara. *Simplicissimus* was a satirical German magazine founded in 1896.

Santa Severa / Santa Severa
Santa Severa is a seaside resort in Lazio near Santa Marinella. Bassani knew the coast along the Via Aurelia well. The Prologue of the *Garden of the Finzi-Continis* begins with a car trip down the Via Aurelia. The group of friends stopped "a few kilometers from Santa Marinella, intrigued by the towers of a medieval castle [...]" (*The Novel of Ferrara*: 245). See comment on "The Depressed Man Speaks" from *In Great Secret*.

Isola Bisentina
Centuries-old trees, native flora, and ancient settlements on the largest volcanic lake in Europe make the Isola Bisentina an extraordinary place. The Swiss painter Arnold Böcklin (1827-1901) is considered one of the founders of Symbolism. Bassani refers here to his most famous painting, *Island of the Dead*, of which the artist made five different versions.

Dalla Sicilia / From Sicily
"Zàgara" means orange blossom or, in general, any citrus tree blossom.

Danse macabre / Danse Macabre
This is also the title of a poem in Baudelaire's *Les fleurs du mal* (Dolfi 2021: 550).

Salto di Fondi / Salto di Fondi
Salto di Fondi is a small village, in the province of Latina in Lazio. The syntagm "life is elsewhere" alludes to the French poet Arthur Rimbaud, whose supposed remark "La vie est ailleurs" or "La vrai vie est ailleurs" is probably among his most famous. But it might also bring to mind the novel by Milan Kundera, which was translated into Italian as *La vita è altrove* (trans. Serena Vitale, Milano: Adelphi, 1973) (see Dolfi 2021: 551). As Kundera writes in Part Four of his novel, Rimbaud's sentence was adopted in May 1968 by Parisian students as a slogan: "Life is elsewhere, the students have written on the walls of the Sorbonne" (Kundera 2000: 237). This is a misquote, since Rimbaud, in the prose poem "L'époux infernal," wrote "absent" and not "elsewhere:" "Quelle vie! La vraie vie est absente. Nous ne sommes pas au monde" (Rimbaud 2003: 492).

Forte Antenne / Forte Antenne
Forte Antenne is one of Rome's fifteen forts, built between 1877 and 1891. Dolfi quotes from a 1975 article where Bassani writes: "After an almost spring-like day, the air has become pungent, and my friend suggests we get the car to go from the historic center to his club where we will dine in a peaceful environment. The walk is quite long through the winding paths of Forte Antenne" (Dolfi 2021: 551-552).

Bocca Trabaria / Bocca Trabaria
Bocca Trabaria is a mountain pass in the Apennines not far from Urbino. In modern Italian poetry, whenever a *ginestra* (broom-plant) is mentioned, it re-

calls Giacomo Leopardi's (1798-1837) famous poem "La ginestra, o fiore del deserto," which the great poet from Recanati wrote in 1836 but was published posthumously in the 1845 edition of the *Canti*. "The genista or flower of the desert" grows on the slopes of Vesuvius, on ungrateful and hard ground, yet it adapts and survives. The poem is considered Leopardi's spiritual testament.

Tennis Club / Tennis Club
The poem is prompted by Bassani's remembering his exclusion from the Marfisa Tennis Club in Ferrara following the 1938 Racial Laws, which is also the *casus belli* at the start of his novel *The Garden of the Finzi-Continis*, where the narrator and his friends are invited to play on the family's private tennis court. For Bassani and tennis, see also comment on "Foro Italico '72."

Odradek / Odradek
In Kafka's short story, "The Anxiety of The Head of Family" (in the collection *A Country Doctor*), Odradek is the name of a spool of thread (however it reminds us of a dust kitten – Italian uses the same image for dust accumulation: "gatti" or "gatte") – it has the same volatile quality) "a flat, stellar spool for thread [...] old torn threads of the most disparate sorts and colors, knotted together, but also ensnarled" (Kafka 1995: 265). In this retelling of Kafka's short story, there is perhaps an influence from the end of *The Metamorphosis*, with the body of Gregor Samsa slipping lifelessly along the floor struck by the cleaner's broom.

Sul Pollino / On the Pollino
The Pollino mountains are located in northern Calabria. The Pollino National Park is now the largest protected area in Italy. Bassani was very fond of animals which often play an important role in his works. In one of his prose pieces, "Di là dal cuore" (Beyond the Heart), which gives its title to his collected non-fiction, *Di là dal cuore* (1984) – and originally introduced the essays *Dalla parte degli animali* (On the Side of The Animals) (Porzio 1972: 7-12) – he wrote: "I have always loved animals: by natural disposition. For some years, however, [...] I have begun to love them more, more and more" (Bassani 1998: 1274).

Saturnia / Saturnia
In Saturnia, Maremma, where the famous thermal baths are located, the painter and sculptor Gastone Novelli (1925-1968) bought a house that was to become a meeting place for artists and writers (Dolfi 2021: 555). In the interview "Meritare il tempo," Bassani recalls this poem to explain how the shape of the epitaph

contains life and death in a single structure: "Saturnia, a poem where I mention a painter, an exquisite aesthete, recently dead, with his house over there, jinxed, mortuary, funerary, and 'and me / still alive'" (Dolfi 2003: 178).

In memoria / In Memory

The addressee of this poem is Francesco Arcangeli (1915-1974), art historian and critic, a close friend of Bassani and his university classmate when they were both students of Roberto Longhi in Bologna and to whose chair Arcangeli succeeded in 1967 (for Roberto Longhi, see comment on "You Too"). Arcangeli is the author of an important monograph on Giorgio Morandi (1890-1964), one of Bassani's favorite artists. Uniquely in Bassani's poetry, the two stanzas of this poem are reprinted identically in another poem addressed to Arcangeli, "A Momi" (Arcangeli's nickname), in *In Great Secret*. The poem "Bareheaded" from *Epitaph* is a recollection of Arcangeli's funeral.

Per una macchiolina / For a Little Spot

Dolfi thinks that the addressee ("my beautiful") of this poem is most likely Anne-Marie Stehlin (see comment on "In the Open"), and that the "little insignificant spot" is from a birthmark on the forehead and hands of his friend, the poet Attilio Bertolucci (1911-2000), hence the reference to the color purple, *la viola d'Attilio* (Dolfi 2021: 556).

La Porta Rosa / Porta Rosa

In 1973, Bassani and Anne-Marie Stehlin visited the archaeological site of Elea-Velia, in the Cilento National Park in Lazio, together with the superintendent Mario Napoli, who had named the "Porta" to the archaeological area "Rosa" after his wife' (Dolfi 2021: 557).

Ars dictandi / Ars Dictandi

This poem is addressed to his friend Agostino Richelmy (1900-1991), poet and translator (according to Bassani's note at the end of the 1974 edition of *Epitaffio*). Horace recommended hellebore as an antidote for madness. Here Bassani says that the gift of hellebore from his friend, instead of making him come to his senses, would make him mad. For Bassani the antidote to madness is, in fact, poetry itself.

Valzer / Waltz

The Lungotevere are the boulevards in Rome that follow the course of the river Tiber through the entire city.

In capelli / Bareheaded

For "Momi," nickname of his friend Francesco Arcangeli, see comment on "In Memory;" see also the poem "To Momi." Francesco Arcangeli died in 1974.

I grandi / The Grown-Ups

In the short note at the end of the 1974 edition of *Epitaffio* (see comment on "Ars Dictandi"), Bassani wrote that this poem was addressed to Cesare Garboli (1928-2004), literary critic, translator and writer, and his close friend in the 1950s and 1960s. Their friendship deteriorated when Garboli, who had appreciated Bassani's first poetic production, harshly criticized his last (Dolfi 2021: 568). See the poem "To a Literary Man," in which the object of Bassani's violent criticism is Garboli himself.

In an interview, Bassani explained the autobiographical content of this poem as "a maximum opening, but a 'funnel' opening", a sort of "balance between saying it all and the epitaph" (Dolfi: 2021 560), clarifying how in poetry form can determine content. All of Bassani's later production uses the epitaph – the two collections, *Epitaph* and *In Great Secret*, the *Without* section of his collected poems – because all of his late poetry is autobiographical. The "funnel" shape allows the autobiography to be filtered, distilling it, and transforming it in memory.

The "dream" begins in Maratea, the symbolic place of his relationship with Anne-Marie Stehlin (for Maratea, see comment on "Letter"; for Anne-Marie, see comment on "In the Open"), and retraces its seaside resorts and beaches (the gulf of Policastro, Filocaio, Cersuta), moves further south (Conca dei Marini, a splendid village on the Amalfi coast), and then comes back toward the center and north of the peninsula (Santa Liberata, Orbetello, a town on Monte Argentario in Tuscany, Salto di Fondi in Lazio, Fiascherino in Liguria). These places are all connected to friends that Giorgio and Anne-Marie visited, including Susanna Agnelli Rattazzi and Mario Soldati (for Soldati see comment on "Angry with His Best Friend"). Not only Maratea, but also the two families, Giorgio's, and Anne-Marie's, are characters in the dream: his younger brother Paolo (Bassani also had a younger sister, Jenny), his mother Dora and her mother – among the few still alive – his grandparents, Cesare (Minerbi) and Davide, their fathers both deceased, an ancestor uncle of hers, a whaler, lost at sea. Of this uncle, Dolfi remembers an amusing anecdote, told by the writer Masolino D'Amico (1939-), who after listening to Bassani recite this poem, and remembering Stevenson's *Treasure Island*, had advised him to replace whiskey with rum, more suitable for a "captain of the British navy, perhaps a half-pirate," a "filibuster" (Dolfi 2021: 561). Bassani complied.

Marg / Marg
Salario, Tiburtino and Trionfale are three of the thirty-five Roman *quartieri*.

In gran segreto / In Great Secret

A Momi / To Momi
Momi was the nickname of the art historian Francesco Arcangeli (see "Bareheaded" and the comment on "In Memory" in *Epitaph*).

Tale e quale / Exactly Like
For Bassani's interest in tennis, see comment on "Foro Italico '72" in *Epitaph*. The image of the "half-broken" tennis shoes can also be found in one of Bassani's early short stories, "I campi da tennis del Dopolavoro Aziendale Elettrico" (The Tennis Courts of the Electric Company after Work) (Bassani 2014: 249-260), in the first edition of the collection *The Smell of Hay* (1972) and in a short story later discarded for the final edition of the *Novel of Ferrara* (1980), "Le scarpe da tennis" (Tennis Shoes).

A Natalia Ginzburg / To Natalia Ginzburg
Natalia Ginzburg (1916-1991) was a novelist, short story writer, theater author, essayist, and a leading figure in twentieth-century Italian literature. Although Bassani and Ginzburg were friends, in a review published in the *Corriere della Sera* on 9 June 1974, under the title "La soddisfazione" (Satisfaction), Ginzburg demolished *Epitaph*. The next poem is also addressed to her; see comment on a third poem, "On Holiday."

A un letterato / To a Literary Man
The "literary man" is Cesare Garboli, see comment on "The Grown-Ups" in *Epitaph*. The next poem is also addressed to him.

Congedo / Farewell
The image of Maratea ("the blue pandering / seas of our beautiful Italian south"), with which the poem opens, bears witness to Bassani's interest in politics and the protection of the natural and cultural environment, resulting in his presidency of the environmental association Italia Nostra between 1965 to 1980. See comment on "Ferrara's Ex-Fascists" in *Epitaph*. For Maratea, see comments on "In the Open" and "Letter" in the same collection.

I congiurati / The Conspirators
The conspirators are the Christian Democrat literary establishment, whose party was ruling Italy during those years (see Dolfi 2021: 571).

Piazza Indipendenza / Piazza Indipendenza
Piazza Indipendenza is a square in Rome, close to the Termini Station. For the description of the "solid and beautiful old boxlike villa," isolated and with its shutters closed, Dolfi evokes the American painter Edward Hopper (Dolfi 2021: 571).

Al critico d'un rotocalco / To a Magazine Critic
Bassani is compared to Catullus thanks to his polemical vein which recalls, precisely, the ferocious invective of the Latin author's poems. The moralistic tone of the collection also derives from Dante's *canzoni morali* which Bassani rightly claims for himself. Dante was one of Bassani's models; in particular, he provided him with a structure for *The Garden of the Finzi-Continis*, the story of a Jewish family from Ferrara descending into hell.

Quartiere Salario / Quartiere Salario
Via di Novella, via di Santa Priscilla, and via Ostriana are Roman streets in the Salario neighborhood. Its name originates from the Via Salaria, so called by the ancient Romans because of the transportation of salt from Ostia to Sabina. It is located north-east of the city and is the smallest neighborhood in Rome.

Dove vivi? / Where Do You Live?
Rome, Ferrara, Maratea are "places" from *Epitaph*, which appear frequently in Bassani's last works.

In collera col più grande amico / Angry with His Best Friend

The "best friend" whom Bassani accuses of superficiality is most likely the writer, journalist, and film director Mario Soldati (1905-1999) with whom he had disagreed about the film director Michelangelo Antonioni (Dolfi 2021: 574). Soldati is a constant presence in Bassani's works. In "Down there, at the End of the Corridor" (the last prose of *The Smell of Hay*, at the very end of *The Novel of Ferrara*), he writes of having been able to complete "The Stroll Before Dinner," one of his most important short stories (*The Novel of Ferrara*: 38-59), thanks to Soldati and his advice to "stop […] gadding around Rome on my bicycle," (*ivi*: 736) an ironic way to invite his friend to concentrate more and to follow up on his writing project; in "Campus" he explicitly mentions Soldati, calling him by his first name. Moreover, Bassani dedicated his first novel, *The Gold-Rimmed Spectacles*, to him.

Benedetto Croce (1866-1952) was among the most important Italian philosophers and historians, one of the theorists of Italian neo-idealism. Like Bassani, Soldati was a friend of Elena Croce (1915-1994), the philosopher's daughter and a writer, translator, and environmentalist.

Domenica mattina / Sunday Morning

The car described by Bassani in this poem is likely a Fiat 500 (Dolfi 2021: 575), one of the most iconic Italian cars, in production since 1957 and still available today. It's a small compact car, often a convertible. Dolfi argues that Bassani looks at this car in the same way Edgardo Limentani, the main character in his last novel *The Heron*, looks at his old Aprilia: "To see it from the sidewalk, a little at a tilt and with the windscreen completely dark, it seemed to him even more ancient: a kind of rusty and useless wreck." (*The Novel of Ferrara*: 641)

Racconto / Story

Fonteblanda is part of Orbetello, a coastal town and popular seaside destination in the Maremma, Tuscany.

15 giugno 1975 / 15 June 1975

On 15 June 1975, Italian administrative elections were held in which the Italian Communist Party (PCI), led by Enrico Berlinguer, performed very strongly. This performance was confirmed the following year on the occasion of early elections for the renewal of Parliament, paving the way for the *compromesso storico* (historical compromise) with the Christian Democrats, a government agreement between the two parties that failed after the kidnapping and assassination by the Brigate rosse of the Christian Democrat party president, Aldo Moro, on 9 May 1978.

Modena Nord / Modena Nord
Modena Nord is an exit near Ferrara off the A1 *autostrada*. An indirect mention of Pier Paolo Pasolini, of whom Bassani was a close friend and to whom the poem is addressed (Dolfi 2021: 578), can be found in the "fireflies," an allusion to Pasolini's famous article published in the *Corriere della sera* on 1 February 1975 ("Il vuoto di potere in Italia," The power vacuum in Italy, now with the title "1° febbraio 1975" in the collection *Scritti corsari*: "In the early Sixties, due to air pollution, and above all, in the countryside, due to water pollution (the blue rivers and the transparent ditches) the fireflies have begun to disappear. The phenomenon has been lightning fast and dazzling. After a few years the fireflies were gone. (They are now a rather excruciating reminder of the past)" (Pasolini 1975: 161).

A casa / At Home
"Valli" refers to the Comacchio valleys, one of the largest wetland areas in Italy, south of the Po Delta and north of the Romagna riviera, between the provinces of Ravenna and Ferrara. They are located within the Po Delta Regional Park, which, over more than 11,000 hectares, is one of the most important protected areas in Europe.

In vacanza / On Holiday
The acronym N.G. stands for Natalia Ginzburg to whom are addressed two poems in *In Great Secret*, "To Natalia Ginzburg" and "To the Same". Ginzburg had written a negative review of *Epitaph*. The terms "satisfaction" along with "vain", "pain" and "tedium" are direct quotations from Ginzburg's article which was entitled "Satisfaction" (a term she employed seventeen times [Ginzburg 1974: 3]; see also comment on "To Natalia Ginzburg").

Ciampino / Ciampino
Ciampino is a municipality in Lazio near Rome where one of the city's two international airports, Roma-Ciampino, is located.

Manuscript version of "Modena Nord" (in *In gran segreto*) on notebook paper with a few variant readings. Bassani uses the centered epitaph form in his initial drafting. (Fondo manoscritti Eredi Paola e Enrico Bassani)

Ut pictura / Ut Pictura

The connection with Vienna, also in the preceding poem "By Postcard", is graphically rendered by the initial ellipsis. However, this ellipsis could also be related to the title, an abbreviation of Horace's famous expression in the *Ars Poetica*, "Ut pictura poesis", and also to the incipit of a poem by Eugenio Montale, "The Fan" (Montale 1986: 219): "Ut pictura... The disconcerting lips." In 1976, Bassani made a trip to Vienna, invited by the Italian Cultural Institute. From there he went to Graz to visit the Pinacoteca (Dolfi: 585). As in the Rolls Royce of the eponymous poem from *Epitaph*, the poet sees the landscape through the windshield of a car (here a Mercedes Benz 220D). This same "ekphrastic" vision is also often adopted in the novel *The Heron*, where the presence of the car is functional to the story and in which the main character, Edgardo Limentani, frequently peers at the world through his windscreen: "'Just as well that we're here' he grumbled, glancing up through the windscreen at the two looming chimneys" (*The Novel of Ferrara*: 571); "He had already backed the car up. Through the windscreen he could see the humped back of the suspension bridge" (*ivi*: 613); and again: "Through the windscreen he saw him [Romeo, the doorman] make his way toward the gate" (*ivi*: 658). And see comment on "Sunday Morning."

Compleanno / Birthday

Numerous poems from the collection *In Great Secret* were written in the United States. This is the first, "written in New York, facing Central Park" ("Meritare il tempo", Dolfi 2003: 195). In the 1970s, Bassani spent several months in the United States and Canada: he was often invited by the Italian Cultural Institute in New York and the Casa Italiana of Columbia University, but he was also visiting professor at a number of American and Canadian universities: in 1975 at Northwestern University in Illinois, in 1976 at Indiana University and Berkeley, in 1979 and 1980 at the University of Toronto, and then in Kingston, at Queen's University. In 1980, he received an honorary doctorate in literature from Notre Dame, Indiana.

Campus / Campus

This poem was addressed from Bloomington (on letterhead paper of the Indiana University Center for Italian Studies) in spring 1976 to his friend Mario Soldati (see comment on "Angry with His Best Friend") who, at the time, was teaching at Columbia University in New York. Bassani had been invited by Edoardo

Lèbano – professor of Italian at Indiana University and a prominent figure in the teaching of Italian language and culture in the US – whom he had met in Bologna in 1973. Lèbano then invited him to teach a course on his own works to doctoral students (Lèbano 2016). Bassani returned to Indiana also in 1979. In 2017, invited by Lèbano, Paola Bassani visited the Indiana campus. For the letters exchange between Bassani and Lèbano, and Bassani's visits to American university campuses, see Cappozzo, 2016. Professor Lèbano died in 2020.

The poem contains a long list of Italian intellectuals of different backgrounds and from different eras, almost an ideal history of Italian culture presented in an ironic and humorous vein. The two seventeenth-century architects Gian Lorenzo Bernini (1598-1680) and Francesco Borromini (1599-1667), and the film director Federico Fellini (1920-1993) are mentioned as representatives of the baroque as both a historical movement and taste. The writer Giovanni Verga (1840-1922) and film director Roberto Rossellini (1906-1977) represent the other end of the spectrum, the one as the main exponent of the literary movement called *verismo* (realism), the other as a founder of neorealism. The romantic composer and senator Giuseppe Verdi (1813-1901) is paradoxically compared with Gershwin; writer and translator Vincenzo Monti (1754-1828) and film director Luchino Visconti (1906-1976) mentioned as exponents of Lombard Catholicism; the painters Lorenzo Lotto (1480-1556/57), Bernardo Bellotto (1721-1780), Giotto (1267- 1337) and the poet Andrea Zanzotto (1921-2011) brought in simply for the comical rhymes. Dante is missing from this list, but as a representative of the so-called three crowns of the Italian *Trecento*, there is Giovanni Boccaccio (1313-1375). Finally, Griso is a character in Alessandro Manzoni's novel, *The Betrothed*, set in Lombardy in the 1600s, under Spanish domination. He is one of the chiefs of the *Bravi*, violent henchmen at the service of a local baron, Don Rodrigo: "'It's hard,' Griso replied, remaining with one foot on the first step, 'it's hard to receive reproaches, after having worked faithfully, and tried to do your duty, and even risked your skin'" (from chapter 11). Alessandro Manzoni (1785-1873) is among Italy's most important writers, his historical novel *The Betrothed* one of the great masterpieces in European literature. Published for the first time in 1823 under a different title, *The Betrothed* appeared first in 1827 and in its final edition in 1840-1842. A symbol of national identity, *The Betrothed* is still included in all high school programs.

Visitando l'Indiana / Visiting Indiana

This poem was also written during Bassani's time in Bloomington in 1976. The "historian of scandals" is probably the author himself, given this poem's draft title "Confiteor" (I Confess), as noted in Dolfi 2021: 588.

Per lettera / By Letter

In manuscript variants, the poem is entitled "From Michigan" and contains instead of the affectionate term "nini" the name of a woman, "Anna" (Dolfi: 589), most probably Anne-Marie Stehlin. This poem was also written in Bloomington.

In gran segreto / In Great Secret

Written in Berkeley in 1976 (see comment on "Birthday"), this is the last of the "American" poems. The Shattuck Hotel (title of the preceding poem), where Bassani stayed during the first month of his visit to Berkeley, has a hard-boiled fiction atmosphere (in his youth Bassani had translated James Cain's novel, *The Postman Always Rings Twice* – see Antognini, 2016).

In Maremma / In Maremma

Maremma is the wild and once uninhabitable marshland of southern Tuscany between Siena and Rome (also extending into northern Lazio). It was plagued by malaria until the marshes were drained in the 19th century. Now the Maremma is a largely agricultural area: vineyards, olive groves and flocks of sheep and cattle define its landscape, rather than marshes and swarms of mosquitoes.

Parla il depresso / The Depressed Man Speaks

Palidoro, not far from Cerveteri, is in the Maremma Laziale, which begins in the north of the province of Viterbo in Lazio and extends as far south as Santa Marinella in the province of Rome. Bassani's readers will remember that the prologue to his novel *The Garden of the Finzi-Continis* tells the story of a day trip to Santa Marinella and the Etruscan necropolis of Cerveteri (see comment on "Santa Severa" in *Epitaph*).

Padre e figlio / Father and Son

Dolfi writes in her comment that Bassani made trips by car with his son Enrico and loved driving up and down Italy (Dolfi: 592), something he often did as President of Italia Nostra. Bassani and his wife Valeria Sinigallia (1918-2013) had two children, Enrico, and Paola. One of his last poems, "To My Daughter for

INDIANA UNIVERSITY
Center for Italian Studies
BALLANTINE HALL
BLOOMINGTON, INDIANA 47401

Dal Campus — *a Mario Soldati*

Richiamandosi imperterriti alla più ormai universalmente riconosciuta opportunità dei confronti infra ed extra senza più la minima remora insomma a questa

libera

— né sto a descriverti le masate Mario mio che quelle puoi di sicuro immaginartele —

consideri più valido Manzoni — intervenga dolcemente — ovvero Antonioni?

Opta per la linea Borromini-Fellini diciamo o per quella Rossellini?

E Verdi? Non pare a lei che Giuseppe Verdi ricordi come fenomeno un po' il nostro Gershwin?

E il lombardo Vincenzo Monti in che rapporto lo mette lei col lombardo Luchino Visconti?

E Lotto
e Belotto

Manuscript version of "Campus" (in *In gran Segreto*) with a few variants, written on the Indiana University Center for Italian Studies letterhead, with a dedication to his friend Mario Soldati. Bassani spent two months in Bloomington as a visiting professor, from March to April 1976. (Fondo manoscritti Eredi Paola e Enrico Bassani)

INDIANA UNIVERSITY
Center for Italian Studies
BALLANTINE HALL
BLOOMINGTON, INDIANA 47401

TEL. NO. 812—337-2302

C2

c Gioco
e
Zanzotto

non sarà il caso che si verifichi se abbiamo davvero qualcosa fra loro da
spartire?
E lei medesimo infine in che rapporto si sente
col Boccaccio?

Questo è più o meno ciò che mi chiedono tutti quanti in giro come se niente
fosse
tolchè più morto che vivo delle due l'una o di
botta ci abbraccio oppure sfuggito
giusto a metà da un gran
tonfo
fronte ai ginocchi ho cura di esprimi bon bene
con entrambe le mani il
viso

Ecco quanto cosicchino può per dirle

INDIANA UNIVERSITY
Center for Italian Studies
BALLANTINE HALL
BLOOMINGTON, INDIANA 47401

C3

TEL. NO. 812—337-2502

col vecchio Guido è
dura

Her Birthday," is addressed to her. Feniglia is a beach in Maremma connecting the Argentario promontory with the mainland. The Uccellina Natural Park was established in 1975 and covers over 10,000 hectares in the province of Grosseto in the heart of Maremma.

La capanna dell'ortolano / The Market-Gardener's Shed
The Argentario is a promontory in the province of Grosseto in Tuscany. Santa Liberata is a beach. The Aurelia is an ancient Roman road leading along the Tirrenean coast from Pisa to Genoa and on into France. The modern Aurelia is 698 km long and is one of the most important roads in Italy.

Raccordo anulare / Raccordo Anulare
The *raccordo anulare* is the ring road around Rome. For Bassani's mother, Signora Dora, see comment on "I Arrive My Mother's Not Well" in *Epitaph*.

A mia figlia per il suo compleanno / To My Daughter for Her Birthday
Paola Bassani, daughter of the writer, was born in Rome on 1 September 1945. She is the first of Bassani's two children. Inheriting her father's passion for the subject, she became an art historian. A tireless supporter of her father's work, she lives in Paris and is President of the Fondazione Bassani.

Gli spettri (*frammento*) / The Ghosts (*Fragment*)
P.P.P. are the initials of Pier Paolo Pasolini (1922-1975), to whom Bassani was very close (see comment on "Modena Nord"). Pasolini was born in Bologna to a noble father from Ravenna and a Friulian mother. The "roggia" that divides them is the Sillaro stream, between Romagna (Bologna) and Emilia (Ferrara). The acronym P.C. stands perhaps for the writer and literary critic Pietro Citati (1930-2022), who was born in Florence into a noble Florentine family and who, like Pasolini and Bassani himself, had moved to Rome.

The story of Bassani's "cousin Arrigo" is interrupted, as was the life of Ferrara's Jews and Bassani's "autobiography" which ends with this poem. It is one of his latest writings, since the last published work was this collection of poems, *In rima e senza*, in 1982 (he was too ill to supervise the 1998 edition of the *Opere* published by Mondadori). The poem is written in the same vein as others such as "The Grown-Ups" or "I Arrive My Mother's Is Not Well" in *Epitaph*, in which the poet's interest in his "Jewish and Ferrarese kinship" is a way of remembering the "forgotten shades" as in "Easter Supper" from *In Rhyme*, or the tragic ghosts of the Easter supper in *The Garden of the Finzi-Continis* ("that grotesque and desperate gathering of ghosts", *The Novel of Ferrara*: 375) where the loss of the narrator's family represents the tragic loss of an entire community.

The Carso is a rocky limestone plateau between Friuli-Venezia Giulia (province of Gorizia and Trieste), Slovenia and Croatia, historically known for having been the scene of violent battles during the First World War between Italian and Austro-Hungarian troops. Born in Ferrara, Italo Balbo (1896-1940) was an Italian politician and aviator. He was a protagonists in the March on Rome in 1922, and one of the most prominent figures in fascist Italy. Balbo was the founder in 1920 of Ferrarese fascism and distinguished himself in the organization of violent beatings. The Caffè and Pasticceria Folchini (now called Europa) is one of Ferrara's historical coffee shops, documented since 1846. It is located on Corso della Giovecca, one of the main arteries of the city. In the poem "Rolls Royce" in *Epitaph*, Bassani's father's friends from his youth stand in front of the Caffè Folchini, "most with wide gray lobbia hats on their heads some even with silver-knobbed / canes in their fists."

Bibliography

Works by Giorgio Bassani

(1940), *Una città di pianura*. Milan: Arte Grafica A. Lucini e C. (under the pseudonym Giacomo Marchi).
(1945; 1946), *Storie dei poveri amanti e altri versi*. Rome: Astrolabio.
(1947), *Te lucis ante (1946-47)*. Rome: Ubaldini.
(1951), *Un'altra libertà*. Milan: Mondadori.
(1956), *Cinque storie ferraresi*. Turin: Einaudi
(1958), *Gli occhiali d'oro*. Turin: Einaudi.
(1962), *Il giardino dei Finzi Contini*. Turin: Einaudi
(1963), *L'alba ai vetri. Poesie 1942-'50*. Turin: Einaudi.
(1964), *Dietro la porta*. Turin: Einaudi.
(1966), *Le parole preparate*. Turin: Einaudi
(1968), *L'airone*. Milan: Mondadori.
(1972), *L'odore del fieno*. Milan: Mondadori.
(1973), *Dentro le mura*. Milan: Mondadori.
(1974), *Epitaffio*. Milan: Mondadori.
(1974; 1980), *Il romanzo di Ferrara*. Milan: Mondadori.
(1978), *In gran segreto*. Milan: Mondadori.
(1982), *In rima e senza*. Milan: Mondadori.
(1984), *Di là dal cuore*. Milan: Mondadori.
(1998), *Opere*, R. Cotroneo (ed.). Milan: Mondadori.
(2005), *Italia da salvare. Scritti civili e battaglie ambientali*, C. Spila (ed.). Turin: Einaudi.
(2014), *Racconti, diari, cronache (1935-1956)*, P. Pieri (ed.). Milan: Feltrinelli.
(2018), *Italia da salvare. Gli anni della presidenza di Italia Nostra (1965-1980)*, D. Cola e C. Spila (eds.). Milan: Feltrinelli.
(2019), *Interviste 1955-1993*, B. Pecchiari and D. Scarpa (eds.). Milan: Feltrinelli.

Translations in English

Caetani Marguerite (ed.) (1950), *An Anthology of New Italian Writers*. New York: New Directions.

McKendrick Jamie (trans.) (2007), *The Garden of the Finzi-Continis*. London, New York: Penguin Books.
– (2012), *The Gold-Rimmed Spectacles*. London, New York: Penguin Books.
– (2014), *The Smell of Hay*. London, New York: Penguin Books.
– (2016), *Within the Walls*. London, New York: Penguin Books.
– (2017), *Behind the Door*. London, New York: Penguin Books.
– (2018), *The Heron*. London, New York: Penguin Books.
– (2018), *The Novel of Ferrara*. London, New York: Penguin Books; Norton & Company.

Quigly Isabel (trans.) (1960), *The Gold-Rimmed Spectacles*. New York: Atheneum.
– (1962), *A Prospect of Ferrara*. London: Faber and Faber.
– (1965), *The Garden of the Finzi-Continis*. New York: Atheneum.

Valente Francesca (trans.) (1982), *Rolls Royce and Other Poems*. Toronto: Aya Press.

Weaver William (trans.) (1970), *The Heron*. New York: Harcourt, Brace & World.
– (1971), *Five Stories of Ferrara*. New York: Harcourt Brace Jovanovich.
– (1972), *Behind the Door*. New York: Harcourt Brace Jovanovich.
– (1975), *The Smell of Hay*. New York: Harcourt Brace Jovanovich.
– (1977), *The Garden of the Finzi-Continis*. New York, London: Harcourt, Brace and Company.
– (2005), *The Garden of the Finzi-Continis*. New York, London: Everyman's Library.

Works Cited

Antognini Roberta (2016), Giorgio Bassani e James Cain. Storia e critica di una traduzione. In: V. Cappozzo (ed.), *Lezioni americane di Giorgio Bassani*. Ravenna: Giorgio Pozzi Editore, 89-121.

– (2020a), Traduzione e ricezione dell'opera poetica di Giorgio Bassani in Nord America. In: V. Cappozzo (ed.), *Dal particolare all'universale. I libri di poesia di Giorgio Bassani*. Ravenna: Giorgio Pozzi Editore, 311-337.
– (2020b), Giorgio Bassani's Poems. Antologia di poesie in traduzione. In: V. Cappozzo (ed.), *Dal particolare all'universale. I libri di poesia di Giorgio Bassani*. Ravenna: Giorgio Pozzi Editore, 365-398.
Antognini Roberta and Blumenfeld Rodica (eds.) (2012), *Poscritto a Giorgio Bassani. Saggi in memoria del decimo anniversario della morte*. Milan: LED.

Bassani Paola (2016), *Se avessi una piccola casa mia*. Milan: La nave di Teseo.

Cappozzo Valerio (2012), Incontri indiani. Lettere inedite di Giorgio Bassani. In: R. Antognini and R. Blumenfeld (eds.), *Poscritto a Giorgio Bassani. Saggi in memoria del decimo anniversario della morte*. Milan: LED, 41-54.
– (2016a), Il viaggio in America di Giorgio Bassani tra poesia e insegnamento. In: V. Cappozzo (ed.), *Lezioni americane di Giorgio Bassani*. Ravenna: Giorgio Pozzi Editore, 15-39.
– (ed.) (2016b), *Le lezioni americane di Giorgio Bassani*, Ravenna: Giorgio Pozzi Editore.
– (2018), Dall'altra parte della luna». Le poesie di Giorgio Bassani tra gli Stati Uniti e il Canada. *Cahiers d'études italiennes* 26, 2018: 1-13 (available online: https://journals.openedition.org/cei/3925).

Cucchi Maurizio and Giovanardi Stefano (eds.) (1994), *Poeti italiani del secondo Novecento 1945-1995*. Milan: Mondadori.

Dolfi Anna (2003), *Giorgio Bassani. Una scrittura della malinconia*. Rome: Bulzoni
– (ed.) (2021), Giorgio Bassani, *Poesie complete*. Milan: Feltrinelli.

Eco Umberto (2003), *Dire quasi la stessa cosa*. Milan: Bompiani.
– (2003b), *Mouse or Rat? Translation As Negotiation*, London: Orion Books.

Gallot Muriel (trans.) (2021), Giorgio Bassani, *Poèmes*. Paris: Cahiers de l'Hôtel de Gallifet.

Ginzburg Natalia (1974), La soddisfazione. *Corriere della Sera* 9 June: 3.

Kafka Franz (1995), The Anxiety of The Head of Family. In *The Metamorphosis, In the Penal Colony and Other Stories*, J. Neugroschel (trans.), New York: Scribner, 265-267.

Kertesz-Vial Elisabeth (2011), Un'intervista a Giorgio Bassani (1984). In: A. Perli (ed.), *Giorgio Bassani: la poesia del romanzo, il romanzo della poesia*. Ravenna: Giorgio Pozzi Editore, 271-283.

Kundera Milan (1973), *La vita è altrove*, S. Vitale (trans.), Milan: Adelphi.
– (2000), *Life Is Elsewhere*, Aaron Asher (trans.), New York: Harper Perennial.

Lèbano Edoardo (2016), Giorgio Bassani a Indiana University. In: V. Cappozzo (ed.), *Lezioni americane di Giorgio Bassani*. Ravenna: Giorgio Pozzi Editore, 11-13.

Litrico Gaia (2020), Giorgio Bassani alla ricerca di "Un'altra libertà" poetica: scrittura, lettere, editori. In: V. Cappozzo (ed.), *Dal particolare all'universale. I libri di poesia di Giorgio Bassani*. Ravenna: Giorgio Pozzi Editore, 243-272.

Mondadori Mimma (1985), *Una tipografia in paradiso*. Milan: Mondadori.

Montale Eugenio (1986), *The Storm and Other Things*. W. Arrowsmith (trans.), New York: Norton.
– (1996), Parole di poeti. In *Il secondo mestiere, I: Prose 1920-1979*. Milan: Mondadori, 634-639.

Mosena Roberto (ed.) (2015), In rima e senza. Una lezione inedita di Giorgio Bassani dal Fondo di poesia P. Tondi. *Nuovi argomenti* 72: 77-91.

Pasolini Pier Paolo (1975), 1° febbraio 1975. In *Scritti corsari*. Milan: Garzanti, 160-168.

Parussa Sergio (2016), Giorgio Bassani's America. In: *New York Lectures and Interviews*, S. Baker (trans.). New York: CPL Editions, 121-145.

Porzio Domenico (ed.) (1972), *Dalla parte degli animali*, Milan: Ferro.

Rimbaud Arthur (2003), *Une saison en enfer*, *Rimbaud Complete*. W. Mason (trans.), New York: Modern Library Paperback.

Robinson Peter (trans.) (2007), Luciano Erba, *The Greener Meadow. Selected Poems*. Princeton & Oxford: Princeton UP.
– (2017), *Collected Poems 1976-2016*. Swindon UK: Shearsman Books.
– (2023), Giorgio Bassani: In rima in inglese. In V. Cappozzo (ed.), *Giorgio Bassani poète. Actes du colloque du 15 octobre 2021*. Paris: Cahiers de l'Hôtel de Galliffet (Troisème série), forthcoming.

Scarpa Domenico (2018), Paperback Writer. In: T. Rimini (ed.), *Giorgio Bassani, scrittore europeo*. Bern: Peter Lang, 197-224.

www.ingramcontent.com/pod-product-compliance
Lightning Source LLC
Chambersburg PA
CBHW030510080526
44586CB00011B/137